Carmela Sophia Sereno, an Italian food writer and cookery tutor, was brought up on a small farm in the north of Bedfordshire. Although she was raised on the outskirts of Bedford town, known by many as 'Little Italy', her family originates from the regions of Puglia and Molise in the south of Italy. Today, Carmela lives in a small Northamptonshire village with her four children and husband, where she balances family life with her work as an Italian food writer, cookery tutor, chef, demonstrator and recipe developer.

Carmela shares her love of Italian food through her work as an Italian cookery author, magazine contributor and fortnightly food columnist for local newspaper *The Chronicle & Echo*. Her writing has brought her to the attention of olive oil producers, Filippo Berio, who sponsor her fortnightly supper club, the success of which sees each session sold out months in advance.

Carmela's first book, *Southern Italian Family Cooking*, was a true labour of love, which showcased the best dishes of Southern Italy. The recipes in this book show her passion for the *cucina povera* (or traditional peasant food) style of cooking and encourage the use of seasonal ingredients in everyday family cooking. Carmela's second book, *A Passion for Pasta*, showcases different regional pastas alongside their complementary sauces.

For more details, please visit www.carmelas-kitchen.com

Also by Carmela Sophia Sereno

A Passion for Pasta
Southern Italian Family Cooking
Northern Italian Family Cooking
How to Make Your Own Pasta

Pasta Fresca:

Mastering the art of fresh pasta

Carmela Sophia Sereno

ROBINSON

ROBINSON

First published in Great Britain in 2022 by Robinson

10 9 8 7 6 5 4 3 2 1

A CIP catalogue record for this book is available from the British Library.

ISBN: 978-1-47214-569-7

Typeset in Great Britain by Mousemat Design Limited

Printed and bound in Great Britain by Clays Ltd, Elcograf S.p.A.

Papers used by Robinson are from well-managed forests and other responsible sources.

MIX
Paper from responsible sources
FSC® C104740

Robinson
An imprint of
Little, Brown Book Group
Carmelite House
50 Victoria Embankment
London EC4Y 0DZ

An Hachette UK Company
www.hachette.co.uk

www.littlebrown.co.uk

How To Books are published by Robinson, an imprint of Little, Brown Book Group. We welcome proposals from authors who have first-hand experience of their subjects. Please set out the aims of your book, its target market and its suggested contents in an email to howto@littlebrown.co.uk

Contents

Introduction   1

  A brief history of pasta   1

  What is pasta?   2

Pasta dough   4

  Basic pasta   4

  Coloured and flavoured pasta   8

  Gluten-free and vegan pasta   23

Making pasta   29

  Rolling out pasta dough   29

  Shaping pasta   33

  Fillings   59

  Cooking and storing pasta   66

Pasta essentials   69

  Pasta kit and equipment   69

  Larder and pantry ingredients   71

  Cook's notes   76

  Online stockists   78

Stocks, sauces and dressings   79

Short pasta and soups   110

Long pasta   152

Gnocchi and gnudi   184

Filled pasta   206

Baked pasta   238

Sweet and celebration pasta   276

Index   300

To my papa Rocco:
thank you for your guidance, support and love
throughout the years. I'll forever miss you, love big pip x

Rocco Sereno, May 1951–September 2021

Introduction – 'Inspire me'

A brief history of pasta

It was once thought that the thirteenth-century Venetian explorer and traveller Marco Polo (1254–1324) returned from China, his arms laden with pasta. Alas, there is no truth in the tale; it is but a myth. Pasta was already being made in Italy when Polo visited China, and in fact many years even before his birth.

There are suggestions that the ancient Romans in the first century AD ate pasta and that ancient Greeks consumed a version of lasagne. The Etruscans, who were ancestors of the Italians, made drawings depicting food that looked like pasta, even including drawings of instruments and tools used to make and cut the dough. There is evidence that they made pasta from durum wheat, which is still used to produce pasta today. It was called *lagane* and, like its modern-day namesake *lasagne*, was dried in sheets to preserve its life until it was needed for cooking.

In the Middle Ages pasta was eaten by the Arabs, who ruled the island of Sicily at the time. An Arabic traveller who settled in Sicily in 1154 described delicate strings made from flour and water, now known to us as spaghetti. The final will of Ponzio Baestone, a Genoan soldier, shows he requested *'Bariscella peina de macarone'* – a small basket full of macaroni. His will was dated 1279, thirteen years before Marco Polo returned from China.

By the 1300s, dried pasta was very popular for its long shelf life and high nutritional value, making it an ideal choice for long ship voyages and other journeys. However, pasta was not regularly featured or included as part of a meal in Italy until the sixteenth century. It was a seen as a luxury item because the durum wheat that was required to make the pasta had to be imported from Sicily or Puglia, and this made it incredibly expensive at the time. Until the eighteenth century, the less financially fortunate in Italy mainly ate a diet based on fresh, seasonally available vegetables, but the availability of durum wheat increased as the concept of large farms took hold and led to more widespread cultivation across the country. This, combined with the development of a kneading machine and press, meant pasta could be produced in factories. If you visit the area, make time to visit the museum of pasta, the *Museo Storico Degli Spaghetti*, in Pontedassio, Italy.

Clearly pasta is an ancient food that is still loved, valued and eaten across the world. So now we have dipped our toes into the myths, tales, legends, and history, let's together learn, share and enjoy the most versatile combination of flour and water you will ever find.

Pasta, anyone?

What is pasta?

'Life is a combination of magic and pasta'
– *Federico Fellini*

The meaning of 'pasta' is 'a simple dough or paste' – an unleavened dough of wheat, made using water. A simple classification into the two main groups of dried and fresh pasta does not do justice to the massive array of shapes, sizes, colours, textures and flavours available.

Pasta can be found on most supermarket and deli shelves. *Pasta secca* (dried pasta) uses a blend of durum wheat semolina (*semola di grano duro*) and water. Mass-produced Italian dried pasta must all be made with 100 per cent durum wheat flour. My larder is always fully stocked to the brim with a variety of dried pasta shapes, but what is paramount is the quality that you purchase.

As an alternative to durum wheat, there is 00 flour (*doppio zero, farina di grano tenero*) which is my preference for egg-based fresh pasta, especially for all filled pasta. Flour in Italy is graded due to its coarseness from very fine 000, through 00, 0, 1 and 2, 3, 4, becoming more textured and with less wheat germ removed. 000 has a very fine talcum powder feel to it, whereas number 4 is verging on wholemeal. For pasta-making, 00 flour makes the perfect flour choice every time, though a combination of both durum wheat flour and 00 can also be used to give a variation in colour, texture and bite.

The number of registered and recognised pasta shapes is staggering with a figure in excess of six hundred. There are multiple names for many shapes, from the famous and widely used penne, farfalle and spaghetti to some lesser-known varieties such as the incredibly delicious strozzapreti, bigoli, chitarra and garganelli. It is not uncommon for the same shape to have several different names across regions of Italy. The tagliatelle of the north becomes the fettuccine of Rome, and what I call cicatelli someone else will refer to as cavatelli. You would be forgiven for being a little confused; I still am to this very day!

Years ago pasta would be made in small establishments and left to air dry on the open streets of cities like Naples on long, wooden poles that bow slightly in the centre. In my pasta room I have a photo depicting this time of days gone by and I look at it with great affection. It's yesterday's beginning that makes today possible.

Nowadays most factory-made pasta is extruded through a bronze die mould and is cut to a specific shape before drying in special chambers. The extruders create shapes that are either smooth in texture (*lisce*) or ridged/ribbed (*rigate*), making varying pasta shapes intended for certain sauces. For the purist, certain shapes are meant for specific sauces – but there's no harm in experimenting.

Regional traditions and preferences can be seen across the entire country. The people in the north of Italy consume more in terms of rice and polenta than the south of Italy; however, in terms of pasta, the northerners prefer a richer combination of 00 flour and eggs, whereas the southerners prefer the firmer bite of semola and water. I have to admit I am with the latter as the firm texture of semola and water wins my heart every time.

Fresh versus dried? Many would assume that fresh is best. Whilst filled pasta such as ravioli, agnolotti and tortellini benefits greatly from being made fresh, in all other recipes, dried pasta would make the ideal choice. I am a huge lover of dried pasta, while always remembering quality is key. There is a huge difference in good quality dried pasta so please be sure to use a reputable brand; no shop own brands please! Try to not be limited by what your local supermarket is able to offer you. Search out an Italian deli or browse online for a new shape or two to fall in love with.

Pasta Dough

Basic pasta

Let us start at the beginning. The foundation of all pasta is flour and water. Master the simple techniques and pasta doughs below first as they will stand you in good stead to go on to develop, colour and blend your own unique preferences. Always remember that mastering how to make a fantastic dough and allowing it to rest at an ambient temperature will allow the gluten to relax, thus gifting you with a dough that will be pliable and have great stretch, lending itself well to rolling and shaping as required.

Semola pasta dough

Semola and tepid water pasta dough, from the south of Italy, is prepared on a wooden surface. This dough would suit many shapes with my favourites being orecchiete, gnocchetti sardi, cavatelli and cicatelli. I use no salt in any of my pasta doughs. I prefer to salt my pasta water to within an inch of its life and I also season my sauces, stocks and dressings well instead.

Preparation time: 15 minutes plus 30 minutes resting at room
    temperature
Makes: 400g/14oz

> 400g/14oz semola di grano duro rimacinata flour
> 200ml/7fl oz tepid water

1. I prefer to use a wooden surface as this gives a little added texture to the dough and helps in the kneading process. Tip the flour onto a wooden board and form a well in the centre with your fingers. Ensure the well is large enough to take the required liquid.
2. Slowly add the tepid water into the well.
3. With your fingertips or a fork gently introduce the flour to the water, being careful not to break the walls of the well and lose any of the liquid mixture.
4. Form the mixture into a soft, pliable dough.

5. Knead the dough using the heels of both hands until it has bec ome smooth and silky with a light spring back when pushed with your fingertip. Kneading by hand will take around 7–10 minutes.
6. If the dough is a little dry, dampen your palms a little and knead; if it is too wet, add a little more flour. Just remember that adding too much flour can lead to a dry and slightly denser final dough.
7. Cover the dough and allow to rest for a minimum of 30 minutes at room temperature.

Egg pasta dough

This pasta dough, from the north of Italy, would be my preference for filled pasta as the eggs give a perfect richness and the 00 flour adds a light tender bite.

Preparation time: 15 minutes plus 30 minutes resting at room temperature
Makes: 400g/14oz

400g/14oz 00 flour
4 eggs

1. Work on a wooden board. Tip the flour onto the board and form a well in the centre with your fingers. Ensure the well is large enough to take the eggs.
2. Crack the eggs into the well.
3. With your fingertips or a fork, gently introduce the flour to the eggs, being careful not to break the walls of the well and lose any of the egg mixture.
4. Form the mixture into a soft, pliable dough. If there is any excess flour that will not incorporate into the dough, add a little water or scrape it away.
5. Knead the dough on a clean debris-free board using the heels of both hands until the dough has become smooth and silky with a light spring back when pushed with your fingertip. Kneading by hand will take around 7–10 minutes.
6. If the dough is a little dry, dampen the palms of your hands and knead; if too wet, add a little more flour. Just remember that adding too much flour can lead to a dry and slightly denser dough.
7. Cover the dough and rest for a minimum of 30 minutes at room temperature.

Enriched egg yolk pasta dough

A pasta dough of true opulence, this is one for a special occasion as it is incredibly rich but well worth the extra calories.

Preparation time: 15 minutes plus 30 minutes resting at room temperature
Makes: 200g

> 200g/7oz 00 flour, plus extra for kneading and dusting
> 140g/5oz egg yolks, roughly 10 egg yolks

1. Tip the flour onto a board and make a huge well in the centre, large enough to take the 10 egg yolks.
2. Add the yolks to the well and retain the whites for later use.
3. Use a fork and gently combine the yolks with the flour. Combine and form a dough.
4. Knead until smooth and elastic. Cover and rest for 30 minutes.

CARMELA'S TIP:
- Freeze the egg whites in pairs for ease.

Standard pasta dough ratios

Use these basic ratios to guide you in making different quantities of pasta dough for use in the recipes later in the book.

Water-based dough:
100g/3$\frac{1}{2}$oz semola di grano duro rimacinata to 50ml/1$\frac{1}{2}$fl oz of your chosen liquid, e.g. tepid water

Egg-based dough:
100g/3$\frac{1}{2}$oz 00 flour to 1 egg (65g/2oz shelled in weight)

A note on pasta dough hydration

To the uninitiated, the word hydration can leave you feeling a little confounded, but please do not allow this word to intimidate you at all. Hydration is a word that is used quite liberally in pasta dough and sourdough recipes, and I am constantly asked to demystify the term and complexity of hydration, so in simple terms, and with no fear, here we go.

Hydration simply refers to how much liquid is added to dry ingredients, whether we're talking about egg, water or another liquid-based solution. For example: 100g/3$\frac{1}{2}$oz semola at 50 per cent hydration would require 50ml/1$\frac{1}{2}$fl oz liquid.

I very rarely use the term hydration and as a *pastaia* the only time we concern ourselves with hydration is when we use an extruder (page 31) to pull and twist pasta dough, forming it with ridges through a brass die. The pasta dough would require less liquid, making it crumbly in texture.

Coloured and flavoured pasta

Developing unique, beautifully mastered and coloured pasta shapes is well worth the time and effort it takes. Patience and time are both essential. I enjoy colouring and creating the dough and developing the recipes much more than eating the rainbow itself.

In this section I will explain to you how to make basic and coloured pasta doughs that you can transform into your chosen shape. I have included various recipes that use vegetables such as beetroot and peppers to colour the dough, as well as spice, fruit and vegetable powders and some more unusual ingredients.

When colouring pasta, the quantities of both dry and wet ingredients will vary greatly. For example, when making spinach pasta, the consistency of the dough will depend on how well you squeeze the water from the blanched spinach. However, have a look at my simple no-blanch vegan spinach pasta dough on page 28; it's a foolproof recipe that will never fail you.

Spinach makes a very delicious green dough; blanched stinging nettles, asparagus, kale, cavolo nero or basil and parsley would also work well. The list of vegetables or leaves you can use to colour pasta dough is endless, so do experiment and try something a little different. There seems over the last few years to have been an explosion across social media of pasta experimentation recipes; some are winners and some are huge fails, so please tread carefully.

When using vegetables, coloured pasta does not necessarily take on their flavour. However, the black cuttlefish pasta does retain the fishy aroma, so always bear this in mind when cooking your pasta.

See page 32 for instructions on making beautiful striped pasta with your coloured doughs.

Vegetable and fruit powders

I was introduced to the diversity and versatility of vegetable and fruit powders at Borough Market in London. You can use powders in your standard cooking or in your morning smoothie drink, if you so wish, for an added nutritional benefit. They are a great source of colour and nutrients. That said, I do not find them all palatable (I have a huge personal dislike for spirulina and wheatgrass); however, most of them are very good. Find the flavours you like and invest in small pots as you will not need much in pasta dough.

Here are some examples of the kinds of powders you can buy:

- Porcini powder
- Spinach powder
- Tomato powder
- Red onion powder
- Raspberry powder
- Blackberry powder
- Spirulina powder
- Wheatgrass powder

Per 100g/3$\frac{1}{2}$oz of either 00 flour or semola flour you will need 5–7g/$\frac{1}{8}$oz of the chosen powder. However, for a deeper, more vibrant colour I would recommend that you increase your dehydrated powder to 10–15g/$\frac{1}{4}$–$\frac{1}{2}$oz.

Here is how you mix your vegetable or fruit powder into your pasta dough:

1. Put your flour in a bowl.
2. Weigh your powder into a small bowl, and sift it into your bowl/board. The sifting will ensure you have an even colour distributed throughout the flour.
3. Use a spoon to mix thoroughly.
4. Add your egg or water to the flour to make your paste.
5. Work the dough into a ball and knead on a wooden surface until smooth and pliable.
6. Cover and rest at room temperature for 30 minutes.

Pasta dough blends for coloured pasta

Here are a few of my foolproof coloured pasta dough recipes for you to try.

Spinach Pasta Dough

Preparation time: 15 minutes plus 30 minutes resting at room temperature
Serves: 2

100g/3½oz fresh spinach (blanched, squeezed weight 50g/1½oz)
1 egg
200g/7oz semola di grano duro rimacinata

1. Blanch the spinach in a dry frying pan on a low heat for 2 minutes or until the spinach is fully wilted. Remove from the heat.
2. Squeeze excess water from the spinach with your hands, then wrap the spinach in a clean tea towel and squeeze tightly again. Do this a few times, making sure you wring it well. Spinach holds a lot of water, so you need to ensure as much of it is removed as possible otherwise you will end up with a wet and unmanageable pasta dough.
3. Tumble the spinach and egg into a food processor and blitz; alternatively, chop the spinach very finely and mix with the egg.
4. Tip the flour onto a wooden board or into a bowl if preferred.
5. Make a well in the centre of the flour and pour in the wet ingredients, being careful to not break the walls of flour.
6. Slowly incorporate the spinach and flour together to form a dough. Work from the inside out, using either your fingertips or a fork if preferred. If the dough is a little wet, add an additional tablespoon of semola flour.
7. Knead the spinach dough for 7 minutes until smooth and elastic. Cover and rest for 30 minutes at room temperature.

Tomato Pasta Dough

Preparation time: 15 minutes plus 30 minutes resting at room temperature
Serves: 2

1 egg
60g/2oz tomato purée
200g/7oz 00 flour

1. Pop the egg and tomato purée into a food processor and blitz for 10 seconds, or use a fork to combine thoroughly.
2. Pour the flour onto a wooden board or into a bowl.
3. Make a well in the centre and add the wet ingredients.
4. Use a fork to slowly incorporate the flour from the inside out into the tomato mixture.
5. When you have a dough, knead it well for 7 minutes until smooth and elastic. Cover and rest for 30 minutes at room temperature.

Avocado Pasta Dough

Preparation time: 4 minutes plus 30 minutes resting at room temperature
Serves: 2

> 1 avocado (100g/3½oz peeled and stone removed weight)
> 150g/5oz semola flour

1. Place the peeled avocado, stone removed, into a blender and pulse for 10 seconds.
2. Pour in the semola and blitz until a ball of dough has formed.
3. If the dough appears a little dry, add a tablespoon of water.
4. Tip the ball of dough onto a lightly floured surface and knead until smooth and elastic. Cover and rest for 30 minutes at room temperature.

Pea Pasta Dough

Preparation time: 15 minutes plus 30 minutes resting at room temperature
Serves: 2

100g/3½oz frozen peas
1 egg
200g/7oz 00 flour

1. Blanch the peas in a saucepan of boiling water for 3 minutes.
2. Drain the peas and blitz in a food processor with the egg. Pulse until you have a textured yet relatively smooth green purée.
3. Pour the flour onto a wooden board or into a bowl.
4. Make a well in the centre and add the pea purée.
5. Use a fork to slowly incorporate the flour from the inside out into the pea mixture.
6. When you have a ball of dough, knead it well for 7 minutes until smooth and elastic. Cover and rest for 30 minutes at room temperature.

Beetroot Pasta Dough

Preparation time: 15 minutes plus 30 minutes resting at room temperature
Serves: 2

1 egg
75g/2½oz beetroot, pre-cooked without vinegar
200g/7oz 00 flour

1. Crack the egg into a food processor and add the beetroot. Blitz for 30 seconds until the beetroot has incorporated fully with the egg and you have a smooth, flecked purée.
2. Pour the flour onto a wooden board or into a bowl and make a well in the centre.
3. Add the deep-purple beetroot mixture to the well and mix with a fork to incorporate slowly, working with the flour from the inside out.
4. Form into a dough and knead for 7 minutes until smooth and elastic, then cover and rest for 30 minutes at room temperature.

Saffron Pasta Dough

Preparation time: 15 minutes plus 30 minutes resting at room temperature
Serves: 2

2 eggs
Pinch of saffron strands
200g/7oz 00 flour

1. Crack the eggs into a bowl and add the delicate saffron strands. Whisk well and set aside.
2. Tip the flour onto a wooden board or into a bowl if preferred.
3. Make a well in the centre and pour in the saffron egg mix.
4. Incorporate the eggs into the flour gently, ensuring the walls of the well remain intact. The saffron will add a light amber colour to the dough with a delicious hint of flavour.
5. Using a fork or your fingers, work the egg mixture with the flour until you can form a dough.
6. Knead the dough for 7 minutes until smooth and elastic. Cover and set aside for 30 minutes at room temperature.

Cuttlefish/Squid Ink Pasta Dough

Preparation time: 15 minutes plus 30 minutes resting at room temperature
Serves: 2

2 eggs
14g/1 heaped tsp cuttlefish ink
200g/7oz 00 flour

1. Crack the eggs into a bowl and squeeze or spoon in the cuttlefish ink. Using a fork, whisk together.
2. Tip the flour onto a wooden board or into a bowl if preferred. Make a well in the centre of the flour.
3. Pour the fragrant onyx mixture into the well.
4. Using a fork, work the squid ink into the flour. Form a dough (your hands will be black and fragrant).
5. Knead the dough for 7 minutes until smooth and elastic. Cover and rest for 30 minutes at room temperature.

Red Wine Pasta Dough

Preparation time: 15 minutes plus 45 minutes allowing the red wine to cool and the dough to rest
Serves: 2

285ml/10fl oz red wine (not cooking wine)
1 egg
200g/7oz 00 flour

1. Pour the red wine into a small saucepan. Please use a good-quality wine as the flavour is important here. Reduce the wine down to roughly half the original quantity over a steady boil.
2. Allow the wine to cool to a tepid temperature.
3. Whisk the egg into the red wine.
4. Tip the flour onto a wooden board or into a bowl if preferred. Make a well in the centre.
5. Pour the red wine and egg mixture into the well. Combine using a fork or your fingertips and form into a dough.
6. Knead for 7 minutes until smooth and elastic. Cover and rest for 30 minutes at room temperature.

Chocolate and Frangelico Pasta Dough

Preparation time: 15 minutes plus 30 minutes resting at room temperature
Serves: 2

2 eggs
1 tbsp Frangelico
2 tbsp cocoa powder
200g/7oz 00 flour

1. Crack the eggs into a bowl and add the Frangelico.
2. Sift the cocoa powder into the eggs and whisk with a fork.
3. Tip the flour onto a wooden board or into a bowl if preferred. Make a well in the centre.
4. Pour the wet ingredients into the well. Use a fork to combine the eggs with the flour until you have a workable dough.
5. Knead the dough for 7 minutes until smooth and elastic. Cover and rest for 30 minutes at room temperature.

Grano Arso Pasta (Burnt Wheat Pasta)

Grano arso is a flour that is used in the region of Puglia to make bread, pasta and pizza dough. It gives a nutty, burnt taste that is reminiscent of days gone by. Cook the semola at a low temperature for a long time to get a light burn, or at a high temperature for a shorter time for a deep burn and darker colour.

Preparation time: 3 minutes
Cooking time: between 25 and 45 minutes. Cook at 220°C/200°C fan-assisted/Gas 7 for 45 minutes for a light burn, or 240°C/220°C fan-assisted/Gas 9 for 25 minutes for a deeper burn.

Semola di grano duro rimacinata, as required

1. Preheat the oven to your chosen temperature above.
2. Take a large oven tray and line it with parchment paper.
3. Cover the tray with semola flour, spreading evenly, and bake as above. Please be aware the oven may smoke a little so leave a window ajar.
4. Every 5 minutes, carefully open the oven and move the semola about with a fork, ensuring an even colour.
5. Once the semola has been burnt for its allotted time, allow it to cool, then pass it through a sieve, knocking out any lumps and bumps.

The grano arso flour can now be used as required or stored in a jar for up to 6 months. The gluten level is much lower now so be sure to blend it with 00 flour or semola: 70 per cent 00 flour or semola to 30 per cent grano arso.

Hemp Pasta

Hemp offers a nutty flavour while being rich in protein, minerals and fibre. I do think hemp is a little like Marmite: you either love it or hate it.

Preparation time: 10 minutes plus 30 minutes resting at room temperature
Serves: 2

200g/7oz semola flour
10g/¼oz hemp flour
90ml/3fl oz tepid water

1. Mix the semola and hemp flours together in a bowl.
2. Tip the flour onto a wooden board and make a well in the centre.
3. Slowly add the tepid water and form a dough. Knead well for 7 minutes until the dough is smooth and elastic.
4. Cover and rest for 30 minutes at room temperature.

Blutnudeln (Italian Pasta Dough Using Pig's Blood)

From the snout to the tail, and beyond, there is no waste at all in this recipe and rightly so. Obviously, this may not be to everyone's taste; however, I embrace the use of blood as people do throughout many regions in Italy. The pasta tastes rich, and with the rye flour, it is robust yet warming, almost autumnal. You can serve this pasta simply with melted butter, but I prefer it with a drizzle of peppery extra virgin olive oil. You can increase the number of eggs and reduce the volume of blood if you prefer.

Preparation time: 15 minutes plus 30 minutes resting at room temperature
Serves: 2

150g/5oz rye flour, spelt or kamut
150g/5oz 00 flour
1 egg
120ml/4fl oz pig's blood (purchased from a good-quality butcher)

1. Pass the pig's blood through a sieve. Mix with the egg and set aside.
2. Combine both flours and tip them onto a wooden board.
3. Make a well in the centre of the flour.
4. Pour the blood mixture into the well and use a fork to combine.
5. Form the pasta into a ball of dough and knead it well for 7 minutes until soft and elastic.
6. Cover and rest the dough for 30 minutes at room temperature.

Flour blending

Blended pasta doughs use a mixture of different flours to add flavour. To make a blended pasta dough that will be well received, you need to use a flour that has a high gluten content. The gluten is what allows you to stretch and roll the pasta dough as required. If you want to use 00 flour or semola flour as your gluten flour, simply reduce the amount to 70 per cent and make up the 30 per cent with one of the flours below. Then make, knead and rest as you would a normal pasta dough.

Per portion, use $70g/2^{1}/_{2}oz$ of either 00 flour or semola flour plus $30g/1oz$ of one of the following gluten-free flours:

- Chestnut flour
- Chickpea flour
- Pea flour
- Fava bean flour
- Quinoa flour
- Lentil flour
- Nut flour such as hazelnut, pistachio or almond

You will also need a liquid ingredient such as an egg, aquafaba (chickpea water), mozzarella milk, pasta cooking water, rice cooking water or potato cooking water, or standard tepid water. (Remember to use a 2:50 ratio of dry to liquid ingredients.)

You could also change the blend of flour by using ancient grains such as farro, spelt, kamut or grano arso. Follow the 70:30 instructions above. This will add texture, aroma, and a welcome alternative bite.

Gluten-free and vegan pasta

What is gluten?

Gluten is the stretchy, glue-like substance that can be found in all grass-related wheat grains, namely wheat, barley, rye and spelt. Gluten allows your freshly made and worked dough to stretch, giving it a wonderful elasticity that makes it incredibly versatile and popular with those who make pasta, bread and pizza, to name but a few. That said, many flours will vary in terms of their percentage of gluten, meaning some flours will be stronger as they house more gluten, while some flours are lighter, having less gluten. Here, we will concentrate on flours that contain no gluten and learn how to make some fantastic pasta doughs.

While most of the ingredients in *Pasta Fresca* are easy to find and readily available, to make gluten-free pasta you may need to purchase a few ingredients ahead of time as some are not staples and may only be stocked by specialist suppliers.

Gluten-free flours and ingredients

These are some gluten-free grains, flours and starches that I like to use and would recommend:

- Almond flour – Made with blanched almonds. A great taste and interchangeable in many recipes.
- Black chickpea flour – Ground black chickpeas, leaving the flour with a speckled finish.
- Buckwheat flour – Buckwheat is a plant cultivated for its grain-like seeds that are then ground down into flour.
- Chestnut flour – A sweet yet mellow flour ground from chestnuts.
- Chickpea flour – Ground from fried chickpeas, this flour is very nutritious and high in protein.
- Cornflour – A starch used to thicken sauces.
- Fava bean flour – Ground fava beans.
- Hazelnut flour – Ground hazelnuts.
- Lentil flour – Ground lentils.
- Pea flour – Ground peas.
- Potato starch – Starch extracted from potatoes. Known in Italian as *fecola di patate*.
- Pumpkin flour – Ground pumpkin.
- Quinoa flour – An ancient grain, high in fibre, calcium and iron.
- Rice flour – Produced from milled rice grains. A thickening agent.
- Spirulina powder – Strong in flavour, use in small amounts.
- Tapioca flour – A sweet flour offering a sense of lightness to dough.
- Wheatgrass powder – Deep and rich in colour with an aroma of hay; use sparingly and in small amounts.
- Xanthan gum – Acts as a stabilizer and binding agent.

These ingredient suggestions will enable you to comfortably blend and work with doughs that you can trust and use repeatedly. Making gluten-free pasta is no easy task; however, gaining experience of how flour behaves when gluten is not present will help you a great deal.

Liquids

Choose your preferred liquid to make and combine your pasta dough. There are many options available to you. By varying the liquids you will also change and modify the flavour.

These recipes are made with large eggs, which weigh approximately 60g/2oz. Feel free to use egg with a combination of any other liquids to change the balance of flavour. Just be aware that as there is no gluten in these doughs, I would advise the use of at least one egg (or aquafaba which is a chickpea protein).

Other liquids you could use include:

- Aquafaba – The water from drained chickpeas (full of protein from the chickpeas).
- Pasta water, potato water or rice water – Salted water from boiling pasta, potatoes or rice.
- Mozzarella water – Liquid from a bag of fresh mozzarella. For each bag containing one portion of mozzarella you will obtain around 100ml/3$\frac{1}{2}$fl oz liquid.
- Stock – Any stock.
- Milk – Full fat or semi-skimmed.
- Butter whey.
- Cheese whey.
- Nut milks – As well as being gluten-free, these are vegan-friendly.

Gluten-free pasta dough

Gluten-free pasta doughs just need to be combined; they do not require kneading for long as there is no gluten to work. Please note the reduced resting time too.

Each recipe below requires only 5 minutes of preparation and kneading time, 10 minutes resting at room temperature and serves two (so multiply as required).

Basic Gluten-Free Pasta Dough

250g/9oz gluten-free flour (I would recommend Doves Farm)
½ tsp xanthan gum
1 tsp baking powder
2 eggs
1 tbsp extra virgin olive oil
3 tbsp water or aquafaba
Pinch of salt

Standard Gluten-Free Pasta

160g/5½oz rice flour
50g/1½oz potato starch
2 tbsp xanthan gum
Pinch of salt
1 tbsp cornflour
1 tbsp extra virgin olive oil
3 eggs

Quinoa Gluten-Free Pasta

60g/2oz potato starch
80g/3oz quinoa flour
70g/2½oz cornflour
1 tsp guar gum
2 tsp xanthan gum
Pinch of salt
2 whole eggs plus 4 yolks

Brown Rice Gluten-Free Pasta

190g/6½oz brown rice flour
60g/2oz tapioca starch
1 tsp xanthan gum
Pinch of salt
4 eggs

1. Choose your recipe, place all the ingredients into a small food processor and blitz to fully incorporate for 1 minute. I would normally make my pasta by hand but the food processor is my preferred choice for gluten-free dough.
2. Turn the dough out onto a wooden board and bring it together. Knead for 2 minutes until smooth. The kneading time is reduced due to no gluten being present.
3. Cover the dough and rest for 10 minutes at room temperature.
4. Cut the dough in half as this makes it much easier to work with. Wrap up one half and set aside.
5. You have two options available to you with regards to rolling the pasta dough: either use a rolling pin and roll the dough to your desired thickness, shape dependent, or use a pasta machine. Start at the widest setting. Take the dough and pat it down into a flat disc. Roll the dough through the widest setting twice. It is not necessary to fold the dough. Gluten-free pasta will react differently and will not be as firm as a traditional pasta dough, so please take your time. Remember there will be no natural stretch in the dough.
6. Change the setting to a slightly narrower width and pass the dough through twice on each setting.
7. Work your way through to the thinnest setting or until you have a pasta dough approximately 3mm/^{1}/$_8$in thick or to your desired thickness, depending on the shape.
8. Shape and cut as required.
9. Cook the pasta until *al dente* or air-dry on racks and freeze.

Vegan spinach dough (food processor method)

There are many pasta doughs that tick the vegan box in *Pasta Fresca* such as a simple semola di grano rimacinata and water dough, or even a 00 flour and aquafaba dough. This spinach dough offers the bonus of leafy greens and no added liquid.

This is a great recipe that requires only two ingredients, and it is totally foolproof. Due to the amount of natural water in spinach, no other moisture or liquid will be required. This method requires a food processor with a sharp blade in situ. Also refer to my avocado pasta dough recipe on page 13.

Preparation time: 5 minutes plus 30 minutes resting at room temperature
Serves: 4

> 300g/10½oz 00 flour or 300g/10½oz semola flour for a firmer dough
> 240g/8½oz spinach, fresh, unblanched

1. Put your chosen flour into the food processor.
2. Top the flour with the fresh spinach leaves and process on full speed for 2 minutes until the mixture fully incorporates and forms a ball of verdant dough; you will see the colour change to a deep yet vivid green.
3. Remove the ball of dough from the food processor and knead on a wooden surface for a few minutes until the dough has become elastic and pliable.
4. Cover the spinach dough with a clean tea towel and allow it to rest for 30 minutes at room temperature.

CARMELA'S TIP:
* The dough freezes well for up to 3 months.

Making Pasta

Rolling out pasta dough

Once you have made and rested your pasta dough, you can either work or roll the dough by hand using a very thin rolling pin (I use a wooden broom handle), or alternatively use a pasta machine. Using a pasta machine allows the dough to become silky and guarantees a smooth finish.

Using a pasta machine

It is always best to work with your pasta dough in smaller portions when using a pasta machine. Cut the dough in half. Take the first half and cover the remaining half to ensure the dough does not dry out and form an outer skin. You can also place a bowl over the dough.

1. Set the pasta machine to the widest setting. Each machine will differ so please follow your manufacturer's instructions.
2. Flatten your rested dough with your palms and knuckles. Lightly flour the dough, then feed it through the pasta machine on the widest setting. Fold the dough back over itself (like an envelope), pushing down once again with your knuckles, and feed through the widest setting again. Repeat this process six times. This will ensure smoothness and elasticity.
3. Increase the setting a notch at a time on the machine and feed the dough through each setting twice. There is no need to envelope the dough at this stage; you are just trying to lengthen it.
4. Continue rolling the dough, narrowing the rollers at every stage.

Remember that the thickness of your sheet will vary depending on your chosen pasta shape. I tend to stop at setting 6 on a Marcato Atlas machine for filled pasta sheets (approximately 2mm/$\frac{1}{16}$in thickness). I find this is the optimum thickness for filled pasta; you should be able to read a newspaper through the pasta sheet. For lasagne or chitarra pasta sheets I would roll to level 4 as you are looking for a thicker sheet.

Hand-rolled pasta sheet – the pasta tablecloth
La sfoglia

'*Sfogline* are known to say that the pasta dough is ready when you hear it sing.' To sing means you hear and feel bubbles popping as you knead the dough with the heels of your hands. *Sfogline* are ladies who specialise in rolling freshly made pasta dough into *una sfoglia*, a large see-through sheet of pasta.

You have the choice and ease of using a pasta machine nowadays, either a hand-cranked one that has pride of place on your kitchen surface or a modern electric machine with a specialist attachment. The *sfoglina* method is the traditional method used and preferred by the older generation of pasta-makers, the pasta-makers that we all look up to with great appreciation and thanks. Rolling with a pin is a great technique to master but requires skill and copious amounts of elbow grease and patience.

1. There is no need to halve the dough into portions when using this rolling pin method. Push the ball of dough into a large flat disc with the palms of your hands.
2. Flour the dough to prevent sticking. Place the rolling pin in the centre of the pasta dough and begin to roll as you would a sheet of pastry, working from the centre.
3. Roll the pasta dough, do not fold it. As the sheet becomes larger, gently hang it over the edge of the table and continue to roll from the centre, rolling outwards, then roll back to the centre. Hanging the sheet over the edge of the table will aid in stretching the dough.
4. Turn the dough sheet around 90 degrees (do this by rolling the pasta sheet around your rolling pin and turning it; this will prevent any careless tearing) and continue to roll it until you have reached the perfect smooth *sfoglia* sheet you require.

The thickness of the *sfoglia* will depend on the pasta shapes you intend to make. I always aim to make my sheet to approximately 3mm/^{1}/8in thick.

How to use a pasta extruder

A pasta extruder is a machine that pushes out a pasta shape with force through a chosen die. A pasta extruder can be a great investment, but the hand-cranked and turned styles can sometimes be tough to use; you need to have the strength and muscles of a superhero. Alas, I struggle with mine somewhat. Thankfully, there are some electric extruders on the market that make the job a pleasure and a whole lot easier.

When using an extruder, you need to manage the consistency of the base dough, which in fact is not a dough; it's more of a textured crumb. You are looking for a crumb that if squeezed together, holds well.

Please note all extruders work differently (refer to the manufacturer's instructions), and you will need to experiment, but a basic dough for you to try is: 100g/3^1/$_2$oz semola di grano duro rimacinata and 33ml/2 tbsp tepid water per person.

You will notice the level of liquid is only 33 per cent hydration. This is what makes the mixture more of a crumb than a standard coherent dough.

I prefer to put the flour in a food processor and slowly drip in the water and pulse. Then I tip the crumb mixture into the extruder.

Edible flower and herb pasta lamination

Soft edible herbs and petals can be gently pressed into pasta dough, creating a beautifully pressed sheet. I prefer to use whatever is seasonal – springtime wild garlic flowers, chive flower petals, violas, borage flowers, daisies and rose petals to name a few. You can also use any soft herbs with no stems. Flat leaf parsley, thyme, sage and basil are my favourites; just stay away from any woody herbs such as rosemary.

1. Make, knead and rest your chosen pasta dough.
2. Prepare your soft herbs or petals by making sure they are stem free and clean.
3. Roll your pasta dough out as you would a standard dough and stop at setting 4 (I use a Marcato Atlas 150 machine) on your pasta machine setting.
4. Lay your herbs or petals over one half the pasta sheet in any format and design you would like.

5. Fold the other half the pasta sheet over the petals and press down with your palms and knuckles to secure.
6. Set the pasta machine on to setting 3. Roll the sheet through the pasta machine once on settings 3, 4 and 5 and twice on number 6, without folding.
7. You should now have a beautifully decorated pasta sheet with a vintage style. Use as required.

Striping pasta

Striping pasta adds an extra creative dimension to the whole colouring pasta experience. Adding stripes to pasta is an art form and one of my favourite pastimes. Whenever I have coloured dough in my hand, a sense of design takes over. I prefer to make a standard egg-based pasta dough (page 6) as the base colour sheet and then use an additional two, three or four colours to add stripes. See pages 8–10 for coloured and flavoured pasta doughs.

Once the dough has rested, halve it with a knife (covering the remaining half in a clean tea towel to prevent it drying out) as this will make it much easier to work with. Roll the dough with either a pasta machine, rolling pin or wooden broom handle and then make your chosen shape.

When striping your pasta dough, you will need to work quickly to prevent the dough from drying out. Once your dough is rolled out, cover it with damp kitchen paper. When you are ready to work with the dough, simply discard the kitchen papers. You can now work at a slightly steadier pace.

You will need:

- Pasta machine (this will ensure precision and perfection)
- Small dough scraper
- 200g/7oz plain 00 fresh pasta dough or semola dough (for the base sheet)
- 100g/3½oz coloured dough of your choice, such as beetroot, tomato or spinach

1. Allow all the dough to rest fully before stretching.
2. Take the plain pasta dough and run it through the pasta machine as if making lasagne sheets. Try to not press the sheets any thinner than 4mm/⅛in. I normally roll my base sheet to level 4

on my Marcato pasta machine. Place the sheet on your work surface and cover with damp kitchen papers to prevent the dough from drying out.

3. Roll out the coloured pasta dough in the same way to level 4 of your pasta machine. Always flour the coloured dough well on both sides before rolling as in some instances this dough may hold a little more moisture than a standard plain pasta dough.

4. Allow the coloured sheets to dry for 10 minutes or so.

5. Run the coloured dough through the tagliatelle cutter on the pasta machine. Alternatively, flour the sheet, fold it like an envelope and manually cut it into tagliatelle strips with a sharp knife.

6. Take the plain dough and trim off both raw edges.

7. Take a strand of the coloured tagliatelle and lay it on the pasta sheet. Continue in this way, leaving small gaps as desired to make stripes. If your pasta is drying out, use a little water to fix the stripes in place.

8. Once the sheet has been fully striped with the coloured tagliatelle, trim the raw edges.

9. Using your palms, gently apply pressure to the striped pasta to ensure the strands are fixed and in place. Starting from the top left, push down with your fingertips and make sure each strand is sitting in place and there is no direct movement.

10. Lightly flour the pasta on both sides.

11. Set the pasta machine to number 3 (a medium setting) and start rolling the coloured sheet, once through on each setting until your desired thickness has been reached, approximately 3mm/^{1}/$_8$in.

12. To alternate the coloured pasta stripes, simply use two or three different colours.

13. Cut and shape the pasta as required.

Shaping pasta

Making pasta shapes by hand – unfilled

Making pasta by hand is such a cathartic task. It allows you to clear your mind and let your creativity flow. Allow plenty of time to make fresh pasta, as there are a few steps to follow in order to achieve a great dough as well as a delicious finished article. Below are a few of my favourite and most used unfilled and hand-formed pasta shapes.

Corzetti

Corzetti pasta is a flat, circular pasta shape from the region of Liguria. Carved wooden stamps are used to obtain the decorative design. Many years ago, affluent families would have their own wooden corzetti with their unique coat of arms embedded into the wooden disc. If you do not have a corzetti stamp, then just use a small glass or biscuit cutter with a diameter of 5–6cm/2–2^{1}/2in. Corzetti work incredibly well with a simple drizzle of pesto, tomato sauce or a heavier meat-based sauce (*sugo*).

Preparation time: 10 minutes plus 30 minutes resting the dough at room temperature
Serves: 4

1 egg
120ml/4fl oz white wine or vermouth
360g/12½oz 00 flour
Semola for kneading and dusting

1. Whisk the egg and wine together.
2. Tip the flour onto a wooden board (or into a bowl) and make a well in the centre.
3. Slowly pour in the wet ingredients.
4. Begin to combine the wet mixture with the flour, using either your fingers or a fork.
5. Form the paste into a ball and work the dough for 7 minutes until smooth. Cover and rest for 30 minutes at room temperature.
6. Roll out the corzetti dough using a large, thin rolling pin to the thickness of a 50p piece, or to setting 4 of your pasta machine.
7. Flour the corzetti stamps to stop the pasta from sticking.
8. Cut discs with the corzetti stamp cutter and then place the pre-cut disc onto the opposite side of the cutter. Take the stamp and push down on the pasta; this will imprint a design. Allow the corzetti to dry for 20 minutes and cook as required.

Malloreddus/gnocchetti sardi

Malloreddus or gnocchetti sardi are from the island of Sardinia.
They are a small, shell-like shape made from a simple dough of
water and semola di grano duro rimacinata flour. I use a gnocchi
board but equally you could use a flat grater, butter pat or sushi mat
to form the ridges. Malloreddus are small nuggets of pasta rolled
with your thumb to form ridges that house a small central funnel.
They are great collectors of sauce and are seriously scrumptious
with sausages, saffron and tomatoes.

Preparation time: 10 minutes
Serves: 4

400g/14oz semola pasta dough (page 4)

1. Flour your gnocchi board or chosen tool.
2. Pinch a blueberry-sized piece of dough. Roll it into a round.
3. Place the dough at the top of the gnocchi board and use your
   thumb to push the dough down; this should create a shell shape
   with a slight indent in the centre. Continue with the remaining
   dough.

Lasagne

Preparation time: 10 minutes, plus 15 minutes to air dry the pasta sheets
Serves: 4

400g/14oz fresh egg pasta dough (page 6)

1. Portion the dough in half and roll out with your pasta machine to setting 5. Cut lasagne sheets approximately 20cm x 10cm/8in x 4in.
2. Air dry the pasta sheets for 15 minutes.
3. Blanch each pasta sheet in a large pan of boiling water for 1 minute. Remove each sheet from the pan and place directly onto a clean tea towel to dry.

Strozzapreti

I was taught to make strozzapreti on a trip to Romagna by a wonderful lady called Nonna Violante. They are simple enough to master but a little time-consuming. This pasta shape is known as 'priest stranglers', as some combination of hunger and gluttony would make the priests eat so quickly that they would choke. I do love a good tale.

Preparation time: 10 minutes plus 30 minutes resting the dough at room temperature
Serves: 4

400g/14oz fresh egg pasta dough (page 6)

1. Halve the dough. Work with one portion of dough at a time to make it easier to roll out. Cover one half the dough and set aside until required.
2. Roll out the pasta dough, either with a thin rolling pin to the thickness of a lasagne sheet or use a pasta machine. I prefer to use my pasta machine and roll to the 5th setting.
3. Cut the pasta sheets into 30cm/12in lengths. Allow the sheets to sit for 5 minutes to air dry a little; this will prevent sticking.
4. Dust and pass each sheet through the tagliatelle attachment of your machine.
5. Take a tagliatelle and hold it at the top in between your palms.
6. Use your palms to roll the tagliatelle. Slide them one way and then the other; this will twist the pasta.
7. Once twisted, pinch the strozzapreti to detach it from the tagliatelle and continue with the remaining strands. Each strozzapreti should be around 8cm/3in in length, I normally suggest the width of your palm.

Sorpresa

Sorpresa resemble unfilled tortellini shaped like tiny belly buttons – there's something slightly erotic about them. Only two simple folds and a light pinch are required. If you have no pasta filling, then this shape is the one to make as the structure is robust and they can withstand a heavier sauce.

Preparation time: 10 minutes plus 30 minutes resting the dough at room temperature
Serves: 4

400g/14oz fresh egg pasta dough (page 6)

1. Divide the dough in half so you can work in sections. Roll out one half the dough either with a rolling pin or through a pasta machine; I roll to setting 5 of my Marcato machine.
2. Cut the dough into 4cm/1^{1}/$_{2}$in squares.
3. Take a square and make a triangle by pinching the opposite two corners together.
4. Then take the other two corners and pinch them together but encouraging the dough the opposite way.
5. Repeat with the remaining squares.

Lorighittas

From the region and island of Sardinia, lorighittas are delicate pasta ropes that take a little skill to master. The important point to follow is to knead the dough very well, as it needs to stretch well, and the pasta ropes need to be incredibly thin. Thick ropes will lead to a heavy pasta. The recipe below makes a 23cm/9in long pasta rope with a diameter of 1.5mm/^{1}/16in.

Preparation time: 10 minutes plus 30 minutes resting the dough at room temperature
Serves: 4

400g/14oz semola pasta dough (page 4)

1. Cut the dough into eight portions. Roll each portion out into long, thin sausages. Aim for a diameter of 1.5mm/^{1}/16in if you can manage it, or the thickness of a pici pasta.
2. Take the long pasta and double loop the dough around three fingers so that you have two pasta bracelets or loops around your three fingers. Pinch the surplus dough away to separate the length so you only have the two loops.
3. Twist the bracelets (or loops) into each other to create a rope effect. Place on a tray that has been lightly dusted with semola. Continue with the remaining dough and repeat as required.

Paccheri tubes

Paccheri is a wide-mouthed, versatile pasta tube. They can be filled and stood up in a bakeware dish like little toy soldiers, topped with sauce and baked, or spooned through a meat ragu. These are well worth learning how to make so you can add them to your pasta-making repertoire.

Preparation time: 10 minutes plus 30 minutes resting the dough at room temperature
Serves: 4

400g/14oz semola pasta dough (page 4)

1. Cut the dough in half and roll with either a rolling pin or a pasta machine to a 3mm/^{1}/8in thickness.
2. Cut the pasta sheet into 9cm x 4cm/3^1/2in x 1^1/2in pieces of dough, using all the dough as required.
3. To form the cylinder I use a dowel (purchased from a DIY shop, that has been cleaned with olive oil) that is approximately 3cm/1^1/4in in diameter and roll each piece of cut-out pasta dough around the dowel. Secure by overlapping the seams a little and applying pressure to fix in place.

Orecchiette

When I think of orecchiete, I think of the pasta nugget being dragged and flipped onto Nonna's thumb; she would then lay them into methodical rows. I long to create orecchiete that meet her quality-control standards. One day, maybe! Orecchiette are known as 'little ears'. Below is also my method for making the flat, textured version called strascinati; if you struggle with orecchiette, then these will hopefully be your saving grace.

Preparation time: 10 minutes plus 30 minutes resting the dough at room temperature
Serves: 4

400g/14oz semola pasta dough (page 4)

1. Portion the dough into four equal amounts and roll each section into long sausages. They should be the thickness of your little finger.
2. Cut each sausage into acorn-sized pieces of dough.
3. Take a knife (I use a large vintage butter knife with a thick blade) and place it on top of the piece of pasta, then drag the knife towards you as you hold the pasta on the back of the knife.
4. This will stretch the pasta as it curls around the knife. Form the dough over your thumb to leave an indent and repeat.
5. Alternatively, take an acorn piece of dough and push down firmly with your thumb indenting the pasta dough. This method is perfect for children to master – that said, I like this method too as my orecchiette are visually unappealing.

Strascinati (flat, dragged orecchiette)

Preparation time: 10 minutes plus 30 minutes resting the dough at room temperature
Serves: 4

400g/14oz semola pasta dough (page 4)

1. Portion the dough into four equal amounts and roll each section into a long sausage shape, the thickness of a sharpie.
2. Cut the sausage into small, acorn-sized pieces and, using your butter knife, drag the pasta towards you in a low, flat manner, grabbing the back piece of dough with your other thumb.
3. This should leave you with a flat, textured piece of pasta. I call these messed-up orecchiette.

Cicatelli/capunti

Cicatelli is the pasta shape I remember eating by the bowlful as a child, more than any other. It is a beautiful rope of pasta that is cut and indented with the tips of your fingers so that it looks very similar to the casing of empty pea pods. Nonna Carmela would make, dry and freeze bags full to the brim with cicatelli for the entire family so that we always had a little pasta *fatto a casa* (homemade pasta) to eat whenever we wanted.

Here is my guide on sizing and pairing:

1.5cm/½in	1 finger indent	soups
3cm/1¼in	2 finger indent	fish or vegetables
4cm/1½in	3 finger indent	fish or vegetables
5cm/2in	4 finger indent	meat

Preparation time: 10 minutes plus 30 minutes resting the dough at room temperature
Serves: 4

400g/14oz semola pasta dough (page 4)

1. Portion the dough into four equal amounts and roll each section into long sausages, the thickness of your little finger.
2. Cut each sausage into your chosen size.
3. Take a piece of your pasta, sit your required number of fingertips above it and push down, pulling slowly towards you, releasing the dough. This should leave you with a small piece of indented pasta. This shape is a great collector of sauce.
4. Repeat with the remaining dough.

Cavatelli/cazzarille/cecatidde/cecatielle

This shape can be made with a knife or a hand-cranked cavatelli machine that can be purchased online. Either method is great. The machine just requires a rope of dough to be continuously fed into its body while you turn the handle. With a knife it is even simpler.

Preparation time: 10 minutes plus 30 minutes resting the dough at room temperature
Serves: 4

400g/14oz semola pasta dough (page 4)

1. Portion the dough into four equal amounts and roll each section into long sausages, the thickness of a pencil.
2. Cut each sausage into 3cm/1¼in lengths.
3. Take each piece of pasta and use a blunt butter knife to drag it across your wooden board, to make a shape like a small butter curl. Repeat with the remaining dough.
4. To add a little extra flavour to the cavatelli dough you could substitute some of the semola for grano arso from page 20.

Autumn leaves (*Foglie d'ulivo*)

These most beautiful leaves will have you falling in love with the season of autumn. When you have mastered the shape, try making them with the spinach dough on page 11.

Preparation time: 10 minutes plus 30 minutes resting the dough at room temperature
Serves: 4

400g/14oz semola pasta dough (page 4)

1. Working with half the dough at a time, portion each half into six and roll into ropes of pasta, the thickness of a thin pencil.
2. Cut each rope into 3cm/1¼in lengths.
3. Take each piece and roll it in between the palms of your hands. This will leave you with a piece of pasta that is thin at both ends and full bodied in the middle.
4. Take the pasta and lay it down lengthways. Use your butter knife and drag down, holding the top of the pasta in place; this will form your leaf.
5. Repeat as required. I'd recommend that you use the spinach or tomato dough to make these, as the leaves look beautifully autumnal.

Trofie

From Liguria with love. Trofie are a semola-based twisted pasta, traditionally served with green beans, boiled potatoes and pesto Genovese.

Preparation time: 10 minutes plus 30 minutes resting the dough at room temperature
Serves: 4

400g/14oz semola pasta dough (page 4)

1. Working with half the dough at a time, portion each half into six and roll into ropes of pasta, the thickness of a thin pencil.
2. Cut each rope into 2cm/³⁄₄in lengths.
3. Take each piece and roll it between the palms of your hands. This will leave you with a piece of pasta that is thin at both ends and full-bodied in the middle.
4. The pasta can be cooked as it is now.
5. Alternatively, take the pasta and lay it down on the slant. Take your butter knife and pull the pasta from the top corner to the bottom – the pasta should twist. For a visual aid have a look at my YouTube channel, Carmela's Kitchen.

Fusilli, busiate, ricci

A very beautiful yet relatively simple pasta shape to master. This pasta lends itself to many names. To form the shape, I twist the pasta strips around my ferro. A ferro is a long piece of metal approximately 30cm/12in in length, the thickness of a piece of spaghetti, but with four sides. You could use long wooden barbecue skewers or a piece of spaghetti to form them. I call this pasta fusilli and this is my foolproof method.

Preparation time: 10 minutes plus 30 minutes resting the dough at room temperature
Serves: 4

400g/14oz semola pasta dough (page 4)

1. Roll out the rested pasta dough using a rolling pin to make a see-through sheet of dough, or use your pasta machine and roll to the 5th setting.
2. Allow the dough to rest again for 10 minutes. Sprinkle with flour and roll up the dough into a loose sausage.
3. Using a sharp knife, cut ribbons of dough the thickness of a tagliatelle.
4. Cut each tagliatelle into 10cm/4in strips.
5. Take a wooden skewer or piece of spaghetti, place it on one corner of the tagliatelle and roll, creating a twisted fusillo.
6. I leave the rolled fusillo on the skewer for 10 minutes to dry, and repeat with another skewer.
7. Remove all the skewers and allow the fusilli to dry for a further hour before cooking.

Maccheroni al ferro

An alternative to fusilli using the same dough.

Preparation time: 10 minutes plus 30 minutes resting the dough at room temperature
Serves: 4

400g/14oz semola pasta dough (page 4)

1. Portion the ball of dough into 10 pieces (cover what you are not using until required) and roll the portions into thin sausages (the thickness of a thin pencil).
2. Cut each sausage into 3cm/1¼in lengths and place the skewer on top of the piece of dough. Apply pressure and roll back and forth with the palm of your hand until the shape is made and you have an enclosed maccheroni with a hole running through the centre.

Grattini/grattoni

This pasta is universally loved and will help you use up any leftover pasta that has become a little dry and unworkable. I always prefer to make pasta scraps into something edible even if it creates only one portion. Grattini comes from the word *grattugiare*, meaning to grate. All you need to do is take leftover pasta, clump it all together, allow it to dry for an hour and grate (I prefer to use a grater with medium-sized holes), being careful to not catch your fingers. Add to soups for a little texture. If, however, you'd like to have a go at a slightly fancier grattini pasta, try this recipe.

Preparation time: 5 minutes
Cooking time: 7 minutes (or 1 hour to air dry)
Serves: 1

> 100g/3½oz semola di grano duro rimacinata,
> plus extra for kneading and dusting
> 1 egg
> 30g/1oz Parmigiano Reggiano, grated

1. Put the semola, egg and Parmigiano Reggiano into a food processor and pulse to a coarse loose mixture.
2. Tumble onto a baking tray and bake for 7 minutes at 190°C/170°C fan-assisted/Gas 5. Alternatively you can air dry the grattini for an hour or so and use as required.

Fregula/fregola

I always find fregula is a tricky recipe to create in specific amounts, so you will need to judge this one as you go. Refer to my Instagram (@carmelaskitchen) for a video guide. Fregula is wonderful in soups and sensationally scrumptious with fresh clams and cherry tomatoes.

Preparation time: 10 minutes, plus 1 hour to air dry
Serves: 2

200g/7oz semola di grano duro rimacinata
Tepid water, as required

1. Take a large bowl with high sides and add your semola.
2. Spray the flour with water (I use a spritz bottle) then make the fingers of one hand into a claw shape and rotate to stir the flour.
3. Alternatively you can drip in small amounts of water, just do this gradually.
4. You are looking for tiny balls of pasta, the size of pink peppercorns. When I make fregula I tend to make varying sizes: small, medium and large (*fino, medio* and *grosso*). Pass the fregula through a small colander. What passes through will be one size and what's left in the colander or sieve will be another size.
5. Leave the fregula to air dry on a tray or piece of muslin for at least an hour.
6. Serve as required. It takes only 2 minutes or so to cook, depending on size of course.

Maltagliati

The idea of maltagliati is that this pasta is made using up the scraps of pasta that are left when you are making another shape – the scrappy bits of pasta that you cut away. These remnants are then cut into small irregular shapes. I like to dry them and freeze them for an instant pasta soup directly from the freezer. However, if you would like to make this shape specifically:

1. Make an egg or semola pasta dough as above (page 4 or page 6).
2. Roll the pasta through your pasta machine or use a rolling pin; roll to 2mm^{1}/16in in thickness.
3. Using a knife or fluted pasta wheel, cut your pasta sheet into irregular shapes as required. You could of course be a little more specific and cut squares, triangles or rectangles. Use your imagination.

Making pasta shapes by hand – filled

What is your favourite filled pasta shape? For me this is an impossible question to answer as there are so many possibilities. Each shape has its own place and identity thanks to their unique shape. Filled pasta is endlessly versatile as you can mix and match pasta shapes, fillings and the sauce, be it a bowl of perfectly pinched tortellini in stock (brodo) or ravioli dressed with a classic tomato sugo.

For these filled pasta shapes, use the wonderful egg dough recipe found on page 6 and pair the dough with a chosen filling that can be found from page 60

For a touch of indulgence, remember that these small, filled pasta parcels can also be baked in the oven. Boil them first, then drain and dress with your chosen sauce and a few handfuls of Parmigiano Reggiano. Bake for 15–20 minutes until golden.

Here are a few classic methods for you to try.

Tortellini

Tiny tortellini remind me of little delicate belly buttons. Beautifully formed, they are delicious in either brodo (stock), browned butter and sage, or a simple seasonal tomato and basil sauce.

Serves: 4

400g/14oz fresh egg pasta dough (page 6)
Chosen filling (from page 60)

1. Cut the prepared pasta dough in half, cover one half the dough, and roll the remaining pasta out with either a pasta machine, rolling pin or broom handle to a thickness of 2mm/^{1}/$_{16}$in. I prefer to use my pasta machine and press the pasta into two large lasagne sheets.
2. Cut the pasta sheets into either 4cm x 4cm/1^1/$_2$in x 1^1/$_2$in squares, or small circles of approximately 5cm/2in diameter.
3. Add a teaspoon of the filling into the centre of each pasta shape.
4. Take the pasta in both hands and fold the pasta square in half to form a triangle. Or if using a circle shape, fold the pasta in half as if you were making a mezzaluna (half-moon).
5. Pinch the pasta dough around the filling, removing any excess air. Take the tortellini with the triangle pointing up towards the ceiling – or if you have made circles, point the curve to the ceiling. Take each corner and attach them together one in front of the other to create unique tortellini.
6. Repeat with the remaining pasta dough.
7. Cook in a medium pan of stock for 3 minutes. Ladle into bowls, then top with a little black pepper and Parmigiano Reggiano.

Ravioli

Simple filled pasta parcels – just choose your favourite filling and shape, from a simple square to a triangle or circle.

Serves: 4

400g/14oz fresh egg pasta dough (page 6)
Chosen filling (from page 60)

1. Cut the prepared pasta dough in half, cover one half the dough and roll out the remaining pasta with either a pasta machine, rolling pin or broom handle to a thickness of 2mm/^{1}/$_{16}$in. I prefer to use my pasta machine as it gives the pasta a silky finish. Press the pasta into two large lasagne sheets, approximately 15cm/6in wide.
2. Take one sheet and place a teaspoon of filling on the dough. Repeat across the length of the dough, leaving a gap of approximately 4cm/1^1/$_2$in between each mound.
3. Dip your finger in a little water and lightly dampen the area around the filling.
4. Place the top layer of pasta directly over the base sheet.
5. Gently use your hands to cup the pasta and filling, pushing out any excess air.
6. Seal the pasta around securely and use a pastry cutter or shaped cutter if you prefer to cut the ravioli.
7. Lay the ravioli on a tray that has been lightly dusted with semola and finish off making the rest with the remaining pasta.

Fresh egg yolk raviolo

Serves: 4

400g/14oz fresh egg pasta dough (page 6)
Chosen filling (from page 60)
XXX eggs

1. Make and roll your dough as the previous recipe and roll it into long sheets 40cm/16in in length, using your pasta machine or rolling pin. Use a 7cm/3in round cutter to cut multiple discs of dough as required.
2. Pipe your filling (I like to use a classic spinach and ricotta filling) onto one disc in a ring, leaving a 1cm/½in gap around the edge and ensuring there is enough room in the centre of the filling to drop in an egg yolk.
3. Break each egg individually and separate the white into a bowl. Drop the egg yolk into the centre of the filling and add a tiny pinch of coarse rock salt to the top of the yolk.
4. If required, dampen around the outside of the pasta disc with the egg white, or just use a slightly wet finger.
5. Place a disc of pasta on top and attach the two layers at one side. Gently pull the top disc and continue to attach all the way round, trying to eliminate any air. Ensure the raviolo is pinched all the way around. One raviolo would make a perfect starter.
6. Cook in salted boiling water for 2 minutes and 40 seconds, then serve with melted butter and sage.

Double ravioli (*Doppio ravioli*)

Serves: 4

400g/14oz fresh egg pasta dough (page 6)
Two chosen fillings (from page 60), half quantities of each

1. Make, prepare, and roll your pasta dough as page 53 into 60cm x 10cm/24in x 4in sheets, using all the pasta dough.
2. Prepare two fillings that would complement each other and place them into piping bags. For example, one could be a ricotta filling; the other a mixed mushroom and thyme filling.
3. Take a long sheet of pasta and pipe one flavour of filling along the length of the dough on one side, 2cm/1^3/4in from the edge.
4. Leave a 1cm/^{1}/2in gap and pipe the other flavoured filling along the inside of the first filling.
5. Fold the pasta sheet over and use a small wooden pin (the thickness of a pencil) to apply pressure in between the fillings, encouraging the pasta to sit proudly over each filling. Secure at the front, removing any excess air.
6. Pinch the dough including the fillings at 4cm/1^1/2in intervals all the way along, top and bottom.
7. Take a pastry roller and cut the dough along the pinched sections of dough. This will leave you with double ravioli –fiddly but truly fantastic.

Anolini

Anolini are in essence ravioli but without the pasta skirt that surrounds them. They are traditionally served on New Year's Eve in freshly made stock. They resemble small coins and are said to bring good luck! You will need a small circular cutter to make these little pillows. Anolini really are pasta dumplings; they are perfect if you are in the mood for filled pasta but would prefer a lighter option.

Serves: 4

400g/14oz fresh egg pasta dough (page 6)
Chosen filling (from page 60)

1. Cut the prepared pasta dough in half, cover and begin rolling the pasta. Roll the pasta out into long lasagne sheets using a pasta machine.
2. Take one sheet and place teaspoons of filling across the length of the dough, leaving an approximate gap of 4cm/1$\frac{1}{2}$in between the mounds.
3. Dip your finger in a little water and lightly dampen around the filling. Place the top layer of pasta directly over the base sheet.
4. Slowly use your hands to cup the pasta and filling, removing any excess air.
5. Seal around the pasta securely and use an anolini cutter (or a small 3cm/1$\frac{1}{4}$in biscuit cutter) to press down around each pasta mound. You will be left with tiny pasta dumplings, less a pasta skirt.
6. Lay the anolini on a tray that has been lightly dusted with semola and finish off the remaining pasta.

Caramelle

Pasta parcels that mimic the vintage style and look of sweeties, caramelle have plump centres and beautifully puckered edges. Versatile and wonderful with a sense of a special occasion.

Serves: 4

400g/14oz fresh egg pasta dough (page 6)
Chosen filling (from page 60) in a piping bag

1. Portion the prepared pasta dough in half, working with one half at a time.
2. Roll out the dough with your pasta machine or rolling pin to 2mm/^{1}/16in in thickness.
3. Cut the pasta sheets into 32cm/13in lengths.
4. Cut rectangles of dough 8cm/3in in length by 6.5cm/2^{1}/2in in width.
5. Using a piping bag, squeeze a tablespoon amount of the filling onto the centre of each square, leaving a 2cm/1^{3}/4in gap at each end.
6. Fold the length of dough over the filling to create a sausage.
7. Pinch the pasta dough where the filling finishes, leaving a frilly edge of pasta on each end.

Agnolotti

These are ravioli from the Piedmont region of Italy but are simply known by a different name, 'agnolotti'. The only difference is the way they are connected and pinched.

Serves: 4

400g/14oz fresh egg pasta dough (page 6)
Chosen filling (from page 60)

1. Cut the prepared pasta dough in half, cover one half the dough with a tea towel and roll the remaining pasta out with either a pasta machine, rolling pin or broom handle to a thickness of 2mm/^{1}/16in. I prefer to use my pasta machine and press the pasta into two large lasagne sheets.
2. Take one sheet and place teaspoon amounts of filling across the length of dough, leaving an approximate gap of 4cm/1^1/2in between the mounds.
3. Dip your finger in a little water and lightly dampen around the filling.
4. Place the top layer of pasta directly over the base sheet and filling.
5. Slowly use your hands to secure the pasta dough around the filling. Pinch the dough in between the agnolotti so that they are all attached.
6. Use a pastry cutter or sharp knife to cut across each attached pinched piece of dough to separate the agnolotti.
7. Lay the agnolotti on a tray that has been lightly dusted with semola and finish off making the remaining pasta.

Cappellacci/cappelletti

Let's finish with these beautifully pinched and pleated cappellacci.
A fold, a pinch and a tease to gently open up the fold. Cappellacci
are traditionally cooked in meat stock (broth).

Serves: 4

400g/14oz fresh egg pasta dough (page 6)
Chosen filling (from page 60)

1. Cut the prepared pasta dough in half, cover one half the dough
   and roll out the remaining pasta using either a pasta machine,
   rolling pin or broom handle to a thickness of 2mm/^{1}/16in. I prefer
   to use my pasta machine and cut the pasta into two large lasagne
   sheets.
2. Cut out 6cm/2^1/2in rounds (or squares) and spoon teaspoon
   amounts of filling into the centre of each disc.
3. Dip your finger in a little water and lightly dampen around each
   disc (only dampen if required). Seal each disc into a mezzaluna
   (half-moon) or into triangles if using squares.
4. Take the mezzaluna in your hand with the curve (or point) facing
   upwards, and gently pull the corners together.
5. Open out the back of the cappellacci a little, by folding the back
   out. Repeat as required.

Pasta fillings
Here are a few simple pasta fillings for you, with the aim of inspiring
you to try a new variety no matter what shape you choose to make.
My pasta fillings and choices are always guided by season, so through
the spring and summer months I enjoy lighter, almost creamy fillings
with a twist of lemon, while through the chilly autumn and winter
months I adore the woody bite of foraged and pan-fried mushrooms,
slow-cooked ragu and slow-roasted pumpkin or squash.

Each of these recipes makes enough to fill 400g/14oz pasta.

Mushroom filling

2 tbsp extra virgin olive oil
30g/1oz butter
350g/12½oz mushrooms, cubed
1 garlic clove, peeled, minced
450g/1lb ricotta, drained overnight
60g/2oz Parmigiano Reggiano, grated
¼ tsp freshly grated nutmeg
Salt and pepper, to season
1 tsp freshly chopped thyme

1. Heat the extra virgin olive oil and butter in a sauté pan over a medium heat.
2. Tumble in the prepared mushrooms and fry for 5 minutes.
3. Add the garlic and stir. Continue cooking for a further 3 minutes. Then remove from the heat.
4. In a bowl, place the ricotta, Parmigiano Reggiano and nutmeg. Stir well to incorporate.
5. Spoon the mushroom mixture into the ricotta mix and stir well. Season with salt, pepper and a little freshly chopped thyme.

Tortellini filling

25g/1oz butter
2 tbsp extra virgin olive oil
200g/7oz pork loin, fat removed, chopped
200g/7oz chicken thigh, boneless, chopped
200g/7oz prosciutto, sliced
200g/7oz mortadella, sliced
70g/2½oz Parmigiano Reggiano, grated
¼ tsp freshly grated nutmeg
Salt and pepper, to season
2 tbsp fresh parsley, finely chopped

1. Heat the butter and oil in a sauté pan over a medium heat.
2. Tumble in the pork, chicken, prosciutto and mortadella.
3. Fry over a medium heat for 15–20 minutes, or until cooked through. If the mixture becomes a little dry, add a tablespoon or two of water.
4. Remove the meat mixture from the heat and blitz in a food processor.
5. Scrape the mix into a bowl, add the Parmigiano Reggiano and nutmeg. Stir well.
6. Season as required with salt and pepper. Add the parsley.

Roasted butternut squash and Gorgonzola

400g/14oz butternut squash, cubed
40g/1½oz soft breadcrumbs
90g/3¼oz Parmigiano Reggiano, grated
70g/2½oz Gorgonzola, crumbled with a fork
2 egg yolks
Salt and pepper, to season

1. Preheat the oven to 200°C/180°C fan-assisted/Gas 6. Roast the butternut squash for 30 minutes or until golden and soft when pressed with a fork. Using a food processor or a potato masher, blitz or mash the roasted butternut squash for 30 seconds.
2. Scrape the butternut squash into a bowl and scatter in the breadcrumbs, Parmigiano Reggiano and crumbled Gorgonzola.
3. Stir well and add 2 egg yolks (retain the whites for meringues or add them to a frittata).
4. Season with salt and pepper, taste and adjust seasoning as required.

Gorgonzola, pear and pecorino

25g/1oz butter
2 tbsp water
250g/9oz pears, peeled, cored, tiny cubes
1 small lemon, zest only
150g/5oz Gorgonzola or Dolcelatte
40g pecorino, grated
Salt and pepper, to season
1 tsp fresh thyme leaves

1. Put the butter and water in a sauté pan and scatter in the tiny cubes of sweet pear. Fry these cubes off for 5–7 minutes or until softened. Add the lemon zest. Slice the remaining lemon and freeze for future use.
2. Remove the pan from the heat and tumble the contents into a bowl. Use a fork to break up the cubes, or use a potato masher for ease.
3. Add in the Gorgonzola and pecorino. Stir and season as required, and finish with the thyme leaves.

Breadcrumb filling

180g/6½oz stale breadcrumbs
40ml/1½fl oz chicken stock or water
120g/4oz Parmigiano Reggiano, grated
1 egg
½ tsp freshly grated nutmeg
1 large tbsp parsley, finely chopped
Salt and pepper, to season

1. Tip the breadcrumbs into a bowl and pour over the chicken stock. The stock can be replaced with water if preferred. Leave the breadcrumbs to steep for 10 minutes.
2. Move the breadcrumbs to a clean bowl, removing any excess stock. Add the Parmigiano Reggiano, egg and nutmeg to the bowl and stir. Scatter in the parsley and season with salt and pepper as required.

Sweet ricotta filling

250g/9oz ricotta, drained overnight
Zest of 1 small orange
50g/1½oz hazelnuts, finely chopped
50g/1½oz dark chocolate buttons
1 tbsp honey
1 tbsp vanilla icing sugar

1. Place the drained ricotta in a bowl and add the orange zest. Stir well.
2. Tumble in the chopped hazelnuts, dark chocolate buttons, honey and icing sugar. Mix well. This is perfect for both filled sweet pasta and also cannoli.

Cooking and storing pasta

In Italy, pasta is normally eaten as part of a four-plus-course meal, served after the antipasti starter, and is known as *primi*. The portions are generally a little smaller than we are used to here in the UK, normally around 70g/2^1/2oz of pasta per person. If, however, you are looking to serve pasta as a main meal, then I always suggest 100g/3^1/2oz per person. Please do not be too strict; the quantities I suggest are only guidelines and not rules.

Pasta is simple enough to cook correctly and yet it can very easily go terribly wrong with many simple factors playing a key role.

How to cook pasta

- Choose the type of pasta according to the sauce and dish you will be making. If you're making a particularly saucy pasta, I adore rigatoni *rigate*, which has a furrowed ridge that runs along or around the body of the pasta. This type tends to absorb the sauce more easily. Pasta that is smooth is known as *lisce*.
- Use a large saucepan, allowing the pasta room to move about.
- Salt the water. For every 100g/3^1/2oz of pasta you will need 1 litre/1^3/4 pints of water and 7–10g of salt, according to taste. No salt will mean no flavour.
- Every type of pasta has a different cooking time. Timings can differ from the brand of pasta to whether you are cooking dried pasta or fresh egg pasta; egg pasta cooks much more quickly than a semola pasta.
- For dried pasta (*pasta secca*) I recommend you follow the cooking instructions on the packet, but stop cooking 2 or even 3 minutes before the time given. This will leave you with an *al dente* bite every time. Remember, sometimes the pasta is also returned to a stove-top pan after draining to combine with a sauce, so this will also give it additional cooking time.
- Portion size is something that most people, especially Italian pasta-lovers, struggle with. I will always cook more because I adore leftovers and, in all honesty, I've been known to dive headfirst into a small bowl at breakfast time. The average standard portion size, as I said above, is 100g/3^1/2oz uncooked pasta per person for a main meal unless you are my mum, in

which case this will easily be doubled – this is another reason I love her so.

- Before we go any further, I think we need to dispel the myth of it being helpful to add oil to pasta water while cooking. Oil is NOT required. It will not stop pasta from sticking. The oil will simply sit on top of the water (as oil and water do not mix). A large pan and intermittent stirring of the pasta with a wooden spoon will prevent sticking. I only use a little oil in pasta water when I make *pastina* or soups such as minestrone. However, drizzle away with a good quality extra virgin olive oil to finish your plated-up dish; this will add flavour.
- Always reserve a cup or ladleful of the pasta water. This liquid is the elixir of life. It contains starch which helps the pasta and sauce come together in a silky finish. Add the pasta to the sauce, stir, add a little reserved pasta water and toss until the pasta is fully coated.

How to store fresh pasta

Storing fresh pasta correctly is vital because so much time and work goes into making it; we then need to make sure it is preserved correctly for longevity.

1. **Freezer** – I prefer to freeze fresh pasta, cooking it directly from frozen if I am not using it on the same day that it has been made. This will ensure the pasta holds its form and then you simply cook from frozen by adding a couple of extra minutes to the cooking time. Lay your ravioli or small pasta shapes on a tray in a layer. Freeze on the tray for 2 hours, then tumble into a container or freezer bags. Label and store for up to 3 months.

2. **Fridge** – Keep fresh pasta stored in the fridge for no longer than 36 hours, wrapped with a top blanket of cling film. Just be aware that the fridge can sometimes lead to a slight discoloration and greying in the pasta dough, especially with an egg-based dough.

3. Any short, unfilled pasta can be left for a few days on trays or tea towels that have been dusted with semola to dry fully. The pasta can then be stored in an airtight container for up to 6 months. Once dried, this type of pasta can also be frozen.

4. Long fresh pasta can be made and left to dry on wooden poles, racks, wooden hangers or on a *tacapasta*. The pasta can also be

rolled into loosely formed bird's nests. The nests need to be turned twice a day to allow plenty of air to circulate around the pasta as it dries. Allow seven days for the nests to dry fully and then store in airtight containers. This type of pasta can also be frozen once dried.

For further information and video aids please refer to my website www.carmelas-kitchen.com.

Pasta Essentials

Pasta kit and equipment

Only a *pastaia* (pasta maker) would feel heart-pounding excitement as much as I do when writing this chapter. I will take you into the depths of my beloved pasta room, sharing with you some of my most treasured pieces collected over the years, some of which I can't live without. Others I own just because I am a keen and passionate collector – some may even say obsessed!

All pasta-makers have certain preferences in how they choose to prepare and make pasta. A few of mine are that I prefer to work and knead on wood if possible. Wood offers a rough yet workable surface, which aids in the kneading of the dough. You can also use marble, granite or stainless steel.

I often use a rolling pin for making my pasta sheets, but I do prefer to use a pasta machine as I will always obtain a beautiful silky dough.

Please do not take this list as gospel or as a total must-have as I will always offer recommendations and alternatives throughout the book for you to use if you don't have these tools to hand.

Taking care of your pasta tools

High-quality pasta tools are not cheap, from boards to stamps and pasta machines. Buying quality means you will hopefully only buy once, but you *must* look after them well with care, and then they will be with you for many years to come.

1. Never fully immerse or wash your wooden boards or corzetti stamps in a sink of water. Allow the pasta to dry on them, then simply brush away. I often use a cocktail stick to get into any intricate spaces.

2. Never clean your pasta machine with a wet cloth or spray. As above, allow the pasta to dry on the machine and simply brush off with a soft brush. Moisture will ruin your equipment.

Pasta tools

- Wooden board – A large board with a wooden lip or ledge to secure and prevent movement on your work surface. Mine vary in size but my most-used board measures 63cm x 50cm x 6cm/25in x 20in x $2^{1}/_{2}$in.

- Rolling pin – I have three different lengths, but my preference is to use a thin broom handle. If you do not have a rolling pin or a clean useable broom handle, then a wine bottle will do the job perfectly too. Always remember, the thinner the rolling pin the thinner the pasta.
- Pasta machine – Not an essential, however I prefer to use a machine in order to achieve uniformity, a level thickness and a smooth, flawless surface. My preferred brand is Marcato and I use their Atlas 150. These machines are available in all manner of colours with a vast range of attachments. An electric motor is also available for this machine.
- Pasta wheel – Also known as a pastry roller. Use either a plain edge or a fluted edge for forming shapes and sheeting.
- Butter knife for forming and dragging pasta (to make orecchiette or strascinati).
- Large flat-blade knife – For slicing and cutting pasta by hand to make tagliolini, tagliatelle and pappardelle.
- Digital scales – For precision weighing.
- Bench scraper (*raschietto*) – For scraping and portioning dough. I prefer a steel blade, not plastic.
- Small brush – Natural hair, to brush and clean tools, boards and machines.
- Cutters – Come in different sizes and different shapes, such as round, square, etc.
- Decorative stamps – Designs and presses to shape your filled pasta.
- Short empty glass bottle – You will use the head of this bottle to form beautiful cappelli pasta hats. Then I store wooden skewers in the bottle.
- Tablecloth – For drying pasta (I use Nonna Carmela's cotton tablecloth).
- Trays or paper trays – For drying pasta.
- Stackable drying racks – Great for a keen pasta-maker.
- Ferro – Square-sided, 30cm/12in in length; or wooden skewers.
- Gnocchetti board – Or use a comb, a sushi mat, the back of a grater or a reed dinner mat.
- Spätzle maker – A flat disc with holes or a grater-style spätzle maker. Alternatively, you can use a colander with large holes.
- Pasta bike – This is a multi-wheeled cutter that can expand and contract with five cutters. Use it to cut your pasta sheet

effortlessly (it is great for precise tortellini squares).

- Raviolamp – Marcato ravioli tablet, for flawless identical ravioli every time.
- Small pin – The size of a thin pencil, to help you form garagnelli pasta.
- Sardinian reed basket (also known as a *ciurili*) – To make traditional gnocchetti sardi.
- Corzetti stamps – Wooden stamps, hand-crafted with many designs. Mine are all handmade by Filippo Romangoli, with designs ranging from an octopus to a floral design and Christmas tree.
- Piping bags – For ease of filling your filled pasta or cannelloni.
- Food processor – To help you make coloured pasta dough.
- Extruder – These come in various styles and sizes, from a hand-turned style to a larger electric version with lots of different changeable dies to extrude pasta shapes.

Larder and pantry ingredients

In order to produce simple, affordable, healthy dishes you will need to have a well-stocked larder, fridge and freezer. Here are my essential ingredients and staples to aid you in your cooking.

Larder
OILS
- Extra virgin olive oil, for light frying, finishing off dishes and salads (I use Filippo Berio)
- Regular olive oil, for drizzling and light frying
- Sunflower oil, for deep-frying

VINEGARS
- An aged balsamic from Modena: I urge you not to buy one from the supermarket, but to search one out independently. I use the Giuseppe Giusti brand. I have visited the farm in Modena and adore the aroma and thickness that comes from every drop.
- Red wine vinegar
- White wine vinegar

TINS AND NON-PERISHABLE INGREDIENTS

A store cupboard full of tinned tomatoes and beans provides a basis for many dishes.

- Passata (I use Mutti and Cirio brands)
- Polpa (tomato pulp – I use Mutti)
- Sun-dried tomatoes
- Tinned beans: cannellini, chickpeas, butter beans, borlotti beans
- Tinned fruit
- Tinned lentils
- Tinned plum tomatoes
- Tomato purée, to add flavour to soups, stocks and sauces

JARRED INGREDIENTS
- Anchovy fillets, in brine, oil and salted: these subtly melt away while leaving a pleasant depth of saltiness to any dish
- Capers, in brine and salted: these berries add texture to dishes
- Mostarda di frutta (Cremona): fruits steeped in a mustard syrup
- Olives (a variety of green and black) with stones, in brine
- Roasted red peppers

DRIED HERBS, SPICES AND STOCK
Dried herbs and spices are essential store-cupboard ingredients. Just always remember that dried herbs have a more concentrated flavour than fresh and should be used sparingly. Also, ideally use them within their 'best before' date, before they lose their intensity.
- Basil
- Chilli flakes
- Fennel seeds
- Marjoram
- Oregano
- Pepper, black, freshly ground
- Salt and rock salt (I use Maldon)
- Stock cubes: chicken, vegetable, beef (use good-quality brands)
- Thyme
- Vanilla: extract and whole pods

FLOUR
- 0 flour, for making bread, pasta and cakes
- 00 flour, an essential flour for making pasta, pizza and cakes
- Self-raising flour: a staple flour for cake making
- Semola/semolina flour (an Italian durum wheat flour): perfect for bread and pasta

- Strong white bread flour: I use this combined with other flours to change the gluten levels and strength of doughs

BAKING
- Chocolate spread: I like Pan di Stelle
- Dried fruit: sultanas, raisins
- Ground almonds
- Hard amaretto biscuits: I crush them and use them as a topping for tiramisu, cakes or ice cream
- Jam (flavour of your choice)
- Leaf gelatine
- Mixed nuts: walnuts, hazelnuts, pistachio nuts, pine nuts, almonds
- Pane degli angeli: a traditional baking powder used in a range of Italian cakes and desserts

DRIED PASTA, SUGAR, PULSES AND GRAINS
- Breadcrumbs, stale/dried
- Lentils: red and green
- Polenta: instant
- Rice: arborio, carnaroli and vialone nano (I use the Riso Gallo brand)
- Spaghetti, bucatini, ditalini, penne, trofie, rigatoni
- Sugar: caster, granulated, golden

Fridge
FRESH HERBS AND SPICES
It is always preferable to use fresh herbs wherever possible, as they add a delicate flavour to any given dish. I use fresh herbs during each stage of cooking. Usually I add the chopped stems to a soffritto, then the leaves midway through cooking and also at the end as a garnish.
- Basil
- Bay
- Fresh red chilli
- Marjoram
- Oregano
- Rosemary
- Sage
- Thyme

DAIRY

- Butter: I use salted butter for all my needs
- Cream: single and double
- Eggs: all the eggs used in this book are large and free range
- Lard: pork lard, known in Italian as *strutto*
- Milk: full fat

CHEESE

- Buffalo mozzarella: torn into a salad – never cooked – as it is delicious simply dressed with a little extra virgin olive oil, salt and balsamic vinegar
- Dolcelatte: the sweeter and younger variety of Gorgonzola
- Fontina: a semi-hard cheese, creamy in texture and perfect for melting
- Grana Padano: not as crumbly as Parmigiano Reggiano, this makes for a great alternative with nutty, sweeter notes of flavour.
- Gorgonzola: mild and creamy cheese with a blue vein
- Mascarpone: perfect for tiramisu, in desserts, stirred through roasted butternut squash and used to fill ravioli
- Mozzarella: made with cow's milk. Ideal to freeze and have in stock for using in layered pasta dishes and for topping pizza
- Parmigiano Reggiano: grate into pasta, risotto and more (never buy it pre-grated). Grated Parmigiano keeps incredibly well in the freezer
- Pecorino Romano: sheep's cheese and an alternative to Parmigiano
- Provolone piccante: a southern Italian cheese that is smooth in texture. Sliced thinly and eaten with bread, this is my father Rocco's and my favourite cheese
- Ricotta: ricotta does not melt ('ricotta' means 're-cooked'). Ideally, buy it from an Italian deli, or from a supermarket. I always choose the Galbani brand
- Stracchino: a soft cheese, delicious scraped onto bread, spooned through pasta or served with a little honey
- Taleggio: made with cow's milk and semi-soft; very delicious
- Tomino: from Piedmont, ideal for baking

CURED MEAT

- Bresaola: air-dried lean beef
- Coppa: thinly sliced, dry-cured whole pork shoulder or neck

- Guanciale: pig's cheek, delicious finely cubed in place of pancetta in a carbonara
- Mortadella: re-formed pork that is very delicious thinly sliced as part of an antipasti platter
- Pancetta: from the pork belly area, thinly sliced or cubed
- Prosciutto cotto: cooked ham
- Prosciutto crudo: Parma ham
- Salami: Milano, Napoli, ventricina, finocchiona
- Speck: a cured and smoked ham, made from the hind leg of the pig, from the Trentino-Alto Adige region of Italy

FRESH VEGETABLES
- Fennel bulb: an alternative to celery, and great in a soffritto
- Garlic: fresh bulbs
- Shallots, celery and carrots: make the perfect soffritto, the base of many Italian sauces. You will notice that throughout this book I have chosen to use shallots instead of onions, as I find them easier to peel and prepare, and they're also a little sweeter.
- Vine tomatoes: cherry and plum, with the vines attached, kept at room temperature

Freezer
- Broad beans
- Gelato
- Mixed berries
- Mozzarella
- Parmigiano Reggiano rinds
- Peas

LIQUOR
- Amaretto
- Frangelico
- Marsala
- Red vermouth
- Tia Maria
- White vermouth

Alongside all the above, you will just need to add leafy vegetables, root vegetables, fresh meat, fish and seafood.

Cook's notes

How to sterilise jars
To sterilise your bottles or jars, wash them and put them in a low oven – about 160°C/140°C fan-assisted/Gas 3) – until ready to fill, or put them in the dishwasher on a hot cycle with no detergent. Wash any rubber seals separately and dry them before filling and sealing the jars.

How to make breadcrumbs
Preheat the oven to 180°C/160°C fan-assisted/Gas 4). Blitz stale bread in a food processor until it forms crumbs, spread out on a baking tray and bake in the oven for 15 minutes. Remove from the oven and allow to cool, then return to the processor to blitz once again. Store in an airtight container for up to 3 months. I also use stale breadcrumbs, that are just blitzed in a food processor and not oven-dried, for ease and speed.

Leftover egg whites
Freeze leftover egg whites for up to 6 months. They are ideal for whipping up meringues or a seasonal frittata.

Carmela's essential cookery tips
- Please do not discard Parmigiano Reggiano rinds: they can be used in stocks, soups and risottos as flavour enhancers, particularly when a dish is slow cooked. They also freeze well.
- Tomato vines can be added to soups, pasta water, *sugo* and standard sauces and stocks for added flavour. Once used, simply discard.
- When cooking fresh pasta, add a tablespoon of semola or 00 flour to the water once boiling point has been reached and prior to salting the water. The reason for this is that fresh pasta only takes 3 or 4 minutes to cook, so the water will have limited flavour, which is not what you want if you require the pasta water to emulsify your sauce. The flour releases gluten into the water, helping the pasta water thicken and emulsify your chosen sauce.
- Do not discard the milky liquid from a bag of fresh mozzarella. Added to flour to make pasta, bread or pizza dough, it gives dough a delicate salty flavour and encompasses the *cucina*

povera style of cooking. Alternatively, add it to stock, soups, or even your pasta cooking water.

General information
A few notes to help you work your way through the book.
- Pasta machine: Please note that the pasta machine I use is a Marcato Atlas 150; other pasta machines may vary in terms of settings.
- Eggs: Are always large and held at room temperature, never fridge cold.
- Season to taste: Add as much salt and pepper as you would like, to your taste.
- Butter: When butter is mentioned I use salted.
- Garlic: Minced means grated, however you can crush and finely chop if preferred.
- Extra virgin olive oil: I prefer to use extra virgin olive oil, but feel free to substitute olive oil, offering a lighter taste.
- Shallots: I use banana shallots, large and long in size as opposed to small, round, fiddly pearl shallots.
- Salt: I use Maldon salt.
- Semola pasta: When checking if semola pasta is ready, simply cut or bite a piece in half. You need to make sure there is not white flour in the centre; the pasta should be translucent all the way through.
- Ricotta: When using ricotta as a filling or in any of my recipes, I prefer to leave the ricotta in a sieve over a bowl in the fridge overnight. This is not necessary with a high-quality Italian ricotta but alas the UK supermarket ricottas seem to be incredibly wet, hence the benefit of an overnight drain.
- Nuts: Please note that sunflower seeds can be used to replace nuts in the recipes.
- Soffritto: When time allows, I prefer to batch-make soffritto, then portion and freeze it. Simply peel and cube shallots, celery and carrots, mix and bag, then freeze. This way you can add more of one vegetable and reduce another according to your own personal preferences, and it makes the primary stages of many dishes a little easier. Cook straight from frozen.
- Lazy garlic: Yes, I cheat on occasion and when I am pressed for time, I find myself cheating most of the time. Sterilise a jar. Peel

a load of garlic cloves and blitz in a food processor. Scrape into the jar and top with extra virgin olive oil. Store in the fridge and use a small teaspoon amount instead of 2 cloves.

Online stockists

Please find below a list of some of my favourite stockists for both Italian ingredients and pasta tools.

Firstly, I must include my local Italian deli, 'The Italian Shop' in Northampton, because without my good friend Adriana Staniscia's shop, I could simply not meet my day-to-day needs.

FOR INGREDIENTS

www.latriestina.co.uk: I adore their guanciale

https://www.melburyandappleton.co.uk: Great for general Italian larder goods

www.vorrei.co.uk: Wonderful range of larder goods

www.natoora.co.uk: Amazing fresh fruit and vegetables

www.seedsofitaly.com: Grow your own seeds and deli goods

www.mydelibox.com: Great Italian brands

www.linastores.co.uk: London deli (My favourite)

www.delitalia.co.uk: Online deli, fantastic selection of goods direct from Italy

www.olianas.co.uk: Sardinian born, Olianas owner Mario now makes a range of award-winning Italian cheeses in Leeds

FOR PASTA TOOLS

www.marcato.it: For the best pasta machines and high-quality pasta attachments and tools. Made 100 per cent in Italy.

www.carmelas-kitchen.com: My own range of ravioli moulds and gnocchi boards.

www.romagnolipastatools.com: Beautifully crafted corzetti stamps and rolling pins from Tuscany

www.tagliapasta.com: Pasta tools and general equipment

www.giordis.com: Pasta boards and moulds

www.etsy.com/shop/44HandMadeTurkey: Handmade wooden pasta moulds and boards

@Wooden_essentials (Instagram): Beautiful wooden boards, pins and corzetti stamps

Stocks, sauces and dressings

The early stages of a dish, the tentative preparation and methodical planning, always excite the constantly hungry girl in me. That said, I am not the best at pre-planning a weekly meal schedule. More often than not, I tend to rescue myself because I always have a sauce or stock bubbling away on the stove.

Sauce, stocks and dressings can make or save the meal. I basically choose a sauce and build my dish around it. I find that, by having a fresh vegetable stock or tomato sauce at hand, you can easily adapt them, just by adding a little browned meat or fish.

This sauces chapter has a diverse range of basic sauces, stocks and dressings that take the bare minimum of effort to master. Simplicity is key in many dishes, and this is true whether you're showcasing the best of the *cucina povera* style of the south, or any other region of Italy.

A note on *La Tassa*:

My mum Solidea speaks very fondly of the worker's lunchtime pasta, *La Tassa* and her childhood memories of my grandfather, Nonno Angelo, eating bowls filled to the brim with pasta and raw red wine, yet you never see it written about. Perhaps they are only fond of it over in the region of Molise where my mum's side of the family are from. All you need to do is boil a little pasta until it's *al dente*; a short shape works best. Drain and tumble the pasta back into the saucepan, reserving a small ladle of pasta water. Pour a small glass of red wine over the pasta and add a little pasta water. Ladle into warmed bowls with no cheese.

Beef stock (*Brodo di carne*)

Beef stock is a classic stock, a foundation that makes a great base for soups. Ask your butcher for any unwanted bones; they tend to give these away happily for stocks and soups. The bones do add a certain something so it's well worth the ask.

Preparation time: 15 minutes
Cooking time: 3 hours
Makes: 3 litres/5¼ pints

1kg/2lb 4oz stewing beef, plus a few bones
4 litres/7 pints water
2 carrots, chopped
3 shallots, quartered
2 celery stalks, chopped
2 bay leaves
Small bunch of parsley, including stalks, chopped
2 tbsp chopped celery leaves
Salt, to season
8 peppercorns (I like to use mixed peppercorns)

1. Lay the beef (and bones, if using) in a large heavy-bottomed saucepan, if using the bones, add them in now. Top with water and bring to a boil.
2. Remove any froth or scum from the top of the pan with a spoon and discard.
3. Add the remaining stock ingredients. I do not peel the vegetables, but if you prefer to, then please go ahead.
4. Cook the stock over a medium simmer for 3 hours, removing scum from the top of the water as you go.
5. Once the stock is ready, remove the beef and set aside for another dish.
6. Drain the stock through a sieve, taste and season.
7. Allow the stock to cool fully at room temperature then remove any settled fat from the top.
8. Refrigerate the stock and use within 3 days, or freeze for up to 3 months.

Chicken stock (*Brodo di pollo*)

Stop press! My children make a weekly request for fresh stock so that they can make and eat their fix of pastina whenever required. I feel as if I have been passed the baton in a race and I have finally taken the lead. Even though Nonna Carmela and my beautiful mamma Solidea still make great stocks, I feel as if my time to shine has finally arrived.

Preparation time: 15 minutes
Cooking time: 2 hours
Makes: 3 litres/5¼ pints

> 1.8kg/4lb chicken pieces – use legs, thighs, wings, breast
> Small bunch of parsley, including stalks, finely chopped
> Small bunch of celery leaves, roughly chopped
> 2 shallots, halved, skins on
> 3 carrots, roughly chopped
> 3 celery stalks, roughly chopped
> 2 medium potatoes, quartered
> 4 litres/7 pints water
> Salt and pepper, to season

1. Place all the ingredients in a saucepan and bring to a boil.
2. Skim off any bubbling froth or scum from the surface with a spoon and discard.
3. Reduce the heat, cover the pan with a lid, leaving a little gap, and simmer for 2 hours.
4. Remove the tender chicken and enjoy with a salad, shredded into soup or eaten as your *secondo*.
5. Pass the stock through a sieve and push the vegetables down using a potato masher or the back of a large wooden spoon.
6. Scrape the base of the sieve and drop the smooth vegetable pulp into the stock. Taste and season.
7. Chill and refrigerate for up to 3 days or freeze in small stock bags for up to 3 months.

Fish stock (*Brodo di pesce*)

A well-made stock can change a basic dish into something truly spectacular, from a wonderful soup to the most extravagant risotto. Remember that all ingredients are totally interchangeable: you can use washed and chopped leeks instead of shallots or onions, or celery instead of rotund and incredibly aromatic fennel. I really prefer the addition of fennel in this stock because the aniseed flavour works so well with fish.

Preparation time: 15 minutes
Cooking time: 1 hour 15 minutes
Makes: 2.2 litres/3³/₄ pints

1.2kg/2½lb white fish (to include heads, bones, etc)
4 litres/7 pints cold water
1 shallot, peeled, quartered
1 bulb fennel, quartered and finely chopped
(including the fluffy fennel fronds)
2 carrots, finely sliced
2 garlic cloves, peeled
4 litres/7 pints cold water
Bunch of parsley, including stems, chopped
1 tbsp celery leaves, chopped
1 tsp fennel seeds
Salt and pepper, to season

1. Prepare the fish by rinsing it well in cold water.
2. Place the fish into a saucepan.
3. Add the shallot, fennel, carrots and garlic cloves to the pan with the fish and add the water.
4. Bring the pan to a rolling boil and add the parsley, celery leaves and fennel seeds.
5. Season with salt and pepper and simmer for 1 hour and 15 minutes.

6. Intermittently you will need to remove the froth or murky scum that sits on top of the water. Just scoop this away with a spoon and discard.
7. Pass the ingredients through a sieve and using the back of a spoon, gently push any excess juice and goodness through the sieve.
8. Discard the fish bones and vegetables.
9. Taste and season the stock and use as required.

CARMELA'S TIP:

• Try and steer clear of oily fish when it comes to making fish stock.

Vegetable stock (*Brodo vegetale*)

In my opinion this is the most used of my stocks as I can cover many bases with it. Simple it may be, but the vegetables are slowly bubbled away with a Parmigiano Reggiano rind and fresh herbs before being pushed through a sieve. There is lots of goodness in this most incredible stock, great for pastina, minestrone bases, risotto, to loosen sauces and to float and carry tortellini in their most favoured way.

Preparation time: 5 minutes
Cooking time: 1 hour 30 minutes
Makes: 1.8 litres/3 pints

2 shallots, unpeeled, quartered
2 carrots, unpeeled, chopped into 3cm/1in pieces
2 celery stalks, chopped into 2.5cm/1in pieces
2 garlic cloves, squashed, skins on
4–6 large ripe tomatoes, quartered
2 potatoes, skins on, quartered
1 Parmigiano Reggiano rind (optional)
Bunch of celery leaves, roughly chopped
Bunch of basil, torn
Parsley stalks, roughly chopped
2.5 litres/4pt 7fl oz water
Salt and pepper, to season

1. Place all the ingredients in a saucepan apart from the salt and pepper.
2. Simmer for 1 hour 30 minutes over a medium heat.
3. Using a potato masher, carefully mash the vegetables in the pan to break them up.

4. Pass the stock through a sieve and once again use the potato masher to push all the goodness through the sieve, leaving the dense pulp behind.
5. Take a spoon and scrape the base of the sieve, adding the puréed pulp back into the stock.
6. Place the stock back onto the heat and cook for a further 15 minutes. Season to taste as required. Prior to serving, remove the Parmigiano Reggiano rind – this is the chef's perk to nibble on.

CARMELA'S TIP:

-   I often form the mashed veg into fritters by adding a couple of tablespoons of flour, a little cheese and some fresh herbs. Fry until golden.

Bolognese ragu, from 'The Accademia Italiana della Cucina' (*Bolognese ragu*)

This first Bolognese recipe is inspired by 'The Accademia Italiana della Cucina', which was registered in the city of Bologna on 17 October 1982. The variations of bolognese are truly endless, and every family, whether they be in the UK or happily living in one of the 20 regions of Italy, will have their own take on this much-loved and respected classic recipe.

Preparation time: 15 minutes
Cooking time: 2 hours 45 minutes
Serves: 4

150g/5oz pancetta, chopped into small cubes
20g/¾oz butter
1 tbsp extra virgin olive oil
50g/1½oz carrots, peeled, finely chopped
50g/1½oz celery, finely chopped
50g/1½oz onion, peeled, finely chopped
300g/10½oz beef, coarsely minced
125ml/4fl oz red wine
300ml/^{1}/2pint/11fl oz passata or pelati tomatoes
150ml/^{1}/4pint/5½fl oz whole milk
Salt and pepper, to season
2 tbsp cream to finish (optional)

1. Put the pancetta into a dry saucepan and fry over a low heat until lightly coloured.
2. Add the butter and olive oil along with the carrot, celery and onion. Cook for 15 minutes over a medium heat until softened and translucent.
3. Add the beef and cook for 10 minutes until seared all over.
4. Pour in the red wine and stir, cooking out the wine until almost evaporated.

5. Add the passata or pelati tomatoes and stir. Season with salt and pepper. Cook for 2 hours over a low heat, remembering to stir intermittently.
6. Stir the pan, slowly add the milk, adjust seasoning as required and cook for a further 30 minutes.
7. If using cream, add this to the sauce and stir, just before serving. Serve with tagliatelle.

Carmela's Bolognese sauce (*Bolognese sugo*)

Here is my beloved recipe that I have been feeding to the masses for years, but I am also forever changing it, from the proportions of the chosen meat and the variety, to the choice of tomatoes and dried herbs. So please feel free to do the same if you so wish. With the 'Accademia' version and my own version, you are sure to find a happy medium.

Preparation time: 20 minutes
Cooking time: 3 hours
Serves: 6

4 tbsp extra virgin olive oil
1 shallot, peeled, finely cubed
1 carrot, peeled, finely cubed
1 stick celery, finely cubed
400g/14oz veal mince
1 tbsp tomato purée
670ml/1^1/$_4$ pints passata
100ml/3½fl oz water
1 Parmigiano Reggiano rind
1 garlic clove, peeled, minced
1 tbsp celery leaves, chopped
¼ tsp dried oregano
Salt and pepper, to season
Small bunch of basil, roughly torn

1. Pour the olive oil into a saucepan and add the shallot, carrot, and celery.
2. Cook over a medium heat for 15 minutes or until tender.
3. Tumble in the veal mince and stir. Sear all over until coloured, about 5–7 minutes.
4. Add the tomato purée and coat the mixture. Stir well.
5. Pour in the passata and rinse out the packaging with the 100ml/3^1/$_2$fl oz water, which also goes into the mixture. Stir the sauce.

6. Lay the Parmigiano Reggiano rind into the sauce and add the garlic, celery leaves and oregano.
7. Stir and season with salt and pepper.
8. Cook over a low heat for 3 hours, uncovered. Add a few basil leaves, reserving a few for serving.
9. Stir intermittently. If the sauce has dried out a little, add a little more water. Prior to serving, remove the Parmigiano Reggiano rind – this is the chef's perk to nibble on.

CARMELA'S TIP:
- Double up quantities for unadulterated happiness.

Crushed cherry tomato sauce
(*Sugo di pomodorini*)

This is my youngest daughter Chiara's favourite sauce. She loves the speed and simplicity of the sauce and enjoys it with a short, firm semola-based pasta such as cavatelli, cicatelli or malloreddus, which are all textured with ridges to grab and carry the sauce. Chiara enjoys making the pasta from my sunny pasta room, music playing in the background, wearing one of my work pinnies and using my small hand-cranked cavatelli maker. *Brava Chiara!*

Preparation time: 5 minutes
Cooking time: 25 minutes
Serves: 4

4 tbsp extra virgin olive oil
1 shallot, peeled, finely sliced
2 garlic cloves, peeled, crushed
800g/1lb 12oz cherry tomatoes on the vine, halved (baby plum tomatoes would also work well)
50ml/1½fl oz vegetable stock (page 84) or alternative (see Tip below)
1 small chilli, finely sliced (optional)
1 tbsp tomato purée
2 Parmigiano Reggiano rinds
Tomato vines (from the tomatoes listed above)
Salt and pepper, to season
1 tsp dried oregano or marjoram
Small bunch of fresh basil, torn
80g/3oz Parmigiano Reggiano, grated

1. Pour the oil into a shallow sauté pan.
2. Tumble in the shallot and garlic, bring the pan to a medium heat and cook for 5 minutes. Take care to not burn the garlic.
3. Tumble in the cherry tomatoes.
4. Cook the tomatoes down for 5 minutes, gently squashing the tomatoes with the back of a wooden spoon.
5. Pour in the stock.
6. Add the chilli (if using) and tomato purée. Stir well.

7. Place the Parmigiano Reggiano rinds into the pan along with the tomato vines, and season with salt and pepper.
8. Add the oregano and half the freshly torn basil.
9. Cook for 20 minutes. Stir intermittently and check the seasoning.
10. Place a large pan of water onto boil for the pasta. Once boiling, salt well and cook the pasta until *al dente*.
11. Drain the pasta, reserving 2 ladles of the starchy pasta water. Add the pasta water to the tomato sauce and stir.
2. Tumble the pasta into the sauce and stir well. Add the grated Parmigiano Reggiano and the remaining basil. Stir and serve in warm bowls. Remember to remove and discard the Parmigiano Reggiano rinds and tomato vines!

CARMELA'S TIP:
- Instead of using stock, a great substitute would also be mozzarella water or aquafaba (chickpea cooking liquid).

Garden tomatoes and honeyed ricotta

(*Pomodorini e ricotta con miele*)

The feel from the warmth of the sun on the back of my neck and back as I gently tend to tying up my forever expanding summer tomatoes. The aroma from the tomato vines and the gentle tug of a ripe tomato from its vine. These are a few of my favourite things, but then there is the bite. The first bite of a warm tomato that has been freshly picked from its vine and the taste of an ambient arrangement of tomatoes tossed through pasta is a revelation to behold. Fasten your seatbelts for what I am sure will be your new summer love.

Preparation time: 20 minutes
Cooking time for pasta: Will depend on which variety you are cooking
Serves: 4

600g/1lb 5oz cherry tomatoes, room temperature
40g/1½oz salted capers, rinsed well and finely chopped
70g/2½oz olives, pitted, chopped
2 garlic cloves, peeled, minced
3 tbsp extra virgin olive oil
Salt and pepper, to season
1 small fresh chilli, seeds removed, finely chopped (optional)
½ tsp dried marjoram
Small bunch of basil, roughly torn

Topping
250g/9oz ricotta, drained overnight
2 tbsp honey (I use borage honey)
Zest of 1 small lemon and the juice of half
70g/2½oz Parmigiano Reggiano, grated
Salt and pepper, to season
Extra virgin olive oil, to drizzle

1. Quarter the tomatoes and pop them into a bowl along with the finely chopped capers and olives. Ensure the capers are rinsed well to eliminate any excess salt. Stir well.
2. Add the minced garlic and extra virgin olive oil to the tomatoes. Season well with pepper. Taste, then salt as required.
3. Leave the tomatoes to sit at room temperature until required. Just before dressing, add the chilli, marjoram and basil, and stir.
4. Into a separate small bowl, spoon in the ricotta, honey, lemon zest and juice. Add 40g/1^1/₂oz of the grated Parmigiano Reggiano, reserving the remainder for serving. Stir well and season as required with a pinch of salt and pepper.
5. Cook your chosen pasta in a pan of salted boiling water until *al dente*. Drain the pasta, reserving 30ml/2 tbsp of the cooking water.
6. Add the pasta to the tomatoes and sprinkle over the reserved Parmigiano Reggiano. Stir well and add a little of the pasta water to emulsify. Spoon into bowls, add a drizzle of extra virgin olive oil and top with a spoonful of the honeyed ricotta.

CARMELA'S TIP:
- Use tomato vines in stocks, pasta water and soups for additional flavour, then discard. Tomato vines freeze well and are great to use for added flavour at a later stage.

Gorgonzola and cream sauce
(*Salsa al Gorgonzola e panna*)

With a cream sauce there must be a little balance because it can be perceived as being too claggy and rich on the palate. Gorgonzola and cream merge so perfectly well together that it needs not much more than that. That said, a little pasta water would be an added benefit if the sauce thickens a little too much. This silky, flecked sauce is a dream if dressed with potato gnocchi.

Preparation time: 5 minutes
Cooking time: 20 minutes
Serves: 4

30g/1oz butter
2 tbsp extra virgin olive oil
1 shallot, peeled, finely chopped
1 garlic clove, peeled, minced
300ml/½ pint/10fl oz double cream
250g/9oz Gorgonzola
¼ tsp freshly grated nutmeg
50g/1½oz Parmigiano Reggiano, grated
Salt and pepper, to season
Small handful of parsley, finely chopped

1. Put the butter and extra virgin olive oil into a shallow sauté pan over a medium heat. Add the shallot and cook for 3–4 minutes until soft and translucent.
2. Scrape in the minced garlic and stir, followed swiftly by the double cream.
3. Warm the cream over a low heat and crumble in the Gorgonzola, stirring and melting with care.
4. Add the nutmeg and Parmigiano Reggiano, taste and season with salt and pepper as required.
5. Cook for an additional 10 minutes and add the parsley just before serving with your chosen pasta.

CARMELA'S TIP:

- If the sauce thickens a little too much for your liking, add a little reserved pasta water, adjusting the seasoning as required. For a little more flavour, you could add 60g/2oz Parma ham, speck or pancetta, fry off with the shallot and continue the sauce as above.

Rich rib ragu (Ragu di carne)

The comfort and immediate richness that comes from slow-cooked tender meat, that simply falls apart when touched with the side of your fork ... I am salivating as I write these words, yet feel fortunate knowing that I will be tucking into this very dish this Sunday lunchtime. My rib ragu takes a little time to prepare but the long slow cooking pretty much takes care of the rest.

Preparation time: 40 minutes
Cooking time: 3 hours 30 minutes
Serves: 4–6

6 tbsp extra virgin olive oil
12 medium pork ribs, sliced into individual ribs
1 shallot, peeled, cut into cubes
1 carrot, peeled, cut into cubes
1 celery stalk, cut into cubes
2 tbsp tomato purée
2 cloves of garlic, peeled, minced
1.2 litres/2 pints passata
300ml/½ pint/10fl oz water
Salt and pepper, to season
1 bay leaf
1 tsp dried oregano
¼ tsp dried chilli
1 Parmigiano Reggiano rind
Large handful of fresh basil, torn

1. Pour 4 tbsp of olive oil into a large shallow saucepan and brown the ribs in batches over a medium heat.
2. Remove the ribs from the heat and set aside.
3. Add the remaining olive oil to the pan and fry off the shallot, carrot and celery until tender and blushing, for about 15 minutes so be patient.
4. Squeeze in the tomato purée and stir, followed by the garlic.
5. Pour in the passata and water, and stir to combine.
6. Lay the seared ribs back into the sauce.
7. Season with salt and pepper. Stir.
8. Add the bay leaf, oregano, chilli and Parmigiano Reggiano rind.
9. Cook the rib ragu over a low to medium heat for 3 hours, making sure to stir intermittently or as required.
10. Add the basil leaves and cook for a further 30 minutes. Prior to serving, remove the Parmigiano Reggiano rind.

CARMELA'S TIP:
- You can serve the ribs as part of your *secondo* dish (after pasta) with salad and potatoes; however, I prefer to pull the tender meat off the ribs and run the meaty sauce through some fresh pappardelle with copious amounts of grated Parmigiano Reggiano.

Ricotta sauce (*Ricotta con pasta*)

So, this is not a sauce recipe, more of a gentle instruction for you to try when you have ricotta to use up. If time is against you, or if you just crave a bowl of pure indulgent pleasure, then this is the dish for you.

Preparation time: 5 minutes
Cooking time: 12 minutes
Serves: 4–6

400g/14oz pasta
300g/10½oz ricotta
Salt and pepper, to season

1. Cook your pasta in a large pan of salted boiling water until *al dente*.
2. Spoon the ricotta into a large bowl and season with salt and pepper as required.
3. Break up the ricotta with the back of a fork and add a ladle of the pasta water. Stir.
4. Drain the pasta, add the pasta to the ricotta, stir and serve in warm bowls.

CARMELA'S TIP:
* You could also add 2 ladles of a basic tomato sauce or a meat-based ragu to the ricotta just before serving.

Simple tomato sauce (*Sugo finto*)

The classics are always the best. Try this with spaghetti for a speedy midweek supper. The sauce keeps well, covered in the fridge for up to a week or in the freezer for up to 3 months. As per many recipes the importance of the ingredients is vital. Here it is all about the tomatoes, so buy the best quality you can afford, making sure you steer clear (if possible) of chopped tomatoes as I find them flavourless, bitter and far too watery. I recommend pelati tomatoes, plum, skinned and beautifully plump.

Preparation time: 5 minutes
Cooking time: 30 minutes
Makes: 750ml/1⅓ pints

2 tbsp extra virgin olive oil
1 shallot, peeled, finely chopped
2 x 400g/14oz tins pelati tomatoes
1 garlic clove, peeled, minced
Salt and pepper, to season
¼ tsp dried oregano
6 basil leaves

1. Pour the oil into a saucepan and add the chopped shallot. Fry off over a low heat to soften the shallots but not to colour them, for 5 minutes.
2. Tumble in the pelati tomatoes and stir, followed by the garlic.
3. Season with salt, pepper and oregano, and cook for 10 minutes over a medium heat.
4. Use the back of a wooden spoon to break up the tomatoes.
5. Cook for a further 15–20 minutes.
5. Add the basil leaves and taste for additional seasoning.

White milk and butter sauce (*Besciamella*)

This foundation for many baked pasta dishes is versatile with all kinds of potential uses. You can add a generous handful of grated hard cheese such as pecorino or Parmigiano Reggiano to the sauce at the end too. Having a trustworthy béchamel sauce in your repertoire will often be your saving grace.

Preparation time: 5 minutes
Cooking time: 10 minutes
Makes: 1 litre/1^3/$_4$ pints

130g/4½oz butter
130g/4½oz 00 flour, sifted
1.2 litres/2 pints milk
¼ tsp fresh nutmeg, grated
Salt and pepper, to season

1. As this is a sauce, I would recommend that you sift the flour to ensure there are no lumps. I never normally sift flour.
2. Melt the butter in a heavy-based saucepan over a medium heat.
3. Whisk in the flour and stir to form a roux.
4. Warm the milk in a small saucepan.
5. Slowly pour the warmed milk into the butter and flour roux mixture, whisking as you go.
6. Stir over the heat until the béchamel has thickened. Season with salt, pepper, and a speckle of nutmeg.

CARMELA'S TIP:
- For a vegan alternative you can easily substitute olive oil for the butter and use a a vegan-friendly alternative milk such as almond or soya.

Wild boar sauce (*Ragu di cinghiale*)

May I introduce you to pure decadence and ultra-satisfaction? Wild boar is so incredibly popular in Italy and is hunted widely, available everywhere and eaten with pure joy, celebration and admiration. Sourcing wild boar in the UK is a little more of a challenge, depending on where you live. Find a good butcher and order directly and in advance.

Preparation time: 30 minutes
Cooking time: 3 hours 30 minutes
Serves: 4

4 tbsp extra virgin olive oil
1 shallot, peeled, finely chopped
1 celery stick, finely chopped
1 carrot, peeled, finely chopped
2 garlic cloves, peeled, minced
500g/1lb 1½oz wild boar, chopped into 2cm/¾in chunks
200g/7oz Italian sausage, skinned, chopped
1 tbsp tomato purée
200ml/7fl oz red wine
Sprig of fresh rosemary
1 bay leaf
600ml/1 pint/20fl oz passata
150ml/5½fl oz water
Salt and pepper, to season

1. Pour the extra virgin olive oil into a large sauté pan over a medium heat. Add the shallot, celery and carrot. Stir and soften for around 15 minutes.
2. Add the garlic and cook for 2 minutes.
3. Tumble in the wild boar meat and skinned sausage pieces. Sear the meat for 10 minutes then add the tomato purée and stir.
4. Pour in the red wine, stir and reduce by half over a medium heat.
5. Add the rosemary and bay leaf.
6. Add the passata and water. Stir and season with salt and pepper.
7. Reduce and cook over a low heat now for $3^1/2$ hours. If the sauce looks a little dry, add some chicken stock or water.

8. Taste and season. Serve as required, remembering to remove the bay leaf and any visible rosemary.

CARMELA'S TIP:
- An ideal pasta pairing would be pappardelle.

Almond, basil and tomato pesto
(*Pesto alla trapanese*)

We thank the region of Sicily and the hungry Genovese sailors who would dock in Trapani many years ago for this fresh-tasting pesto. They chose to change the ingredients up from the classic basil and pine nut pairing, and used what they had to hand, hence the *pesto alla trapanese* was born. A summer favourite of mine, especially when made and pounded with my homegrown ruby tomatoes. It is traditionally served with busiate pasta (page 47), but farfalle, cavatelli or trofie would work just as well.

Preparation time: 10 minutes
Serves: 2–4, depending on use

80g/3oz basil
220g/7½oz cherry tomatoes, quartered
100g/3½oz almonds, whole, skinned
2 garlic cloves, peeled, roughly chopped
200ml/7fl oz extra virgin olive oil, as required
Salt and pepper, to season

1. Pound the basil in a pestle and mortar until bruised.
2. Add half the cherry tomatoes and a handful of the almonds, and pound together with the basil and a pinch of salt.
3. Add half the garlic along with the remaining cherry tomatoes and continue to pound in circular movements.
4. Tumble in the remaining almonds along with the remaining garlic and pound with half the extra virgin olive oil.

5. Pour in the remaining oil until you have a loose dropping consistency (you may not need all of the extra virgin olive oil) and season to taste.
6. Alternatively, you can put all of the ingredients into a food processor along with half the extra virgin olive oil and blitz until it reaches the consistency described above.
7. Pour in the remaining extra virgin olive oil and continue to blitz until creamy and to your preferred texture. Season to taste.
8. Serve with pasta as required.

CARMELA'S TIP:

- The almonds turn this pesto into a wonderful, textured yet creamy sauce as they release their natural fats. I tend to reduce the amount of extra virgin olive oil I use and supplement it with starchy pasta water, leaving you with a wonderfully perfumed and emulsified sauce.

Asparagus pesto (*Pesto di asparagi*)

An incredible pesto, especially when made in the height of the British asparagus season. The asparagus always tastes that little bit sweeter and it seems to retain its colour too. Asparagus pesto keeps very well in the fridge for up to a week if the pesto remains topped up with extra virgin olive oil and you remember to maintain the rules of no double dipping!

Pesto is every cook's store-cupboard essential, quick to toss into pasta, spread over hot bread or drizzle over fish or a juicy steak. When making pesto, use olive oil as opposed to a heavy pepper-based extra virgin olive oil, and if you can source a Ligurian olive oil, that is even better, as it's lighter and has back notes of herbs and almost floral scents. However, I love the peppery notes of extra virgin olive oil.

Preparation time: 5 minutes
Cooking time: 5 minutes
Serves: 2–4 depending on use

150g/5oz asparagus spears, chopped
50g/1½oz pine nuts
30g/1oz basil
30g/1oz Parmigiano Reggiano, grated
Zest of 1 small lemon
Olive oil, as required (or extra virgin if you prefer a strong peppery aroma)
Salt and pepper, to season

1. Lightly fry off the chopped asparagus in a little olive oil for about 5 minutes or until the spears are just tender.
2. Once cooked, leave to cool and blitz in a food processor for 30 seconds.
3. Into the blitzed asparagus tumble in the pine nuts, basil, grated Parmigiano Reggiano, lemon zest and 3 tablespoons of olive oil, then blitz again for 30 seconds. It will resemble a thick paste at this stage.
4. Taste and season with salt and pepper.
5. Continue to pour in the olive oil a little at a time and pulse at 10-second intervals until the pesto has a dropping consistency.

- I tend to reduce the amount of olive oil I use and supplement it with starchy pasta water, making a versatile and wonderfully emulsified sauce.

Basil pesto (*Pesto Genovese*)

Basil pesto is one of the more widely recognised and popular dressings that Italy has gifted the world. The traditional version is wonderful, but once you master the simplicity of this verdant dressing you can add a few extra flavours such as lemon zest or a change of nuts. I prefer not to toast my pine nuts but please feel free to (in a dry pan for a couple of minutes). A Ligurian olive oil would be my chosen liquid gold; however, use what you have available, just remember that extra virgin olive oil has a strong, peppery flavour.

Preparation time: 5 minutes
Serves: 2–4 depending on use

70g/2½oz basil leaves
1 garlic clove, peeled
30g/1oz pine nuts
60g/2oz Parmigiano Reggiano, grated
110ml/4fl oz olive oil, or as required
Salt and pepper, to season

1. I am opting for the food processor method for ease but feel free to use a pestle and mortar for the more traditional feel.
2. Put the basil leaves, garlic, pine nuts and grated Parmigiano Reggiano in the food processor.
3. Add 2 tbsp of olive oil and blitz.
4. Slowly add the remaining oil until you have a beautiful dropping consistency; you may not need all the olive oil.
5. Season with salt and pepper as required.

CARMELA'S TIP:
- The pesto will keep for 2 weeks in the fridge, topped with a little olive oil, or in the freezer for up to 3 months.

Breadcrumb textured pesto (*Pesto di mollica*)

I am such a huge fan of pesto; it is versatile and pretty much universally loved. Within this chapter I have included a few of my most used pesto recipes to give you mid-week alternatives, however, this one is the crowning glory. There are no nuts present and it is a little heavier in density, so it can benefit from pasta water being stirred through to loosen it prior to dressing your chosen pasta.

Preparation time: 5 minutes
Serves: 4

250g/9oz basil leaves
70g/2½oz stale breadcrumbs
1 garlic clove, peeled, crushed
85ml/3fl oz extra virgin olive oil
115g/4oz Parmigiano Reggiano, grated
Salt and pepper, to season

1. Put the fresh basil leaves, breadcrumbs, crushed garlic and half the olive oil into a food processor and blitz for 20 seconds.
2. Scatter in the Parmigiano Reggiano and gently pour in the remaining oil. Blitz to incorporate.
3. Scrape into a bowl and season with salt and pepper as required.
4. Set aside at room temperature until needed. Remember to loosen the pesto with a little reserved pasta water as you serve.

CARMELA'S TIP:
- Use on the day you make it.

Cavolo nero pesto (*Pesto di cavolo nero*)

I just adore cavolo nero. A favourite way to cook it is to slow cook the stripped leaves in stock, then drain and add the heavily wilted leaves to a sauté pan with a little extra virgin olive oil, crushed garlic, chilli flakes and a handful of halved cherry tomatoes. Bread for dipping is an absolute necessity. However, my pesto takes these prehistoric leaves to another level. Textured, deep in colour and robust. Stir through a pasta of your choice.

Preparation time: 10 minutes
Cooking time: 10 minutes
Serves: 4

> 12 large cavolo nero leaves
> Small bunch of basil
> 1 garlic clove, peeled
> 60g/2oz pine nuts, untoasted
> 70g/2½oz Parmigiano Reggiano, grated
> Extra virgin olive oil, as required
> Salt and pepper, to season

1. Wash the cavolo nero.
2. Tear the leaf away from the very firm centre stem. You can also use a knife or a pair of kitchen scissors if preferred.
3. Place the cavolo nero into a pan of lightly salted water and boil for 10 minutes until just tender.
4. Strain the cavolo nero (retaining 30ml/2 tbsp water) and squeeze the leaves in a clean tea towel to remove excess water.
5. Put the cavolo nero in your food processor along with the basil, garlic, pine nuts and Parmigiano Reggiano. Pour in the reserved cavolo nero water and whizz for 10 seconds.
6. Slowly add the olive oil until you have reached the perfect dropping consistency. Taste and season with salt and pepper.

CARMELA'S TIP:
- The pesto freezes well for up to 3 months. It also keeps in the fridge if topped with olive oil for 14 days (just keep the pesto topped up with olive oil as and when required). Add the cavolo nero stems to stocks and discard after boiling.

White pesto (*Pesto bianco*)

Pesto bianco is light and rich. Hailing from the stunning north-western region of Liguria, this intense pesto is pure and almost virginal in colour, like olive oil, while being a little complex in flavour. Pesto bianco makes not only a great base to spread liberally over pizza or toasted crostini and to use as a dip, but it also offers a light blanket of sauce when stirred through *al dente* pasta – all with simplicity and speed.

Preparation time: 5 minutes
Serves: 4–6, depending on use

180g/6½oz walnuts, halved and quartered
2 garlic cloves, peeled, halved
15 fresh basil leaves
Sprig of fresh marjoram or oregano, leaves removed from stems
Salt and white pepper, to season (black pepper would also suffice)
2 tbsp Ligurian extra virgin olive oil
350g/12½oz ricotta, drained overnight

1. Using either a pestle and mortar or a food processor, pound or blitz the walnut halves for a minute or until they have become smaller fragments.
2. Add the garlic cloves and blend them with the walnuts.
3. Add the fresh basil leaves and marjoram leaves. If using a pestle and mortar, continue to work them together, adding a little salt and white pepper. You can substitute black pepper for the white pepper if necessary. If using a food processor, blitz for 30 seconds.
4. Pour in the olive oil, pound and stir to combine.
5. Put the ricotta in a bowl.
6. Pour the pesto base mixture into the ricotta and beat with a wooden spoon until incorporated.
7. Taste and season as required.

CARMELA'S TIP:
- Loosen with a little milk prior to adding to pasta or emulsify with a little starchy pasta water. Alternatively, you could add a yolk for extra richness. If possible, pesto should always be made with a lighter olive oil; one from Liguria would be preferable but not essential.

Poor man's Parmesan (breadcrumb topping) (*La mollica*)

This is hardly a recipe; it is more of a suggestion or alternative. 'La Mollica' is the soft centre from a loaf of bread and was always referred to as 'poor man's Parmesan'. In the south of Italy, when purse strings were tight, these seasoned breadcrumbs would make a perfectly acceptable stand-in. Traditionally La Mollica was made on 19 March for San Giuseppe Day as the breadcrumbs depict the wood shavings from his workshop. Nowadays, La Mollica can totally hold its own dusted liberally over pasta, fish or vegetables.

Preparation time: 2 minutes
Cooking time: 4 minutes
Serves: 4

> 3 tbsp extra virgin olive oil
> 150g/5oz soft breadcrumbs
> Salt and pepper, to season

1. Pour the oil into a frying pan and bring to a medium heat.
2. Sprinkle in the breadcrumbs and toast lightly all over.
3. Season with a pinch of salt and pepper.

CARMELA'S TIP:
- For added flavour, and depending on what you will be adding the mollica to: add a sprinkle of oregano, chilli, minced garlic or anchovy fillets; also, some finely chopped soft herbs would add freshness, as would lemon zest and juice.

Short pasta and soups

Whether they're semola-based or egg-based, short pasta shapes make me want to pour a glass of wine and eat from a bowl with nothing more than a spoon and a rumbling belly.

In this chapter you will find many of my favourite short shapes that use a combination of flours. Each shape is designated to its own sauce, but feel free to make your own judgement as to pairings. My family adore a heavy, mixed meat Bolognese sauce with rigatoni or conchiglie shells. I love the pasta to store the sauce in between its valleys, crevasses and ridges, cupping the slow-cooked ragu as I stir.

This chapter covers everything from garganelli tubes to breadcrumb pasta and fantastically frugal grattoni (grated) pasta. Some recipes require time and patience while others require a mere few minutes. I would suggest you make the pasta fresh on the day you wish to eat it, while making the sauce (if it's a slow-cooked variety) a few days in advance. I always prefer a pre-made sauce as the flavours intensify in the fridge. Just delicious.

Stock can make a quick meal a whole lot easier (it does for me, anyway) so every Sunday evening I prepare either a vegetable or chicken stock and pop it in the fridge. You will have a meal almost instantly.

Badly cut pasta with radicchio, speck and cream (*Maltagliati con radicchio, speck e crema*)

I have chosen to make maltagliati (page 51) for this recipe because I just love the simplicity of using up leftovers and scraps. You can substitute this shape with any short shape you prefer. Some dainty, fresh egg farfalle would work beautifully, as would hand-rolled garganelli or even some autumn leaves in the shape of foglie d'ulivo.

Preparation time: 10 minutes
Cooking time: 20 minutes
Serves: 4

1 small radicchio
2 tbsp extra virgin olive oil
30g/1oz butter
1 shallot, peeled, finely chopped
80g/3oz speck, sliced
400g/14oz maltagliati pasta (page 51)
150ml/5½fl oz single cream
Salt and pepper, to season
80g/3oz Grana Padano, grated

1. Place a large pan of water on to boil. Once boiling, salt well.
2. Cut the radicchio into quarters and slice into thin strips.
3. Put the oil and butter in a large sauté pan and fry the chopped shallot over a low heat until softened but not coloured.
4. Add the speck along with the radicchio and stir.
5. Cook for 5 minutes and season with a little salt and pepper.
6. Cook the pasta until *al dente*.
7. Add the cream to the radicchio and stir to fully incorporate. Check for seasoning.
8. Drain the pasta (reserving 50ml/1½fl oz pasta water) and toss the pasta with the radicchio and cream, then add the reserved pasta water.
9. Sprinkle in half the Grana Padano. Stir and serve in warm bowls with an additional and immensely gratifying sprinkle of the remaining cheese.

Biscuit soup (*Zuppa imperiale*)

From Emilia Romagna with love. I have enjoyed two different versions of this soup before and love and enjoy it a little more every time. A pasta soup with a difference, it oozes comfort and health, and when I eat it with a spoon, I feel like I am being held tightly and kissed on the top of my not-so-angelic head. It is traditionally served with capon stock, which is a pure joy but I also love and enjoy it equally with my basic chicken or vegetable stock on page 84.

Preparation time: 10 minutes
Cooking time: 25 minutes
Serves: 4

4 eggs
60g/2oz butter, softened
90g/3oz Parmigiano Reggiano, plus extra for serving
80g/3oz semola di grano duro rimacinata
¼ tbsp freshly grated nutmeg
Salt and pepper, to season
1.5 litres/2¾ pints stock

1. Preheat the oven to 190°C/170°C fan-assisted/Gas 5. Line a 20cm x 30cm/8in x 12in baking dish with butter and baking parchment.
2. Put the eggs and butter into a bowl and beat with a wooden spoon.
3. Sprinkle in the Parmigiano Reggiano and the semola, stir, and then add the nutmeg.
4. Season with salt and pepper.
5. Spread the mixture into your prepared baking dish and bake in the middle of the oven for 25 minutes or until lightly golden in colour.
6. Warm the stock, then adjust and check the seasoning as required.
7. Remove the pasta biscuit from the oven and lift onto a wooden board.

8. Allow the pasta to cool slightly.
9. Using a sharp knife, cut the room-temperature pasta biscuit into symmetrical little squares of approximately 1cm/$\frac{1}{2}$in.
10. Add the cubes to the stock. Warm for 5 minutes and ladle into warm bowls.
11. Top with extra Parmigiano Reggiano and a little black pepper.

CARMELA'S TIP:
- Add a handful or two of frozen peas and a little lemon zest just before you serve, for a touch of sweetness and freshness.

Bread pasta dumplings and borlotti beans (*Pisarei e fasò*)

I am a collector of pasta tools and love the historical value of well-used and etched wooden boards, knives and rolling pins. These tools, however, are unnecessary here, as all you need is a willing, able and flexible thumb. Hailing from the province of Piacenza in the rich and wonderful region of Emilia Romagna, this pasta combines breadcrumbs with flour and tepid water, and is served with beans. Your thumb is the star here; the pasta is extruded and formed with the side of it. When it is made often you may form a firmness almost like a callus on the working side of your thumb. This callus would please any future mother-in-law because she would know that you can not only make the pisarei but also that her apron-grabbing son or daughter will not go hungry!

Preparation time: 10 minutes plus 30 minutes resting at room temperature
Cooking time: 1 hour
Serves: 6

Pasta
400g/14oz 00 flour
150g/5oz stale breadcrumbs
300ml/½ pint/10fl oz tepid water

Sauce
2 tbsp extra virgin olive oil
70g/2½oz lardo (cubed pork fat, or use lard)
1 shallot, peeled, finely chopped
1 x 400g/14oz tin borlotti beans (or beans of your choice)
240g/8½oz passata
1 sprig rosemary, finely chopped
1 Parmigiano Reggiano rind (optional)
Salt and pepper, to season
80g/3oz Parmigiano Reggiano, grated

1. Tip the flour and breadcrumbs onto a wooden board, stir to combine and make a well in the centre.
2. Gradually pour in the water and form a dough. Knead until smooth. Cover and allow the pasta to rest at room temperature for 30 minutes.
3. Once the pasta has had time to rest, cut the dough into six portions. Roll each portion into long ropes, pinching off bean-sized pieces of dough.
4. Roll each piece of pasta away from you, using a short pushing action, to form a shell. I prefer to make pisarei on a smooth surface, using a standard board with no ridges. If you prefer, feel free to use a gnocchetti board and have them *rigate* (ridged).
5. Use all the dough. Once the pisarei are made, cover them with a clean tea towel and make your bean sauce.
6. Roughly chop and crush the lardo, making a rough paste.
7. Into a saucepan place the olive oil and softened lardo along with the shallot. Cook over a medium heat for about 5 minutes. Add the beans and stir.
8. Pour in the passata. Season with salt and pepper.
9. Add the rosemary and Parmigiano rind. Allow the bean sauce to cook for 20 minutes or so.
10. Fill a large pan with water. Once boiling, salt well.
11. Cook the pisarei for 5 minutes or until *al dente*; they will bob to the top when ready.
12. Strain and add the pisarei into the bean sauce. Remove the Parmigiano Reggiano rind. Stir and serve in warm bowls.
13. Top with grated Parmigiano Reggiano.

CARMELA'S TIP:
- This pasta freezes incredibly well. Double up on the recipe and stash some in the deep freezer for a later date.

Bread pasta in stock (*Passatelli in brodo*)

A small handful of ingredients and yet another dish where my pasta floats away in a warming bowl of stock. A pasta that embraces stale bread will always make it into my top five pasta dishes. I was taught with passion by a wonderful lady called Nonna Violante from Romagna how to make passatelli. Her hands made the entire process look effortless as she combined, kneaded, and extruded the pasta through a wide-holed passatelli press.

Preparation time: 30 minutes plus 10 minutes to rest the dough at room temperature
Cooking time: 5 minutes
Serves: 4

300g/10½oz stale breadcrumbs
200g/7oz Parmigiano Reggiano, grated
4 eggs
Zest of ½ lemon
1 tsp freshly grated nutmeg
Salt and pepper, to season
50g/1½oz 00 flour
Semola for dusting, as required
2 litres/3½ pints beef stock (page 80)

1. Place the breadcrumbs and Parmigiano Reggiano onto a wooden board. Stir with your hands to combine, and make a well in the centre.
2. Crack the eggs into the centre of the well.
3. Add the lemon zest, nutmeg and a pinch of salt.
4. Using a fork, slowly work the eggs around, incorporating the breadcrumb mixture, and knead for 3–5 minutes. If the dough is wet, add a little 00 flour until the dough comes together.
5. Cover the dough with a tea towel and allow to rest for a minimum of 10 minutes.
6. Place your stock on to boil whilst you prepare the passatelli pasta. Taste and check the stock for seasoning.
7. Cut the dough into small, workable sections.

8. Flour and press each section of dough through a traditional passatelli press or use a potato ricer with holes that are approximately 5mm/^{1}/$_4$in in diameter (larger than a standard potato ricer).
9. Pass the passatelli through the press and cut them with a sharp knife to 4cm/1^1/$_2$in in length. Lay them onto a tea towel or a tray dusted in semola and continue until you have used all the prepared dough.
10. Cook the passatelli directly in the stock for around 3 minutes. Ladle into bowls and scatter with additional Parmigiano Reggiano.

CARMELA'S TIP:
*   When making passatelli it is essential that the breadcrumbs are stale and the bread contains no olive oil, as this will affect the overall preparation and cooking of the passatelli by making them fall apart.

Pasta crackers

These baked pasta crackers are such a treat and are speedy to make. When you fancy a light bite or an evening of fine cured meats and cheeses, these crackers would make the perfect pairing. You can use leftover pasta sheets or make a little dough especially for these crackers.

Preparation time: 30 minutes plus 30 minutes to rest the dough at room temperature
Cooking time: 10 minutes
Makes: 25

Leftover pasta sheets
Or:
100g/3½oz 00 flour
1 egg
20g/½oz Parmigiano Reggiano, grated
1 tsp nigella seeds

1. Place the flour onto a wooden board, make a well and crack in the egg.
2. Work the egg into the flour and combine to form a dough.
3. Knead for 5 minutes, cover the dough and allow to rest for 30 minutes at room temperature.
4. Preheat the oven to 210°C/190°C fan-assisted/Gas 6 and line a baking tray with parchment paper.
5. Roll the pasta dough through your pasta machine to level 4.
6. Cut the pasta sheet into 5cm x 8cm/2in x 3in pieces.
7. Place on the baking tray. Sprinkle over the Parmigiano Reggiano and the nigella seeds.
8. Bake for 10–12 minutes.
9. Store in an airtight container for up to 5 days.

CARMELA'S TIP:
- You can change the toppings by swapping the nigella seeds for crushed fennel seeds, dried marjoram or chilli flakes.

Cavatelli, mushrooms and sausage
(*Cavatelli con funghi e salsicce*)

From Molise to mamma. Cavatelli are also known in the region as 'cuzze' or 'cuzzettielle'. They are made from a simple dough of semola flour and water, embracing autumnal mushrooms and succulent sausages. Perfect for a chilly autumn evening, and incredibly easy to make and prepare ahead of schedule.

Preparation time: 40 minutes
Cooking time: 25 minutes
Serves: 4

> 500g/1lb 1½oz mushrooms, mixed varieties of your choice
> 4 tbsp extra virgin olive oil
> 250g/9oz soft Italian sausages, skinned, roughly chopped
> 150g/5oz prosciutto, finely sliced
> 2 garlic cloves, peeled, finely sliced
> 670ml/1¼ pints passata
> 150ml/5½fl oz water
> ½ tsp dried oregano
> Small bunch of basil, roughly torn
> Small bunch of parsley, chopped
> Pinch of dried chilli (optional)
> Salt and pepper, to season
> 400g/14oz cavatelli (page 44)
> 70g/2½oz Parmigiano Reggiano, grated

1. Brush the mushrooms with a clean cloth. Do not wash them as they absorb moisture, similar to tiny sponges. Slice the mushrooms.
2. Pour the extra virgin olive oil into a large shallow pan and bring to a medium heat. Add the sausage and cook until browned all over, 5–7 minutes or so.
3. Scatter the sliced prosciutto into the sausages and stir. Cook for 2 minutes then add the mushrooms and garlic to the pan. Stir and cook for an additional 5 minutes.

4. Pour in the passata along with the water. I normally swirl out the passata jar with the water.
5. Add the oregano, half the fresh herbs and a sprinkle of chilli. Season well with salt and black pepper. Cook for 20 minutes.
6. Place a large pan of water on to boil for the pasta. Once boiling, salt well and cook the pasta until *al dente*.
7. Drain the pasta, reserving a ladle of pasta water.
8. Add the pasta to the sauce along with the reserved water, then stir.
9. Scatter over the remaining fresh herbs. Stir and serve with a sprinkle of Parmigiano Reggiano.

CARMELA'S TIP:
- I love ricotta salata (salted ricotta) with this dish; it creates a perfect pairing.

Farfalle pasta bows with asparagus pesto and spears (*Farfalle [stricchetti] con pesto di asparagi*)

Farfalle pasta from Emilia Romagna. This pasta, which is made with egg dough, was traditionally only ever made to use up leftover scraps of dough from other pasta dishes. The simplicity of creating something delicious from not very much echoes the *cucina povera* methods from the south of Italy that I love and stand by so proudly. Best known as farfalle, these bows have a multitude of different names depending on the region you happen to be in, and whether they are straight-edged or decoratively edged. Obviously, as with all the pasta shapes in *Pasta Fresca*, they are interchangeable.

Preparation time: 1 hour plus 30 minutes resting for the pasta dough at room temperature
Cooking time: 5 minutes
Serves: 4

300g/10½oz egg pasta dough (page 6)
or use chestnut or chickpea dough (page 23)

Semola flour, for kneading and dusting, as required
1 quantity asparagus pesto (page 104)
2 tbsp extra virgin olive oil
12 asparagus spears, sliced lengthways (giving you 24 lengths)
Juice of ½ lemon (you'll have one left over from making the pesto)
40g/1½oz Parmigiano Reggiano, grated

1. Roll the pasta dough out with your pasta machine to level 5 or with a rolling pin to 3mm/^{1}/$_8$in in thickness.
2. Using a straight-edged or fluted wheel, cut the dough into 3cm x 6cm/1in x 2^1/$_2$in rectangular pieces.
3. Place a finger in the middle and place a finger at each edge widthways and pinch them together, forming a small pinched bow.
4. Repeat with the remaining pasta dough.
5. Lay the beautifully pinched bows onto a tray that has been lightly dusted with semola flour to prevent sticking.
6. Place a large pan of water on to boil for the pasta. Once boiling, salt well.
7. Fry the sliced asparagus in the extra virgin olive oil for 2 minutes.
8. Cook the farfalle for 2 minutes.
9. Spritz the lemon juice over the asparagus and toss with a little salt and pepper.
10. Drain the farfalle and reserve 50ml/1^1/$_2$fl oz of the starchy pasta water.
1. Scrape the pesto into a large shallow bowl, tumble in the drained pasta and add the reserved pasta water. Stir and toss until every bow has been coated.
12. Sprinkle over the remaining Parmigiano Reggiano. Plate up, laying 6 asparagus lengths onto each plate.

CARMELA'S TIP:

• The above pasta is best known as farfalle (butterflies or bows). The smaller variety, used for pastina and soups, is farfalline, while farfalloni is the larger, slightly more robust member of the family. Regional names are fiocchetti, stricchetti, sciancon, nocchette and nocheredde, to name a few. I tend to use farfalle or stricchetti.

Fregola with fish stock and clams
(*Fregula al vongole in bianco*)

I feel like I am constantly harping on about how important fresh stock is to a dish. Italian dishes are born out of simplicity, which makes every single ingredient important. Again, the stock here is fundamental to the overall appeal and flavour of the final dish. Freshly made fish stock instantly reflects the aroma of the Mediterranean.

Preparation time: 30 minutes (make the stock in advance as per page 82)
Cooking time: 15 minutes
Serves: 4

6 tbsp extra virgin olive oil
2 garlic cloves, peeled, left whole
1 small chilli, de-seeded, finely sliced
Small bunch of parsley, including stems, finely sliced
800g/1lb 12oz clams, washed
80ml/3fl oz white wine or vermouth
400g/14oz fregola (fresh, page 50, or dried)
400ml/¾ pint/14fl oz fish stock (page 81)
Rustic bread, to serve (optional)

1. Pour the extra virgin olive oil into a large sauté pan.
2. Add the garlic cloves and allow them to infuse the oil for 5 minutes over a low heat.
3. Add the sliced fresh chilli and half the chopped parsley. Stir.
4. Tumble in the clams along with the white wine and clamp on a lid. Cook the clams until each shell has popped open and the wine has evaporated. Remove any clams that remain closed.
5. Remove and discard the garlic cloves (if you can find them).
6. Cook the fregola in a pan of salted water until *al dente*.
7. Pour the fish stock into the clams. Check and adjust the seasoning as required.
8. Drain the fregola and tumble it into the clam soup. Stir, taste and season.
9. Spoon into warm bowls with a little rustic bread for dipping.

Fried pasta (*Pasta fritta*)

It's Friday night and you have had a busy week and are looking forward to a large glass of trebbiano and a savoury snack. Fried pasta is a game changer, especially with the addition of chilli flakes, pounded fennel seeds, celery salt or coarse black pepper and salt. All I will say is, make lots as they are delicious, especially if accompanied by a bowl of olives and a little salami and spicy provolone piccante!

Preparation time: 1 hour including resting of the pasta dough
Cooking time: 15 minutes
Makes: Lots (approximately 60)

200g/7oz 00 flour
2 eggs
1 tbsp extra virgin olive oil
1 tsp chilli flakes, celery salt, black pepper or garlic granules (you choose)
Olive oil, as required, to fry
Cured meats, cheeses and olives, to serve

1. Tip the flour onto a board and make a well in the centre. Add the eggs, extra virgin olive oil and your chosen seasoning.
2. Incorporate all the ingredients in the well with a fork, then use your fingers and hands to work the ingredients and dough together.
3. Knead for 7 minutes, then cover with a tea towel and rest the dough at room temperature for 30 minutes.
4. Heat the olive oil in a wide, heavy-based saucepan to 170°C.
5. Roll out the dough to a thickness of 2–3mm/$^1/_{16}$–$^1/_8$in.
6. Use a fluted pasta wheel to cut the pasta sheets into strips roughly 15cm/6in in length and 4cm/1$^1/_2$in in width.
7. Fry the pasta strips until golden.
8. Place on kitchen paper to remove any excess oil and serve with the cured meats, cheeses and plump olives.

Garganelli with pork cheek ragu
(*Garganelli al ragu di miale*)

Garganelli are tubes of fresh egg pasta that has been cut into small
squares and formed around a tiny pin, the thickness of a pencil, and
rolled down a gnocchi board or sushi mat. Once dried a little they
hold their form perfectly and are similar to dried rigatoni or
tortiglioni. Garganelli in fact refers to the gullet and throat of a
chicken, and they are generally served with a duck ragu, but I just
could not resist my favourite slow-cooked pork cheek ragu.

Preparation time: 1 hour 20 minutes
Cooking time: 4 hours
Serves: 4–6

5 tbsp extra virgin olive oil
1.5kg/3lb 5oz pork cheek, chopped into small bite-sized cubes
2 shallots, peeled, cubed
1 carrot, peeled, cubed
1 fennel bulb, finely chopped, plus fluffy fronds
3 garlic cloves, peeled, finely chopped
Small bunch of parsley, finely chopped, stalks and leaves kept separate
50g/1½oz tomato purée
150ml/5½fl oz red wine
1 tsp fresh freshly chopped thyme
3 rosemary sprigs
2 x 400g/14oz tins mutti polpa (or pelati tomatoes)
500ml/18fl oz beef stock (page 80)
1 bay leaf
Salt and pepper, to season
400g/14oz egg pasta dough (page 6)
Semola for dusting
50g/1½oz Parmigiano Reggiano, grated, plus rind

1. Put 3 tbsp extra virgin olive oil in a large, heavy-bottomed
   saucepan and cook the pork cheek in batches until seared and
   lightly golden in colour.
2. With a slotted spoon remove the pork cheek and set aside.

3. Add the remaining extra virgin olive oil and, over a medium heat, fry the shallots, carrots and fennel until softened, around 15 minutes.
4. Add the garlic and parsley stalks and stir, then follow with the tomato purée and stir well.
5. Spoon the seared pork cheek back into the saucepan.
6. Pour in the red wine and over a medium heat, allow the wine to cook away until it has almost evaporated.
7. Add the remaining ingredients for the sauce into the pan including the Parmigiano Reggiano rind and season well to taste. Add half the parsley leaves. Slowly cook the sauce over a low heat for 3 hours with no lid, stirring and tasting intermittently.
8. Prepare the pasta: cut the pasta dough in half, cover one half with a tea towel and set aside. Roll the pasta through your pasta machine or with a rolling pin to 2–3mm/^{1}/$_{16}$–^{1}/$_8$in in thickness. I prefer 2mm/^{1}/$_{16}$in.
9. Cut the pasta sheet into squares measuring 5cm x 5cm/2in x 2in with a knife.
10. Using your gnocchi board and a tiny rolling pin that is the thickness of a pencil, place each square on the gnocchi board (dusted with semola) with the tip pointing up and roll the pasta around the pin, pushing down with a little pressure as you go. Place the garganelli onto a tray that is lightly dusted with semola to air dry. This will ensure the pasta holds its shape while cooking. Continue making the garganelli.
11. When the sauce is rich and deep in colour, it is ready. Add the remaining parsley leaves and remove the Parmigiano Reggiano rind.
12. Cook the garganelli in a pan of heavily salted water until they are *al dente*.
13. Drain the pasta and place on a large serving platter.
14. Dress with half the sauce and toss, top with a little more sauce and sprinkle with the grated Parmigiano Reggiano.

CARMELA'S TIP:

- Make the ragu a few days in advance and refrigerate; somehow it intensifies the richness of the sauce, taking it to another level.

Grated egg pasta in stock
(*Grattini all'uovo in brodo*)

I always say simplicity is key and this *cucina povera* pasta soup highlights just that. Grated pasta has never looked so damn good. Instant comfort and warmth, this soup most certainly is one that's at the top of my list. The point here is that fresh stock is more important in this recipe than the pasta itself. A cube will simply not do.

Preparation time: 15 minutes plus 30 minutes resting and 30 minutes air drying
Cooking time: 30 minutes
Serves: 4

250g/9oz 00 flour
50g/1½oz Parmigiano Reggiano, grated, plus extra to finish
1 egg
1 yolk
1.5 litres/2¾ pints fresh stock (page 81)
Black pepper, to season

1. Into a bowl or onto a wooden board place the flour and Parmigiano Reggiano. Combine and stir with your fingertips.
2. Make a well in the centre and crack in the whole egg and yolk. (Freeze the egg white for future use).
3. Combine the ingredients together and form a dough. Knead for 5 minutes until smooth.
4. Rest the pasta dough at room temperature for 30 minutes, uncovered.
5. The best way to prepare the pasta is with a box grater. Place the grater onto a clean tea towel or tray.
6. Using the side of the grater with the large holes, take the dough and grate the pasta dough (be mindful of fingertips).
7. Lay the grattini onto trays to air dry for a minimum of 30 minutes.
8. Warm the stock.
9. Add the pasta to the stock and cook for 2 minutes.

10. Ladle into bowls with a little grinding of black pepper and a little extra Parmigiano Reggiano.

CARMELA'S TIP:
- For an additional flourish of texture and flavour, crack an egg into the pasta and stock, and whisk before serving.

Italian pancakes bathed in stock with celery leaves (*Scrippelle m'busse*)

I love a story, a fable or a fairy tale, anything that can take my mind to a whimsical and faraway place. It is said that many years ago a chef was making a pancake-based dish for a regal visitor and the chef accidentally dropped the pancakes that he had prepared into a large pan of freshly made bubbling stock. Scrippelle m'busse was born. Instead of being filled and baked, this version of pancake is fried, sliced, and warmed in a bowl of comfort. Make the batter in the morning before you go to work and simply fry, toss and warm in stock when you have the time. Fresh stock would be a welcome pleasure, but a good quality stock or cube would suffice too.

Preparation time: 15 minutes plus 30 minutes chilling of batter
Cooking time: 20 minutes
Serves: 4

4 eggs
240ml/8½fl oz milk, full fat
100g/3½oz 00 flour
1 tbsp celery leaves, finely chopped
Salt and pepper, to season
Pinch of freshly grated nutmeg
3–4 tbsp butter
1.5 litres/2¾ pints chicken stock (page 81)
200g/7oz Pecorino Romano, grated
2 tbsp celery leaves, roughly chopped

1. Crack the eggs into a large bowl and whisk until light and pale in colour.
2. Pour in the milk and whisk. Spoon in the flour a little at a time, whisking as you go.
3. Tumble in the celery leaves, seasoning with salt, pepper and nutmeg.
4. Warm a little butter in a crêpe pan or frying pan, ensuring it's non-stick.
5. Add a small ladle of batter and swirl it around. Fry for 3 minutes

over a medium heat, flip and cook for a further 30 seconds. Repeat with the remaining batter. This batter should make 10–12 pancakes.

6. Warm the chicken stock and taste, seasoning as required.
7. Roll each pancake up and lay three each into pre-warmed, wide-mouthed bowls.
8. Sprinkle liberally with the grated pecorino and top with a ladle of chicken stock and a scattering of celery leaves.

CARMELA'S TIP:

• Freeze excess pancakes or double the mixture. Once cooled, wrap in foil and freeze for up to 3 months, making an even quicker meal possible.

Leftover pasta with rocket and speck
(Maltagliati con rucola e speck)

Maltagliati (malfatti) means badly cut or badly made pasta. This is a perfect dish to make with scraps of leftover or forgotten pasta. That said, you can easily substitute the maltagliati with another favourite.

Preparation time: 15 minutes
Cooking time: 15 minutes
Serves: 4

5 tbsp olive oil
25g/1oz butter
1 shallot, peeled, finely chopped
300g/10½oz rocket leaves
200g/7oz speck, sliced into 1cm/½in strips
2 garlic cloves, peeled, finely sliced
400g/14oz maltagliati, dried or fresh (see note below or page 51)
1 small red chilli, de-seeded, finely sliced
Salt and pepper, to season
Zest and juice of 1 small lemon
80g/3oz Pecorino Romano, grated

1. Pour the oil and butter into a sauté pan over a medium heat and add the shallot. Stir and soften for 10 minutes.
2. Blanch the rocket leaves in a little water for 2 minutes. Drain and pat the rocket dry with a clean tea towel or kitchen paper to remove excess water, trying to not damage the leaves.
3. Tumble the speck into the pan and colour; at this point the aroma will be amazing. Add the garlic and stir. Be careful to not burn the garlic as it can easily catch.
4. Place a large pan of water on to boil for the pasta. Once boiling, salt well and cook the pasta until *al dente*.
5. Add the rocket to the pan and warm through with the shallots. Cook for 2 minutes. Season with the fresh chilli, salt and pepper.
6. Drain the pasta and add it into the sauté pan. Stir, adding the zest and juice of the lemon, and toss.

7. Serve with a generous sprinkle of Pecorino Romano.

CARMELA'S TIP:
- If you would like to make the maltagliati (malfatti) by hand, make your pasta dough, using either an egg or water-based dough. Roll the dough out into a thin sheet 2m/$\frac{1}{16}$in in thickness and cut it with a pastry cutter into small shapes of your choice. Alternatively, farfalle would be equally delicious here.

Little hats with broad beans, summer peas and pistachio

(Cappelli con piseli e pistacchio)

I love this shape of pasta so much with its incredibly intricate folds, pointy tops and funnelled grooves that hold and cling on to the sauce and dressing so very well. The pasta making takes a little time but when it comes to fresh pasta you need to invest time, and these are a pure joy to make. Visually they are just gorgeous. These cappelli are very similar (just a little shorter in body) to the famous 'Cappellacci dei Briganti' from Molise, which mimic a pointed hat with an upturned brim.

Preparation time: 1 hour plus 30 minutes resting of pasta dough
Cooking time: 15 minutes
Serves: 4

300g/10½oz semola pasta dough
90g/3oz pistachio nuts, shelled
120g/4oz Grana Padano, grated
1 garlic clove, peeled, crushed
Small bunch of basil
35g/1oz butter
Zest and juice of 1 lemon
175g/6oz fresh broad beans (frozen if out of season)
225g/8oz fresh peas (frozen if out of season)
4 tbsp extra virgin olive oil
Salt and pepper, to season
Semola, for dusting

1. To make the pasta hats, take the dough and use either a rolling pin or a pasta machine to roll it to setting 5 on a pasta machine or, if using a rolling pin, to the thickness of a penny piece.
2. Cut out discs to the diameter of 7cm/3in then cut each disc in half.
3. Fold and form a small cone shape, like a witch's hat, and place the tip of the hat into a small empty glass bottle.
4. Fold the edges of the pasta around the lip of the bottle and apply pressure to form a pleat.
5. Tip the hat out of the bottle and repeat with the remaining dough. For a better visual understanding please have a look at my Instagram or YouTube for video inspiration.
6. Place each hat, point up, onto a tray that is lightly dusted with semola. Allow the pasta to sit for at least 30 minutes to dry a little.
7. Place a large pan of water on to boil. Once boiling, salt well.
8. Toast the pistachio nuts in a dry pan for 5 minutes to release their natural oils and aroma.
9. Sit the pistachio nuts to one side and allow them to cool a little.
10. Put 75g/2$\frac{1}{2}$oz of the pistachio nuts into a food processor along with 80g/3oz of the Grana Padano, the garlic clove, basil leaves, butter and lemon juice. Blitz to a textured paste. Taste and season with salt and pepper. Set aside for 10 minutes.
11. Cook the cappelli pasta hats along with the broad beans and peas until the pasta is *al dente*.
12. Drain the pasta (reserve 60ml/2fl oz pasta water) and place the pasta into a large warm bowl. Add the pistachio paste to the pasta along with the pasta water and stir well to emulsify the sauce – it will become creamy and rich in texture.
13. Roughly chop the remaining pistachio nuts.
14. Spoon the pasta onto warmed plates with a scattering of the chopped nuts, a sprinkle of the lemon zest and a little extra Grana Padano.

CARMELA'S TIP:
- Fusilli, orecchiette or farfalle would make great alternatives.

Minchiareddhi/maccaruni with mixed seafood (*Minchiareddhi alla pescardore*)

Minchiareddhi is a homemade pasta also known as 'little willies' from the area of Salento which is located right at the heel of the region of Puglia. They are made using a combination of barley and soft wheat flour, rolled into tiny sausages using 'Lu Ferro', a traditional wire. Lu Ferro is a wire 30cm/12in in length and is used to manipulate and roll the pasta. I use Nonna Carmela's ferro which is more than 75 years old. It was an old spoke from an umbrella, and as she tells me with nostalgia in her eyes, back in the day the umbrella wires were not circular, they were square. This square shape is what helps define the pasta, making it easier to roll. It has now been passed down to my mum Solidea, and I will be honoured to receive it one lucky day.

Preparation time: 1 hour plus 30 minutes resting and 1 hour drying of the pasta dough at room temperature
Cooking time: 20 minutes
Serves: 4

Pasta
250g/9oz barley flour
150g/5oz 00 flour
200–250ml/7–9fl oz tepid water, alternatively aquafaba or mozzarella water

Sauce
4 tbsp extra virgin olive oil
1 shallot, peeled, finely sliced
6 large tomatoes, roughly chopped
2 garlic cloves, peeled, finely sliced
¼ tsp chilli flakes
1.5kg/3lb 5oz mixed clams, mussels, sliced calamari, sliced and cleaned octopus (including tentacles)
100ml/3½fl oz white wine or vermouth
Salt and pepper, to season
Small bunch of parsley, roughly chopped
2 tbsp fennel fronds, roughly chopped

1. Start by making the pasta. Due to the ratio of barley flour to soft wheat flour this pasta is a little difficult to work with; it tends to crumble and become unruly. The secret is to keep working it by hand and just persevere.
2. Pour both the barley flour and 00 flour onto a wooden board and mix with your hand to combine. Make a well in the centre and slowly add a little water. Begin to combine, working the flour into the water inside the well.
3. Add more water as required until all the flour has been combined into a workable dough.
4. Knead the dough for around 8–10 minutes until smooth. If the dough is a little dry add a little more water. Cover and allow to rest for 30 minutes at room temperature.
5. Take the dough and cut it in half, making it a little more manageable to work with. Cover one half with a tea towel and set aside until required.
6. Roll the dough into a large sausage then continue to roll it into a thin sausage.
7. Cut acorn pieces of dough off the sausage. Place the ferro onto the top corner of the acorn and roll it vigorously with your palm, forming a sausage with a hole that runs through the centre.
8. Repeat with the remaining dough.
9. Lay the minchiareddhi onto trays. Allow them to dry for one hour before cooking.
10. Place a large pan of water on to boil; once boiling, salt well. Add the pasta and cook until *al dente*.
11. Pour the extra virgin olive oil into a large shallow saucepan and add the shallot. Fry lightly over a medium heat for 3 minutes.
12. Tumble in the tomatoes, garlic and chilli flakes. Cook down for 5 minutes over a medium heat.
13. Add the seafood and stir. Cook for 2 minutes over a medium heat and add the white wine, salt, pepper and half the parsley. Stir and clamp on a lid for 4 minutes until all the mussels and clam shells have opened and the wine has evaporated. Discard any that remain closed.
14. Taste and check for additional seasoning.
15. Drain the pasta, retaining a ladleful of pasta water.
16. Tumble the pasta into the seafood pan along with the ladle of reserved pasta water and stir well.

17. Tumble in the fennel fronds and the remaining parsley.
18. Spoon into warmed bowls or onto a large platter and enjoy.

CARMELA'S TIP:
• Minchiareddhi are also delicious with a heavy tomato sauce and lots of freshly grated ricotta salate. This pasta is normally made with an 80 per cent barley and 20 per cent 00 flour combination. However, I think this mix works better, is easier to handle and does not break up when boiled.

Orecchiette with chickpeas, smoked pancetta and celery leaves
(*Orecchiette con ceci, pancetta affumicata e sedano*)

An ode to my mum, *mia mamma, cara* Solidea. When I think of chickpeas, I immediately think of my chickpea-obsessed mum: she will most certainly turn into a chickpea if she is not careful. I have mentioned before that she eats them directly from the tin and this is one of her favourite combinations when using them in a dish: the salty pancetta paired with chickpeas and a firm bite of fresh pasta. This dish improves with added flavour and if you are ever lucky enough to have leftovers, I tend to warm it up with a ladle of vegetable stock for good measure.

Preparation time: 15 minutes
Cooking time: 15 minutes
Serves: 4

250g/9oz dried chickpeas (soak overnight in a bowl of water with a pinch of bicarbonate of soda)
1 shallot, halved with skin on
1 carrot, halved
1 celery stick, roughly chopped
3 tbsp extra virgin olive oil
300g/10½oz smoked pancetta, chopped into 1cm/½in pieces
2 garlic cloves, peeled, finely chopped
12 cherry tomatoes, halved

Salt and pepper, to season
¼ tsp dried chilli flakes (optional)
2 tbsp celery leaves, finely chopped
300g/10½oz fresh orecchiette (page 41) or dried
30g/1oz ricotta salata, grated (optional)

1. Drain your chickpeas and place in a pan, covering with water and a pinch of salt. Add the shallot with the skin on, carrot and celery. Simmer over a medium heat for 30 minutes or until the chickpeas are tender.
2. Drain the chickpeas. Retain the liquid and remove the vegetables; I like to keep these to nibble on.
3. Into a sauté pan pour the olive oil and over a low heat add the pancetta. Cook for 5 minutes until almost coloured all over.
4. Add the garlic and tomatoes. Stir. Cook for a further 5 minutes.
5. Pour the reserved stock water into the pancetta pan along with salt, pepper, a sprinkle of chilli and the celery leaves.
6. Tumble in the chickpeas and check the water for additional seasoning.
7. Cook the orecchiette in the pan with the chickpeas until the pasta is *al dente*.
8. Ladle into warm bowls and add a sprinkle of pepper and a little ricotta salata.

CARMELA'S TIP:

- For chickpeas, it's worth doubling up on the soaking, prep and cooking, and then just pop the chickpeas in the fridge so you can add them to another meal in the week. Alternatively, squash them with a fork, add a little butter and oil and spread them onto toasted Pugliese bread. Substitute if you so wish the dried chickpeas with a tin; I would most certainly soak ahead of time, but if you're pushed for time then the tins are perfect!

Paccheri tubes with a veal ragu

(Paccheri al ragu di viletto)

If I could eat this dish every day until the day I die, I most certainly would. The sauce is dense while the pasta is large and yet fragile. It's a dish full of options: the sauce alone would complement any strong pasta, from rigatoni to pappardelle, while being baked and topped with mozzarella would make it a contender for Sunday family pasta. You could of course make the paccheri fresh, but I would always opt for a bag of dried for their firm bite.

Preparation time: 20 minutes
Cooking time: 3 hours
Serves: 6

4 tbsp olive oil
1 shallot, peeled, finely diced
1 carrot, peeled, diced
1 small fennel bulb, finely chopped
800g/1lb 12oz veal mince
2 garlic cloves, peeled, roughly chopped
100ml/3½fl oz red wine
1 tbsp tomato purée
900ml/1½ pints passata
150ml/5½fl oz water
Small bunch of basil leaves, torn
1 tbsp celery leaves, finely chopped
Parmigiano Reggiano rind (optional)
Salt and pepper, to season
500g/1lb 1½oz paccheri, dried (or fresh, see page 40)
80g/3oz Parmigiano Reggiano, grated

1. Pour the olive oil into a pan and place over a medium heat.
2. Tumble in the diced shallot, carrot and fennel. Stir with a wooden spoon until softened. Cook for approximately 15 minutes.
3. Add the veal mince and stir, breaking up any lumps. Colour all over. This will take about 10 minutes or so.

4. Add the garlic and stir.
5. Pour in the red wine and allow the wine to evaporate; this will only take a few minutes.
6. Squeeze in the tomato purée and coat the mince all over.
7. Pour in the passata along with the water. I normally add the water to the passata bottle and rinse it out into the *sugo*, so no passata is left behind or wasted. Season with salt and pepper. Add half the basil leaves, all the celery leaves and the Parmigiano Reggiano rind (optional).
8. Leave the *sugo* to bubble away over a low heat for 3 hours. Stir occasionally and check for seasoning. Prior to serving, remove the Parmigiano Reggiano rind – this is the chef's perk to nibble on.
9. Place a large pan of water on to boil. Once bubbling, salt well.
10. Cook the paccheri until *al dente*.
11. Drain the pasta and place them back into the saucepan. Add a sprinkle of Parmigiano Reggiano and a ladle or two of the *sugo*. Stir gently to incorporate.
12. Spoon the paccheri into large warm bowls. Add a little more *sugo* to the bowls and sprinkle with the remaining Parmigiano Reggiano and fresh basil leaves.

CARMELA'S TIP:
- If you would like to try your hand at making fresh paccheri, just add an extra 90 minutes to the preparation time (page 40).

Pancake pasta (*Testaroli al pesto*)

A totally underrated pasta. I was told by the waiter in the quaint restaurant near the leaning tower of Pisa that I had to give the testaroli a go; I did and now teach this dish as part of my regional pasta courses in London. Testaroli are made in the Lunigiana valley area of Tuscany on the border of Liguria. They are made with flour and water into a loose pancake batter. They are then fried like pancakes, sliced into large triangles then boiled and served with sauce. Traditionally testaroli are made in large cast iron pans with huge domed lids which would have been heated over a wood fire.

Preparation time: 10 minutes plus 30 minutes resting in the fridge
Cooking time: 30 minutes
Serves: 4

Pasta batter
150g/5oz semola flour (semola di grano duro)
250g/9oz 00 flour
Pinch of salt
450ml/15fl oz warm water
olive oil, for frying

Pesto
Large bunch of basil, including stalks
50g/1½oz pine nuts, untoasted
Zest of 1 lemon
1 garlic clove, peeled
Salt and pepper, to season
60g/2oz Parmigiano Reggiano, grated, plus a little extra to sprinkle
Olive oil, as required, to obtain a dropping consistency

1. In a bowl combine the semola flour, 00 flour and salt.
2. Slowly pour in the water and stir; you are looking for a loose pancake batter consistency. Use a fork to ensure any small lumps are removed and dispersed. Cover and set aside for a minimum of 30 minutes in the fridge.

3. Place a large pan of water on to boil. When boiling, salt well.
4. Place the basil, pine nuts, lemon zest, garlic, salt, pepper and Parmigiano Reggiano into a food processor and blitz. Slowly add the olive oil until you have a loose dropping consistency. Taste and check for additional seasoning.
5. Add a tablespoon of olive oil to a 17.5cm/7in frying pan and rub with a little kitchen paper.
6. Spoon in a small ladle of batter and swirl to ensure the batter has coated the bottom of the pan fully. Cook for 2 minutes on each side. Remove and set aside.
7. Repeat until all the batter has been used up. Place the pancakes into an oven at a low temperature to keep warm.
8. Once the pancakes are all cooked, slice them into diamonds or short ribbons.
9. Drop them all into the boiling water and allow to reheat for 2 minutes.
10. Drain and serve the testaroli on plates with a drizzle of pesto and an additional sprinkle of Parmigiano Reggiano.

CARMELA'S TIP:

- Testaroli can be served with a simple tomato sauce (page 99) or with browned butter and sage. To make a gluten-free version of testaroli use 250g/9oz rice flour along with 250ml/9fl oz water and a pinch of salt.

Pasta and bean soup (*Pasta e fagioli*)

My good friend Adriana runs one of the best Italian delis in my home county of Northamptonshire. It is a deli with a vast array of fresh offerings as well as fresh bread, tinned and jarred goods and a room dedicated to pasta. Yes, you heard me correctly, a room full of dried pasta, a totally perfect shopping experience. When I pop into 'The Italian Shop', if Adriana has a Parma ham end or knuckle, she will always ask if I want it to make a sauce at home. That is the best kind of friend, right? If you are not as lucky as I am, then pancetta or lardons will do just as well.

Preparation time: 20 minutes
Cooking time: 1 hour 30 minutes
Serves: 4

300g/10½oz dried cannellini beans, soaked overnight
Small bunch of celery leaves
5 tbsp extra virgin olive oil
Parma ham knuckle, meat cut off and chopped into 1cm/½in pieces, or
200g/7oz pancetta, chopped
2 garlic cloves, peeled, sliced
12 cherry tomatoes, halved
1 Parmigiano Reggiano or Grana Padano rind (optional)
½ tsp dried chilli
1 litre/1¾ pints chicken stock (page 81)
200g/7oz small pasta shells or maccherioni al ferro
Small bunch of basil
Salt and pepper, to season
Drizzle of extra virgin olive oil, to finish
Rustic bread, to serve (optional)

1. Drain your cannellini beans and pop them into a saucepan with the celery leaf tops and boil until the cannellini beans are tender, around an hour or so.
2. Once cooked, drain the beans. Take a quarter of the beans along with the wilted celery leaves and blitz them in a food processor to form a smoothish yet textured purée. Set aside until required.

3. Into a saucepan pour the extra virgin olive oil and add the knuckle pieces and bone (or pancetta).
4. Fry off over a medium heat for 5 minutes, stirring occasionally.
5. Add the garlic, stir and tumble in the tomato halves and optional cheese rind. The rind really does make all the difference.
6. Cook the tomatoes for 5 minutes until just softened.
7. Remove the knuckle bone, add a sprinkle of chilli followed by the stock, and stir.
8. Time to now introduce the beans to the stock, both the whole beans and the purée, and stir.
9. Season the stock with salt and pepper. Remove the Parmigiano Reggiano rind and tumble into the pasta.
10. Cook the pasta until *al dente*.
11. Roughly tear the basil and add it to the pasta.
12. Ladle into warmed bowls with a drizzle of extra virgin olive oil and a little extra black pepper. Serve with rustic bread.

CARMELA'S TIP:
• Make extra if possible as leftovers always taste better than the main event.

Pasta and potato soup (*Pasta e patate*)

A combination loved by many, but not my dad Rocco. He reminisces with me that as a boy he would hide in the garden shed (which had a strong aroma of red wine) so that he wouldn't have to eat pasta e patate. I laugh because my nonno Giuseppe would always find him hiding in the same place and pull him to the family table by his now elongated ear lobe, and urge him to eat up because in the 1960s it was that and nothing else. Now he eats it with a smile on his face. I adore this dish. I always overcook the potatoes because I prefer the texture, it somehow turns the soup wonderfully thick. I prefer to use a small pasta for pasta e patate as I just want to scoop it up with a spoon. An instant hug. If you'd like to use fresh pasta, then make a semola dough and make either cavatelli, farfalle or sorpresini.

Preparation time: 15 minutes
Cooking time: 30 minutes
Serves: 4

2 tbsp extra virgin olive oil
150g/5oz pancetta
2 garlic cloves, peeled, minced
380g/13½oz potatoes, peeled, boiled, cut into small cubes
2 tbsp celery leaves, finely chopped
1.5 litres/2¾ pints stock (chicken or vegetable, see page 81/84)
300g/10½oz ditalini (or make a short semola pasta)
Salt and pepper, to season
40g/1½oz Parmigiano Reggiano, grated (optional)

1. Put the extra virgin olive oil and pancetta into a large saucepan. Fry over a medium heat for 5 minutes before adding the garlic.
2. Keep an eye on the garlic, making sure it doesn't catch and burn.
3. Add the cubed potatoes (small cubes) along with the celery leaves and stir.
4. Add the stock and season as required. Cook for 15 minutes.
5. Tumble in the pasta and cook until *al dente*.
6. Ladle into warm bowls with an optional sprinkle of Parmigiano Reggiano and a little extra black pepper.

Pasta coins with ricotta and honey
(*Corzetti con miele*)

This pasta is an egg-based dough that has a little white wine in it and is rolled out into a sheet (not too thin) and pressed with beautifully hand-crafted wooden stamps. Each stamp depicts a family coat of arms, name or decorative pattern. My stamps range from an octopus to the regional coat of arms from Puglia to my name, a Christmas wreath and many more. My mood, as well as the season, choice of ingredients and sauce, determine the corzetti press that I will use on any given day.

Preparation time: 30 minutes plus 30 minutes resting of the dough at room temperature
Cooking time: 5 minutes
Serves: 4

400g/14oz corzetti pasta dough (page 34)
3 tbsp extra virgin olive oil
Zest and juice of 1 lemon
40g/1½oz pine nuts
300g/10½oz ricotta
Salt and pepper, to season
Drizzle of borage honey
50g/1½oz Parmigiano Reggiano, grated
1 tbsp marjoram leaves
Semola for dusting

1. Take the corzetti dough and, using a rolling pin or wooden broom handle, roll it into a large flat circle to the thickness of a 50p piece.
2. Using either your corzetti stamp or a glass tumbler, press out circles of corzetti dough, then place the circle onto the decorative side of the corzetti stamp and press to imprint. Place each decorative disc onto a tray that has been lightly dusted with semola.
3. Repeat until all the dough has been used.
4. The sauce is not really a sauce per se but it's a favourite

combination of mine that I use on many short pasta shapes. Warm the extra virgin olive oil in a large sauté pan then add the lemon juice. Tumble in the pine nuts, cook for 3 minutes, then remove from the heat.

5. Bring a large pan of water to the boil. Once it's boiling, salt well.
6. Cook the corzetti for a couple of minutes until *al dente*.
7. Mix the ricotta and lemon zest in a bowl. Add a little salt and pepper.
8. Drain the corzetti, reserving 50ml/2fl oz of pasta water, add them to the oil and lemon dressing and toss.
9. Serve on warm plates with quenelles of ricotta and a drizzle of borage honey.
10. Top with a final flourish of grated Parmigiano Reggiano and a few marjoram leaves.

Pasta with aubergine (*Pasta alla Norma*)

One of the most loved and favoured vegetables in Italy, aubergines are incredibly versatile, inexpensive and wholesome. Parmigiana is a classic and timeless dish that takes a little time to prepare. Filled and baked aubergines remind me of my childhood, while pasta alla Norma encompasses everything I love about food. Instead of frying the cubed aubergines, you could also oven bake them for 15 minutes then add them to the tomato sauce. Traditionally served with penne, this sauce would love any fresh pasta. I would recommend garganelli (page 124).

Preparation time: 1 hour and 10 minutes plus 1 hour (salting of aubergines)
Cooking time: 30 minutes
Serves: 4

3 medium aubergines
Maldon salt to sprinkle
3 tbsp extra virgin olive oil
1 shallot, peeled, diced
1 garlic clove, peeled, minced

300ml/11fl oz passata
Salt and pepper, to season
500g/1lb 1½oz penne (dried) or freshly made garganelli (page 124)
150g/5oz ricotta salata, grated

1. Take a vegetable peeler and peel strips of the aubergine skin away, leaving gaps so that the aubergines have a zebra-like appearance. This will remove a little of the bitterness.
2. Cut the aubergines into 2cm/1in cubes.
3. Optional: place the aubergines into a colander and sprinkle liberally with salt to remove any excess liquid and bitterness. After an hour, brush off the salt.
4. Into a large sauté pan pour the olive oil and gently fry the aubergine cubes until they are a light golden colour.
5. Once coloured, add the shallot and the garlic. You may need a further tablespoon or so of olive oil. Stir.
6. Add the passata, taste and season as required. Go steady with the salt if you have followed step 2.
7. Cook the aubergines for 25 minutes.
8. Place a large pan of water on to boil. Once boiling, salt well and cook the pasta for 2 minutes less than the packet instructions, or if you have made the garganelli from page 124 cook them for 3 minutes.
9. Drain and add the pasta to the aubergine sauce. Stir and check for seasoning once again. Add a little of the pasta water if the sauce requires it.
10. Serve with a generous grating of the wonderful ricotta salata.

CARMELA'S TIP:
- Ricotta salata is the most delicious Italian cheese made from the whey of sheep milk. It is pressed and salted then aged for a minimum of 90 days. It is a firm cheese with an intensity that you will just love. It also lasts well in the fridge for a couple of months. Substitute it on pasta dishes instead of Parmigiano Reggiano. It is equally wonderful on a risotto, grated on filled and baked vegetables and in salads.

Pinched triangle pasta with n'duja
(*Fusi Istrani con n'duja*)

N'duja is a spreadable, spicy pork salami that is versatile while offering the much-adored chilli heat of the south of Italy. It has a rich, warm flavour from the chillies and a depth of flavour from deliciously cured pork fat. An essential and welcome treat in any Calabrese's store cupboard. Here I have chosen to pair the sauce with a pasta from the Friuli Venezia Giulia region of Italy. The north meets the south. The pasta is a little different and fun to make, even though patience and time are required.

Preparation time: 1 hour plus 30 minutes to rest the pasta dough at room temperature
Cooking time: 30 minutes
Serves: 4

400g/14oz egg pasta (page 6) plus semola for dusting
170g/6oz pancetta, cubed
1 tbsp extra virgin olive oil
100g/3½oz n'duja
1 garlic clove, peeled, minced
70g/2½oz sundried tomatoes, finely sliced
30g/1oz olives, pitted, finely sliced
1 tbsp tomato purée
1 x 400g/14oz tin plum tomatoes
Large bunch of basil, roughly torn
Salt and pepper, to season
100g/3½oz Pecorino Romano, grated

1. Make the pasta as per page 6. Roll the pasta out with the pasta machine to the level 5 setting or to the thickness of 10 pence piece.
2. Cut the pasta into small triangles measuring 5.5cm/2in on each side.
3. The easiest way to form them is to pinch and secure the three points together, leaving the sides open. I find the best way is to slide a small pin onto the triangle and attach the points together with a gentle push.

4. Set the pasta onto a lightly floured tray and prepare the spicy sauce.
5. Put the pancetta into a sauté pan with no oil and fry off over a low heat for 5 minutes, until golden.
6. Add 1 tbsp extra virgin olive oil and then the n'duja and garlic. Stir and cook for 5 minutes, then tumble in the sundried tomatoes, olives and tomato purée.
7. Stir well. Add a tin of plum pelati tomatoes followed by half the fresh basil and a good twist of salt and pepper. Cook over a low heat for 20 minutes. Check for seasoning after 10 minutes.
8. Place a large pan of water on to boil for the pasta. Once boiling, salt well and cook the pasta until *al dente*.
9. Drain the pasta, reserving a small ladle of starchy water.
10. Add the pasta into the sauce with the ladle of pasta water. Stir well to incorporate.
11. Add the remaining basil and 30g/1oz of Pecorino Romano. Stir and serve in warm bowls with an additional sprinkle of Pecorino Romano if required.

CARMELA'S TIP:

- You could substitute the fusi Istrani with any other store-cupboard favourite.

Polenta quadretti [squares] with a bean and anchovy sauce

(Polenta quadretti con fagoli e acciuga [cresc'tajat])

This pasta lends itself well to being a leftover dish, so you should double up on your polenta the day before and reserve half for this terrific peasant-style pasta dish. Polenta pasta is a Northern Italian treat using up the bounty of leftover polenta. As the polenta will be a little wet, the best flour to pair it with is semola as it will add the correct balance and give you a workable texture.

Preparation time: 15 minutes plus 30 minutes resting of polenta dough at room temperature
Cooking time: 30 minutes
Serves: 4

300g/10½oz pre-made polenta (removed from the fridge at least 60 minutes before use)
100g/3½oz semola di grano duro rimacinata, plus extra for dusting and kneading
3 tbsp extra virgin olive oil
1 shallot, peeled, finely chopped
125g/4½oz pancetta, sliced or cubed
1 garlic clove, peeled, grated
3 anchovy fillets
Small bunch of parsley, finely chopped
1 x 400g/14oz tin pelati tomatoes
1 x 400g/14oz tin borlotti beans
1 x 400g/14oz tin chickpeas
Salt and pepper, to season
50g/1½oz Parmigiano Reggiano

1. Take the polenta and use the back of a fork to break it up.
2. Slowly work in the semola flour until you have a ball of dough. Please bear in mind that the consistency of the polenta will vary depending how you made it the previous day. So you may need a little more flour to firm up the dough or water to loosen the dough.

3. Form and knead the dough. Cover and rest for 30 minutes at room temperature.
4. Lightly flour your board and cut the dough in half. Using a rolling pin or broom handle roll the polenta dough out into a large circle, dusting with flour as required, to a thickness of about 3mm/^{1}/$_8$in. Using a sharp knife cut strips of dough into 4cm/1^1/$_2$in squares. Lay each square on a clean tea towel dusted with semola and repeat with the remaining dough. Set aside until required.
5. Put the oil and shallot into a sauté pan. Over a medium heat soften the shallots until almost translucent, 5 minutes or so, followed by the pancetta. Stir, and cook the pancetta for 5 minutes.
6. Add the garlic and anchovies.
7. Stir well to incorporate and allow the anchovies to almost melt away.
8. Add half the chopped parsley including the stalks.
9. Tip the pelati tomatoes into a medium bowl. Using either a potato masher or your hands, break up the whole tomatoes; this will give the sauce a helping hand.
10. Pour the tomato pulp into the pancetta sauce and stir. Taste and season with a little addition of salt and pepper.
11. Add the borlotti beans and the chickpeas along with the liquid from both tins. Stir and cook for 15 minutes.
12. Fill a large saucepan with water and when boiling salt well.
13. Cook the polenta pasta for 3 minutes or so until *al dente*.
14. Remove the pasta with a slotted spoon and add it to the sauce along with the remaining parsley and half the Parmigiano Reggiano. Toss together and serve on warm plates with an additional sprinkle of the remaining Parmigiano Reggiano.

Long pasta

Spaghetti Bolognese is loved by most in the UK, but venture to Italy and you'll be mocked by all. Spaghetti has its place at the dinner table, but it must be treated and dressed with care, affection, and a light kiss of a sauce. Thanks to its dainty physique, spaghetti is suited to light sauces as opposed to heavier meaty sauces. But if that's what floats your boat then enjoy it, we all have our own quirks and that's what makes us unique.

Long pasta is easy and speedy to prepare and make. That said, feel free to substitute a high-quality dried pasta in any of the recipes in this chapter. To remind you: make, knead, and rest your pasta. Roll it to the 5th setting of your pasta machine and cut it into 30cm/12in sheets. Then grab a glass of wine and have a sit down, allowing your pasta sheets to dry for at least 15 minutes, as this will prevent sticking.

Leftover pasta? Never fear, because the quick frittata will help you to make a perfect lunchtime alternative, or a scrumptious breakfast. The spinach tagliarini are just incredible and the semola pici are thick, hand-rolled pasta worms that quite frankly pair with anything you throw at them. Experiment and try something a little different.

Bucatini with a spicy ragu and whipped ricotta (*Pasta al ragu piccante*)

A pasta dish packed with warmth and flavour. I have opted for dried bucatini with this recipe, but you can easily substitute them with any pasta you'd prefer. For a short pasta, cavatelli or gnochetti sardi would work wonderfully here, as would a fresh tagliatelle.

Preparation time: 20 minutes
Cooking time: 1 hour 15 minutes
Serves: 4

2 tbsp extra virgin olive oil
2 shallots, peeled, sliced
300g/10½oz veal mince (alternatively beef or pork)
150g/5oz spicy fresh sausage
50g/1½oz tomato purée
30ml/1fl oz white wine
Pinch of dried chilli
1 tsp fennel, roughly ground
400ml/¾ pint/14fl oz passata
1 tbsp fennel tops, chopped
400g/14oz bucatini, dried
Salt and pepper, to season
90g/3oz Pecorino Romano, grated
80g/3oz ricotta, drained overnight

1. Pour the olive oil into a sauté pan and fry off the shallots along with the veal mince for 10 minutes.
2. Peel the sausages and discard their skins, chop the sausage meat filling and add it to the mince.
3. Fry the sausage with the veal mince for another 10 minutes or until golden in colour.
4. Add the tomato purée and stir, followed by the white wine; fry for 3 minutes.
5. Add the chilli and ground fennel. Cook for 5 minutes.
6. Pour in the passata. Season with salt and pepper and add the fennel tops; stir and cook for 45 minutes.
7. Place a large pan of water on to boil. Once boiling, salt well and cook the pasta until *al dente*.
8. Drain the pasta and add it to the sauce, stir and scatter in the Pecorino Romano.
9. Add a little salt and pepper to the ricotta and stir well, until a little lighter in texture.
10. Tong the bucatini into a warm bowl with the meaty sauce and a teaspoon of the ricotta spooned over each bowl.

CARMELA'S TIP:
- I like to stir the ricotta through the bucatini and sauce before I tuck in with my fork, but each to their own.

Bucatini with walnut sauce

(Bucatini alla salsa di noci)

To create bucatini by hand you will need a pasta extruding machine with a specific bronze die, as bucatini are long, thin and cylindrical with an internal hole that reaches all the way from one end to the other. So, with that in mind, feel free to substitute bucatini with fresh spaghetti or linguine. Bucatini are available in most Italian delis and online. I adore their firm bite and sturdy structure.

Preparation time: 10 minutes
Cooking time: 12 minutes
Serves: 4

250g/9oz walnuts, shelled
300g/10½oz bucatini pasta
4 tbsp olive oil
3 tbsp double cream
30g/1oz Parmigiano Reggiano, grated
Salt and pepper, to season

1. Place the walnuts in a heatproof bowl and cover with boiling water.
2. Wait for 5 minutes, then drain the walnuts and place them on a clean tea towel.
3. When cool enough to handle, rub the walnuts between your palms to remove any loose skins. There is no need to be to fastidious with the outer skins.
4. Cook the pasta in a large pan of salted boiling water until *al dente*.
5. Tumble the walnuts into a food processor and blitz for 20 seconds.
6. Transfer the walnuts to a clean bowl and add the olive oil, double cream and grated Parmigiano Reggiano.
7. Stir well to incorporate and season with salt and pepper.
8. Drain the pasta. Reserve 50ml/1¹/₂fl oz of the pasta water.
9. Add the pesto to the pasta and stir well. Slowly add the pasta water to emulsify your sauce.
10. Serve with a little black pepper.

Frittata of leftover pasta (*Frittata di pasta*)

I adore a frittata, and when it's paired with leftover pasta I could happily be left to my own devices and eat it entirely. Leftover pasta would be ideal for this recipe, but equally if you fancy a 'Frittata di pasta' then certainly cook and cool your pasta; one should never miss out on a slice of carby goodness. I prefer to use a dried pasta (*secca*) as opposed to freshly made pasta as the texture is firmer and there will be no danger of the pasta breaking up. This is my standard 8-egg frittata, but you can obviously adjust the measurements by increasing or decreasing the size of your frittata depending on your frying pan.

Preparation time: 5 minutes
Cooking time: 12 minutes
Serves: 4

125g/4½oz pancetta
8 eggs
Small bunch of parsley, finely chopped
Pinch of chilli (optional)
¼ tsp dried marjoram
Salt and pepper, to season
150g/5oz leftover pasta

1. Tumble the pancetta into a dry 20cm/8in frying pan and fry over a medium heat until lightly coloured.
2. In a bowl whisk together the eggs, parsley, chilli, marjoram and a twist of salt and pepper.
3. Add the leftover pasta to the pancetta and stir well.
4. Add the egg mixture and stir well to coat the pasta.
5. Leave the frittata to cook over a medium heat for 5 minutes.
6. Place a plate on top of the frittata and, with care, flip over the frittata, sliding it back into the frying pan for a further 3 minutes or so.
7. Slice and serve with a leafy salad or sliced and squashed into a panino and eaten in satisfied silence.

Handkerchiefs dressed in sugar, clementine and poppy seeds

(Fazzolette al papavero)

A beautifully embroidered handkerchief, whether detailed with masculine, bold initials or pretty roses, resembles all that is good and vintage in our world. When I think of fazzolette pasta I immediately imagine Antonio Carluccio cutting the pasta sheets by hand, almost ripping them with his fingers and dressing them with some freshly foraged buttery mushrooms and a few thyme leaves. I have chosen to take them to a sweet taste of heaven instead.

Preparation time: 1 hour plus 30 minutes resting of the pasta dough at room temperature
Cooking time: 10 minutes
Serves: 4

> 400g/14oz fresh egg pasta dough
> Semola for dusting, as required
> 50g/1½oz poppy seeds
> 2 tbsp sugar
> 120g/4oz butter
> Zest and juice of 1 clementine

1. Roll the pasta dough out to a thickness of 2mm/^{1}/₁₆in or until you can see your hands through the pasta sheet.
2. Cut the pasta sheet into 7cm x 10cm/3in x 4in pieces. Allow the pasta to dry for 15 minutes on trays dusted with semola.
3. Into a pestle and mortar put the poppy seeds and sugar. Combine and grind into a textured rubble.
4. Place a large pan of water on to boil. Once boiling, salt well and cook the pasta until *al dente*.
5. Melt the butter in a small frying pan until just browned and add the clementine juice.
6. Drain the pasta and place it back into the pan.

7. Add the butter and toss, adding the clementine zest.
8. Serve the pasta with a sprinkle of the poppy seed and sugar blend.

CARMELA'S TIP:
- Drizzle a teaspoon of locally grown honey over each plate.

Hay and straw pasta with peas and prosciutto (*Paglia e fieno*)

Hay and straw pasta is a combination of verdant green and sunshine yellow pasta, cut into ribbons and combined. That said, you could use this sauce with any preferred pasta.

Preparation time: 1 hour plus 30 minutes resting of the pasta dough at room temperature
Cooking time: 20 minutes
Serves: 4–6

200g/7oz spinach pasta dough (page 11)
200g/7oz egg pasta dough (page 6)
2 tbsp butter
2 tbsp extra virgin olive oil
120g/4oz pancetta, small cubes
250g/9oz prosciutto, thin strips, cut lengthways
175ml/6fl oz double cream
150g/5oz Parmigiano Reggiano, grated
¼ tsp fresh nutmeg, grated
100g/3½oz peas
Salt and pepper, to season

1. Roll each pasta sheet out into a circle with a rolling pin to a 2mm/^{1}/₁₆in thickness. Try to roll the sheets to the same circumference if possible.
2. Dust each sheet with a sprinkle of semola and air dry for 15 minutes.
3. Lay the spinach sheet on top of the egg pasta sheet, sprinkle liberally with semola and roll both sheets into a sausage.
4. Using a sharp, straight-edged blade, cut the pasta into 5mm/^{1}/₄in sections. Lift the pasta and twist it, forming a rough nest shape, then place the pasta ribbons onto a lightly dusted tray while you prepare the sauce.
5. Into a sauté pan put the butter and extra virgin olive oil. Add the pancetta and fry gently over a medium heat until the pancetta has become burnished and golden in colour.
6. Add the prosciutto to the pan and stir.

7. Pour in the cream and reduce the heat to a borderline simmer. Stir intermittently so that the cream does not catch on the base of the pan. Add half the Parmigiano Reggiano and the freshly grated nutmeg.

8. Add the peas to the cream and stir. Season with salt and pepper to taste.

9. Cook the pasta in a pan of salted boiling water until *al dente*, approximately 3–4 minutes.

10. Drain the pasta while retaining 100ml/3$\frac{1}{2}$fl oz of the pasta water.

11. Add the pasta to the pancetta, stirring well to incorporate fully. If you need to loosen the sauce, add a little of the reserved pasta water.

12. Add the remaining Parmigiano Reggiano and serve in loosely twisted nests.

Linguine with anchovy and grapes

(*Linguine con acciughe e uvetta*)

I have four children so my fridge, for obvious reasons, is always full of food – from plates of roast chicken that need nothing more than a sprinkle of salt and a slice of buttery bread and bowls of pasta for Santino, to Chiara's essential carb-loading breakfast. I guarantee that without a doubt you'll find a bowl of grapes that look like they've seen better days. So, I roast them and add them to salads or squash them and top a fresh focaccia or pizza with them. Here they are paired with anchovies and breadcrumbs. Salty and sweet with pasta equals instant happiness. What's more is that this dish is ready in around 15 minutes if you use dried pasta.

Preparation time: 5 minutes
Cooking time: 15 minutes
Serves: 4

350g/12½oz linguine
60ml/2fl oz extra virgin olive oil
25g/1oz butter
120g/4oz anchovies (rinsed well)
2 garlic cloves, peeled, finely sliced
50g/1½oz grapes, halved
250ml/9fl oz passata
Salt and pepper, to season
90g/3oz breadcrumbs (slightly stale)
1 tbsp celery leaves, finely chopped

1. Place a large pan of water on to boil; once boiling, salt well.
2. Into a sauté pan put 40ml/1½fl oz extra virgin olive oil along with the butter and 90g/3oz of well-rinsed anchovies. Stir and warm over a low heat for 3 minutes.
3. Add the garlic and grapes. Stir and pour in the passata. Taste and season with salt and pepper. Cook for 15 minutes.
4. Cook the linguine until *al dente*.

5. Put the remaining oil and anchovies into a small frying pan. Fry off for 1 minute and add the breadcrumbs and finely chopped celery leaves. Add a pinch of pepper and stir. Cook for 4 minutes until the breadcrumbs are lightly toasted.

6. Drain the linguine and add them to the tomato sauce. Stir well and serve with a sprinkle of the aromatic breadcrumbs.

CARMELA'S TIP:

- For fresh linguine, make an egg dough as per page 6. Roll it out with a pasta machine to the 5th setting and lay the sheets (30cm/12in in length) out on your work surface. Allow the dough to dry for 15 minutes with a light dusting of semola flour. After 15 minutes roll each sheet up into a loose sausage that has been lightly dusted with semola and cut 5mm/^{1}/14in-wide ribbons.

Mafaldine with pistachio pesto
(*Mafaldine al pesto di pistacchio*)

Mafaldine are also known as reginette and are the same thickness as tagliatelle with the only difference being their beautifully scalloped and decorated edges. A pasta with regal origins mafaldine is said to be named after Princess Mafalda of Savoy. The pasta has a delicate shape with a robust figure and beautifully scalloped and ruffled edges. The edges give the pasta a sense of luxury and occasion. Marcato have an attachment for cutting the shape that slots onto the back of your machine, but a fluted pasta rolling wheel works just as well. Mafaldine love a heavier, meat-based sauce too, but here I have opted for a taste of Sicily with a textured pistachio pesto. For added freshness, add a spritz of lemon as well as some soft herbs.

Preparation time: 5 minutes
Cooking time: 12 minutes
Serves: 4

> 400g/14oz egg pasta dough (page 6), or dried mafaldine
> 200g/7oz pistachio nuts, unshelled
> 60ml/2fl oz extra virgin olive oil
> 40g/1½oz Parmigiano Reggiano, grated, plus extra for serving
> Salt and pepper, to season

1. If making fresh mafaldine, roll out your pasta sheets to level 5 on a Marcato pasta maker or to the thickness of a 10-pence piece. Cut the sheet into 30cm/12in lengths, and using a fluted pastry wheel, cut it into 1cm/¹⁄₂in strips. This will create beautiful scallop-edged mafaldine.
2. Place a large pan of water on to boil; once boiling, salt well and cook the pasta until *al dente*.
3. In a food processor pulse the pistachio nuts, then add the extra virgin olive oil and the Parmigiano Reggiano. Season with salt and pepper to taste.
4. Drain the pasta, reserving 100ml/3¹⁄₂fl oz of pasta water.

5. Spoon the pistachio pesto into the linguine and stir. Carefully pour in a little of the reserved pasta water to emulsify the pasta and pesto together.

6. Serve on warm plates with a little extra Parmigiano Reggiano.

CARMELA'S TIP:

- Use olive oil for a lighter taste and for a traditional feel pound the pistachio pesto in a pestle and mortar for a textured consistency. To make and roll the fresh pasta add an extra 70 minutes to your preparation time.

Pici with cauliflower, leaves and breadcrumbs (*Pici al cavolfiore con la mollica*)

To infinity and beyond. This pasta has many names, pici being the most recognised, but my favourite name has to be umbricelli (earthworms). Semola pasta dough or an egg dough for richness is made, kneaded, and rolled into long ropes of slightly chewy pasta. A pleasure to make and effortless to eat.

Preparation time: 1 hour plus 30 minutes resting of pasta dough at room temperature
Cooking time: 20 minutes
Serves: 4

300g/10½oz semola pasta dough (page 4)
½ tsp dried marjoram
1 large head cauliflower, separated into florets
6 tbsp extra virgin olive oil, plus extra to serve
120g/4oz breadcrumbs, slightly stale
3 anchovy fillets, rinsed, chopped
1 red chilli, de-seeded, finely sliced
2 garlic cloves, peeled, minced
1 tbsp capers, rinsed, dried, finely chopped
3 tbsp cauliflower leaves, finely chopped
Salt and pepper, to season
40g/1½oz Pecorino Romano, grated

1. Prepare the semola pasta dough as per page 4. Add a sprinkle of your chosen dried herb to the semola dough; I adore the notes of dried marjoram.
2. Work, knead and rest the pasta dough, covered with a tea towel and at room temperature for 30 minutes.
3. Once the pasta has rested, cut the ball of dough into quarters.
4. Roll each quarter of dough into long ropes of pasta, thickish bucatini with bite. Cut them into 30cm/12in lengths. Set onto a lightly floured tray and prepare the dressing.
5. Separate the cauliflower into small florets and boil in salted water for 5 minutes. Drain and set aside.

6. Reserve half the cauliflower and blitz the other half. Scrape the cauliflower purée into a bowl.
7. Heat the olive oil in a sauté pan and tumble in the breadcrumbs. Stir and cook for 4 minutes until golden and lightly toasted.
8. Add the whole florets to the breadcrumbs along with the chopped anchovies, chilli, garlic, capers and finely chopped cauliflower leaves. Cook for 10 minutes until the cauliflower has a golden hue.
9. Stir and season with salt and pepper.
10. Cook the pasta until *al dente*, approximately 6 minutes, drain and reserve 50ml/1^{1}/2fl oz of the pasta water.
11. Emulsify the pasta water with the puréed cauliflower and stir the purée through the pici pasta.
12. Dress with the remaining cauliflower and breadcrumbs. Toss and sprinkle in the grated Pecorino Romano.
13. Serve with a drizzle of extra virgin olive oil.

Pici with Gorgonzola and romanesco
(*Pici con Gorgonzola e romanesco*)

Here is an alternative way to make and prepare your pici pasta.
Perfectly prepared pici is such a simple and forgiving pasta. Make,
rest and portion the pasta dough and roll long, thin, uneven worms.
They have a great texture with a tender yet firm bite. Pairing it with
a pointy-nosed romanesco cauliflower and Gorgonzola gives you a
great combination of flavours, because when Gorgonzola is melted
it becomes clingy, but not in an overbearing fashion. Sliced
mushrooms would also make a welcome addition, as would the
lighter variation of Dolcelatte cheese.

Preparation time: 40 minutes plus 30 minutes resting of the pasta
dough at room temperature
Cooking time: 30 minutes
Serves: 4

300g/10½oz semola pasta dough
250g/9oz cauliflower florets
40g/1½oz butter
3 tbsp extra virgin olive oil
175g/6oz Gorgonzola
1 garlic clove, peeled, minced
80ml/3fl oz double cream
1 tbsp fresh thyme, finely chopped
Salt and pepper, to season
40g/1½oz Parmigiano Reggiano, grated

1. Make and rest your pasta dough as per page 4.
2. Halve the dough and roll it with a rolling pin to a sheet,
   approximately 1–1.5cm/^{1}/2–^{5}/8in in thickness.
3. Cut the sheet into 1cm/^{1}/2in strips and roll each strip into a
   round, thick spaghetti roughly 3mm/^{1}/8in in width.
4. Lay the prepared pici onto a tray dusted with semola until
   required.
5. Make the rest of the pici pasta as needed.

6. Add salt to a pan of boiling water and parboil the cauliflower florets for 7 minutes (depending on the floret sizes). Remove with a slotted spoon and reserve the cooking water.

7. Into a sauté pan put the butter, two tablespoons of extra virgin olive oil and the Gorgonzola with the minced garlic. Using a wooden spoon, stir until the Gorgonzola has melted and become sticky and gooey.

8. Add the cream and freshly chopped thyme. Stir.

9. Cook the pici in a large pan of salted water (ideally the cauliflower water) until *al dente*.

10. Add the parboiled florets to the Gorgonzola. Season with black pepper and combine. Drain the pici and add them to the Gorgonzola cream.

11. Add the remaining extra virgin olive oil and the Parmigiano Reggiano. Toss well and serve on warm plates.

CARMELA'S TIP:

- You can substitute milk for the cream to create a lighter sauce. Also, you could make the pici using an egg-based dough or even the spinach dough on page 11.

Scialatelli with yellow bell peppers, cherry tomatoes and walnuts

(Scialatelli con peperone, pomodorino e noci)

There are many names for scialatelli pasta depending on the region you are standing in. These scialatelli are from the region of Campania and are a speciality of the beautiful town of Minori on the stunning coastline of Amalfi. This pasta is thicker than a tagliatelle and half the length with the occasional addition of Parmigiano Reggiano or lemon zest in the pasta dough. My scialatelli would pair beautifully with any of the sauces from the sauce chapter, in particular the pistachio or asparagus pesto.

Preparation time: 45 minutes plus 30 minutes resting of pasta dough at room temperature
Cooking time: 45 minutes
Serves: 4

Pasta
200g/7oz 00 flour
200g/7oz semola, plus extra for kneading and dusting
40g/1½oz Parmigiano Reggiano, grated
10 basil leaves, finely chopped
120ml/4fl oz milk, tepid
1 egg
2 tbsp extra virgin olive oil

Dressing
2 yellow peppers
3 tbsp extra virgin olive oil
300g/10½oz cherry tomatoes, halved
2 garlic cloves, peeled, finely sliced
3 tbsp stale breadcrumbs
30g/1oz Parmigiano Reggiano, grated
Zest of 1 small lemon
Small bunch of basil, chopped
Small bunch of parsley, chopped
45g/1½oz walnuts, roughly chopped
Salt and pepper, to season

1. Make the scialatelli pasta. In a bowl mix together the 00 flour and semola flour. Sprinkle in the grated Parmigiano Reggiano and combine.
2. Tip the flour onto a wooden board and make a well in the centre, wide enough to take the liquid.
3. In a bowl combine the chopped basil leaves, tepid milk, egg and extra virgin olive oil.
4. Slowly add the liquid to the well and combine with the flour. Form into a ball and knead for 8–10 minutes until smooth and elastic.
5. Press the ball of dough down into a flat disc, cover with a tea towel and rest at room temperature for 30 minutes.
6. Place the (whole) peppers on the wire racks of a preheated oven and bake for 25 minutes.
7. When the peppers are slightly browned remove them from the oven and wrap them in a clean tea towel for 10 minutes. This will allow the peppers to sweat, making it easier to peel them.
8. Peel the outer skin of the peppers (I love this job) and discard them. Slice the peppers lengthways and discard the centre core. Set aside until required.
9. Roll out the pasta dough with a rolling pin or pasta machine to 3mm/^{1}/$_8$in in thickness.
10. Cut strips of the pasta sheet, 10cm/4in in length by 1cm/^{1}/$_2$in in width; a short, wide ribbon.
11. Place the cut scialatelli onto a semola-dusted tea towel or tray.
12. Pour the extra virgin olive oil into a sauté pan. Add the halved cherry tomatoes and fry over a low heat for 5 minutes.
13. Add the garlic and sliced roasted peppers. Cook for 10 minutes. Season with salt and pepper to taste.
14. Mix the stale breadcrumbs with the Parmigiano Reggiano and lemon zest.
15. Place a large pan of water on to boil. Once boiling, salt well and cook the pasta until *al dente*.
16. Add a small ladle of pasta water to the tomatoes and add the fresh herbs and walnuts. Season with salt and pepper.
17. Drain the pasta and add it to the sauté pan and toss.
18. Serve in warm bowls with a scattering of the breadcrumb mixture.

CARMELA'S TIP:
- Any colour pepper will do, but I would always steer clear of green peppers as they are a little bitter for this recipe.

Spaghetti carbonara (*Spaghetti alla carbonara*)

I could not leave this regal classic out of *Pasta Fresca*, even though I prefer my carbonara with a high-quality dried spaghetti instead of fresh. You can of course make your own pasta, but I would suggest dried as it then makes this dish a speedy mid-week supper. Spaghetti carbonara is said to have been created in Rome just after the Second World War. A dish born out of simplicity with just a few key ingredients and NEVER any cream, that was me raising my voice. Spaghetti was made for a classic, light carbonara but equally leggy linguine or bendy bucatini would be nice.

Preparation time: 5 minutes
Cooking time: 12 minutes
Serves: 4

400g/14oz spaghetti, dried
450g/1lb guanciale (pig cheek) or pancetta, cubed
2 garlic cloves, peeled, crushed (optional)
100g/3½oz Pecorino Romano grated, plus extra to serve
1 large egg plus 5 large egg yolks
Salt and pepper, to season

1. Cook the spaghetti according to the packet instructions in salted boiling water, less 2 minutes ensuring it remains *al dente*.
2. Fry the guanciale or pancetta in a dry sauté pan until lightly golden and blush in colour.
3. Add the crushed garlic and stir. Cook for 1 minute but be careful to not burn the garlic. Take the pan off the heat.
4. In a bowl mix 80g/3oz of the Pecorino Romano, the whole egg and yolks together, seasoning with salt and pepper. Reserve 20g/^{1}/$_2$oz of the Pecorino Romano for serving
5. Drain the spaghetti (reserving 70ml/2^1/$_2$fl oz pasta water) and tumble the bendy strands into the bronzed guanciale (which is now off the heat), stirring well. Stir the egg sauce into the spaghetti and pour in the pasta water. Stir vigorously off the heat; this will help to emulsify the sauce.
6. Serve in large bowls with the reserved grated Pecorino Romano sprinkled over the top and a little black pepper.

My papa Rocco's spaghetti with garlic, oil and chilli intensity

(Spaghetti, aglio, olio e pepperoncino)

Spaghetti: the simplest of all pasta shapes and dressings. Uncomplicated to make yet complex in flavour, this is an essential dish, and as per many of my simple recipes these instructions are fairly straightforward. Whenever my mum Solidea was away from home and I phoned up my papa Rocco to ask what he was cooking, he would always say spaghetti aglio, olio with far too much pepperoncino, quickly followed by 'don't tell your mum'. I can still imagine him sitting at the kitchen table twirling his spaghetti with beads of sweat dripping down his forehead; the homemade red wine would always have helped I am sure.

Preparation time: 5 minutes
Cooking time: 12 minutes
Serves: 4

400g/14oz spaghetti, dried
70ml/2½fl oz extra virgin olive oil
5 garlic cloves, peeled, finely sliced
1 red chilli, seeds removed, finely sliced

1. Place a large pan of water on to boil. Once boiling, salt well and cook the pasta until *al dente*.
2. Pour the extra virgin olive oil into a sauté pan, followed by the garlic and chilli.
3. Fry over a low heat and season with salt and pepper.
4. Try to not burn the garlic, as it has a tendency to catch very quickly when your back is turned.
5. Drain the spaghetti (reserving 50ml/1½fl oz pasta water) and toss into the dressing, adding a little of the pasta water to emulsify the sauce.
6. Simply serve with no cheese.

CARMELA'S TIP:
- Add some anchovies for a salty hit of flavour.

Square-cut pasta ribbons with chicken dumplings in stock

(Spaghetti alla chitarra con polpettine di pollo)

Fresh pasta, stock and chicken meatballs – a perfect threesome that comes together in a hearty bowl of textured pleasure. A little preparation would be advised: make the stock the day before, then that leaves just the pasta and chicken polpettine to make on the day. Spaghetti alla chitarra (maccheroni) is a pasta from the region of Abruzzo that is extruded through a tool that is layered with wires, known as a guitar, but my children still call it the pasta harp. In fact, I have a video of Chiara when she was little singing in the kitchen whilst strumming away on said pasta harp.

Preparation time: 1 hour
Cooking time: 30 minutes
Serves: 4

3 litres/5¼ pints chicken stock (page 81)
4 chicken thighs
½ tsp freshly grated nutmeg
1 garlic clove, peeled, sliced
Small bunch of parsley, including stalks, chopped
1 tbsp celery leaves, plus extra to serve
4 tbsp breadcrumbs, slightly stale
1 egg
40g/1½oz Parmigiano Reggiano, grated, plus extra to serve
300g/10½oz egg pasta dough (page 6)
Salt and pepper, to season

1. Pour the chicken stock into a saucepan and simmer the chicken thighs for 15–20 minutes until cooked through.
2. Remove the thighs and place the stock to one side. When the thighs have cooled slightly, remove the meat from the bones. (You could use boneless thighs here for ease.)
3. Blitz the chicken meat in a small food processor along with the nutmeg, garlic, parsley, celery leaves and breadcrumbs.

4. Scrape into a clean bowl and crack in the egg. Sprinkle in the Parmigiano Reggiano and stir, seasoning with salt and pepper.
5. If the mixture is a little wet, add some flour; if the mixture is a little dry, add a tablespoon of stock.
6. Dampen your hands and roll walnut-sized amounts of the chicken mixture into balls. Place them onto a tray dusted with a little semola flour.
7. Prepare the pasta as per page 6 and roll. If you do not have a chitarra press, just roll the pasta to level 4 of your pasta machine and cut 30cm/12in lengths of pasta into sheets. Allow the sheets to dry for 10–15 minutes then pass through the spaghetti attachment.
8. Warm the stock and gently place the chicken balls into the stock. Cook for 4 minutes then add the pasta.
9. Cook the pasta until *al dente*. Use tongs to create spirals of pasta in warm bowls along with a few chicken balls and a ladle of stock.
10. Top with a few celery leaves and a further grating of Parmigiano Reggiano.

CARMELA'S TIP:
*   Other names for this pasta are tonnarelli, crioli and stringhetti.

Strozzapreti pasta with octopus and cherry tomatoes
(*Strozzapreti pasta, polpo e pomodori*)

My love affair with octopus continues. When cooked well, octopus can transport you to the warmth of your most recent holiday. It is opulent, delicate to look at, yet incredibly robust in flavour. I have included this recipe from my last cookbook *Northern and Central Italian Family Cooking* because I love both the shape and the sauce. The sauce and pasta work beautifully together, but the polpo sauce could also be spooned onto warm soft polenta.

Preparation: 20 minutes
Cooking time: 1 hour
Serves: 4

Octopus preparation
800g/1lb 12oz fresh octopus
Pinch of salt
2 bay leaves
Parsley stalks (see below)
5 pink peppercorns

Sauce
4 tbsp extra virgin olive oil
1 small carrot, peeled, finely cubed
1 celery stalk, peeled, finely cubed
1 shallot, peeled, finely chopped
2 garlic cloves, peeled, crushed, finely chopped
300g/10½oz fresh cherry tomatoes, halved
300ml/11fl oz passata
50ml/1½fl oz water
1 tbsp celery leaves, finely chopped
Salt and pepper, to season
Pinch of chilli flakes (optional)
350g/12½oz strozzapreti
Small bunch of parsley, finely chopped (stalks are for the octopus above)
Rustic bread, to serve (optional)

1. Place a large pan of water on to boil – the pan must be large enough to boil the entire octopus. Season with a pinch of salt.
2. Take the octopus and shock it three times in the water as this will aid in tenderising it. Dip the octopus in the boiling water, hold it there for 20 seconds and lift. Repeat this action three times then immerse the entire octopus into the pan.
3. Add the bay leaves, parsley stalks and pink peppercorns.
4. Clamp on a lid and place on a medium heat, then boil for between 30 and 40 minutes until knife tender.
5. Into a shallow but wide saucepan put the extra virgin olive oil along with the carrot, celery and shallot. Cook for 15 minutes until softened but not coloured.
6. Add the garlic and stir.
7. Tumble in the cherry tomatoes and cook for 5 minutes.
8. Once the octopus is cooked, drain and chop the legs (tenacles) into small bite-sized pieces and add them to the tomato sauce.
9. Stir and add the passata and water, along with a generous pinch of salt and pepper and the celery leaves.
10. If you like a little heat then sprinkle in a few chilli flakes. Stir and cook the sauce for a further 15 minutes.
11. Place a large pan of water on to boil for the pasta. Once boiling, season well with salt and cook the strozzapreti as per packet instructions, less 3 minutes ensuring the pasta remains *al dente*.
12. Drain the pasta (retaining a small ladle of pasta water) and toss into the sauce. If needed, add a little of the pasta water, stir, check for seasoning and sprinkle in the chopped parsley.
13. Serve in warm bowls with a little rustic bread.

CARMELA'S TIP:

• It may be necessary to pre-order your fresh octopus from your local fishmonger so please ensure you allow time for this. To make strozzapreti add an extra 1 hour and 10 minutes to your preparation time (page 37).

Tagliarini with spring nettles and egg yolk (*Tagliarini al ortiche*)

Typically, from Piedmont, tagliolini are similar to the well-known tagliatelle but they are much thinner in width. Tagliolini are an egg yolk-based pasta that makes them rich and opulent in colour, too. Foraging soft-tipped spring nettles to go with long, leggy pasta is a tradition as well as a favourite pastime of mine. I take a small basket and head to my parents' farm. Gloves on, I pick the new, tender, prickly nettle leaves with gusto, always remembering it's best to over-pick as when blanched they wilt in a similar way to spinach. If you pick too many, you can also blanch and freeze them for future use.

Preparation time: 30 minutes plus 30 minutes resting of pasta dough at room temperature
Cooking time: 4 minutes
Serves: 4

Pasta dough
60g/2oz nettles
4 egg yolks
200g/7oz 00 flour
50g/1½oz semola di grano duro

Sauce
2 tbsp extra virgin olive oil
30g/1oz butter
150g/5oz nettles, fresh, washed
½ tsp freshly grated nutmeg
Salt and pepper, to season
80g/3oz Parmigiano Reggiano, grated
4 egg yolks

1. Rinse the nettles in cold water. Blanch them in boiling water for 90 seconds, drain and rinse in cold water. Blitz the blanches nettles an and egg yolks together in a small food processor until you have a smooth green liquid.
2. Mix the nettle liquid with the 00 and semola flour and form a dough. Knead for 7 minutes until soft and elastic. Cover the dough in a clean tea towel and allow to rest at room temperature for 30 minutes.
3. Using a pasta machine roll the pasta out to level 5, or use a rolling pin and roll the dough as thin as possible.
4. Cut the long pasta sheets into 25cm/10in rectangular lengths. Lightly dust the pasta sheets with semola and roll into a loose sausage roll.
5. Using a sharp knife slice the pasta into 2mm/$\frac{1}{16}$in laces. Place the tagliarini onto a tray dusted with semola until required.
6. Place a large pan of water on to boil. Once boiling, salt well.
7. In a medium shallow pan put the extra virgin olive oil and butter and sauté the nettles for 3 minutes. Add the nutmeg and stir. Season with salt and pepper.
8. Cook the pasta for 90 seconds, until *al dente*.
9. Drain (reserving 50ml/1$\frac{1}{2}$fl oz of the cooking water) and add the tagliarini to the sauce. Toss and stir together and add the grated Parmigiano Reggiano.
10. Add the reserved pasta water and fully emulsify so that the sauce takes on a creamy finish.
11. Plate up your pasta into loose nests, making a shallow dent in the centre and adding a yolk to the centre of each nest. Top with a little salt and enjoy.

CARMELA'S TIP:
- Retain the whites to make sweet meringues, amaretti biscuits or an egg white omelette. The egg whites freeze well too.

Tagliatelle with mushrooms, thyme and mascarpone

(Tagliatelle con funghi, timo e mascarpone)

Tagliatelle never fails to satisfy. Simple to make, quick to cook and robust in length, it has the capability and pleasing nature to cling joyfully to whatever sauce is passed its way. This mushroom, thyme and creamy mascarpone sauce is no exception.It is fantastic any time of the year but with seasonal wild mushrooms this dish longs for lazy autumn days.

Preparation time: 30 minutes plus an additional 15 minutes resting of pasta dough
Cooking time: 20 minutes
Serves: 4

400g/14oz egg pasta dough (page 6)
2 tbsp extra virgin olive oil
25g/1oz butter
450g/1lb mushrooms, sliced (use your favourites)
2 tbsp fresh thyme, finely chopped (stalks removed)
½ tsp chilli flakes (optional)
Salt and pepper, to season
125g/4½oz mascarpone
150g/5oz Grana Padano, grated

1. Portion your dough into two. Roll out your first half of pasta dough using your pasta machine. I roll to level 5 of my Marcato machine, cutting each length into 25cm lengths. Allow the sheets to air-dry for 15 minutes before feeding the sheets through the tagliatelle section of your pasta machine.
2. Heat the extra virgin olive oil and butter in a large sauté pan over a medium heat.
3. Add the sliced mushrooms and stir. Try to not overcrowd the mushrooms in a tight pan otherwise they will not colour; use a large, medium-sided pan.
4. Fry the mushrooms for 15 minutes.

5. Add the chopped thyme and chilli flakes, if you are using them. Stir well and season with a generous pinch of salt and pepper.
6. Fill a large saucepan with water and once boiling, salt well. Cook the pasta until *al dente*.
7. Add the mascarpone to the mushrooms and stir, along with half the Grana Padano.
8. Using tongs, introduce the tagliatelle to the mushroom pan. Do not be afraid if you add some pasta water as this would be a welcome addition to the sauce.
9. Stir together and add a little more pasta water if required.
10. Spoon onto plates and top with the remaining Grana Padano cheese.

Wholewheat spaghetti with duck offal
ragu (*Bigoli con l'anara*)

This dish requires a little forward planning and a handy duck carcass for stock making! Venetian bigoli are thick, coarse spaghetti strands of pasta that are extruded through a special bronze press called a '*bigolaro*. This dish calls for a duck carcass (once I've roasted a duck, I stash the carcass in my deep freeze to make stock later on). You can order the offal from your butcher or farm shop. Alternatively, you could boil a small duck and use the meat for a second dish. Any long pasta would work well here; I particularly like bucatini if bigoli are unavailable.

Preparation time: 15 minutes
Cooking time: 1 hour 20 minutes
Serves: 4

1 duck carcass, chopped (all offal must be kept)
1 shallot, skin on, quartered
1 large carrot, 2cm/1in pieces
2 sticks of celery including the leaves, chopped
2 large ripe tomatoes, quartered
1 garlic clove, unpeeled, squashed
65g/2oz butter
4 sage leaves
Salt and pepper, to season
400g/14oz bigoli or bucatini, dried
Small bunch of parsley, finely chopped
60g/2oz Grana Padano, grated (optional)

1. Prepare the duck stock by adding the duck carcass to a large saucepan with the shallot, carrot, celery stalks, leaves, tomato and garlic.
2. Top the pan up with water and add a pinch of salt. Boil the duck for around an hour until cooked. Taste and season the stock after an hour and adjust the seasoning, if required, to your personal taste.

3. Put the butter in a small sauté pan and add the sage leaves and duck offal, ensuring all sinew is removed. Cook gently over a medium heat. Add a ladle of the duck stock, place a lid on the pan and simmer for approximately 25 minutes.
4. Strain the stock through a sieve and discard the vegetables. Check the stock for further seasoning.
5. Bring the stock back to the boil and add the bigoli pasta to the pan. Cook for 10 minutes until *al dente*.
6. Drain the pasta (retaining the stock). Add the bigoli to the offal and stir, adding a little more stock if required.
7. Sprinkle in the chopped parsley, stir and serve with Grana Padano.

CARMELA'S TIP:
- Alternatively, you could substitute the dried pasta with pici (page (164). If duck offal is impossible to source, I cheat and use chicken offal instead.

Wide pasta ribbons with autumn mushroom Bolognese

(*Pappardelle al funghi Bolognese*)

Paired with a robust autumnal mushroom and thyme sauce, these wide pasta ribbons feel reassuringly rich and decadent, yet incredibly flavourful and simple. This dish seems to tick all the boxes on a cold winter's day. Pair with pappardelle (which means to gobble up) or you can substitute the pappardelle with any preferred fresh pasta; I just love pappardelle.

Preparation time: 30 minutes
Cooking time: 1 hour
Serves: 4

400g/14oz fresh egg pasta dough (page 6)
Semola, for kneading and dusting
25g/1oz dried porcini
Parmigiano Reggiano rind (optional)
3 tbsp extra virgin olive oil
30g/1oz butter
1 shallot, peeled, finely chopped
2 small carrots, peeled, finely cubed
1 large celery stalk, finely cubed
1.5kg/3lb 5oz mushrooms, diced
2 garlic cloves, peeled, minced
50g/1½oz tomato purée
200ml/7fl oz red wine
800ml/1⅓ pints passata
Salt and pepper, to season
Pinch of dried chilli
1 tbsp fresh thyme, finely chopped
1 tbsp celery leaves, finely chopped
Small bunch of parsley, including stalks, finely chopped
50g/1½oz Parmigiano Reggiano, grated

1. Roll the dough to the 5th setting of your pasta machine. I do, however, prefer a thinner pasta, so I roll to level 6 on my Marcato, taking the pasta to 2mm/^{1}/16in. Cut the ribbons to 2.5cm/1in in width and 25cm/10in in length.
2. Set the pasta aside on a tray dusted with semola until required.
3. Tumble the dried porcini mushrooms in a bowl with the Parmigiano Reggiano rind. Top with boiling water and allow the porcini to plump up for 15 minutes.
4. Heat the extra virgin olive oil and butter in a large saucepan over a medium heat.
5. Add the shallot, carrots and celery. Cook over a medium heat for 15 minutes until softened and just coloured.
6. Add your chosen mushrooms and stir, along with the minced garlic.
7. Squeeze in the tomato purée and add the red wine.
8. Cook the red wine and allow it to evaporate, burning away the alcohol. Stir.
9. Drain the porcini and roughly chop them. Add the porcini to the already cooking mushrooms along with the Parmigiano Reggiano rind.
10. Run the porcini liquid through a little kitchen paper or a small-holed sieve to remove any grit. Add the liquid to the pan. Stir.
11. Add the passata and season with salt and pepper and a little dried chilli and thyme.
12. Cook for 40 minutes over a medium heat.
13. Taste the mushroom sauce and add seasoning if necessary.
14. Cook the pasta in a large pan of water that has been salted until the pappardelle are *al dente*.
15. Scatter the celery leaves and parsley into the sauce. Combine.
16. Drain the pasta and tumble the wide ribbons into the mushroom Bolognese. Remove the Parmigiano Reggiano rind.
17. Tong onto plates and top with a little grated Parmigiano Reggiano.

Gnocchi and gnudi

Truth be told, I always have three packets of pre-made gnocchi in my fridge or freezer. These have saved me on many an evening, when I'm taxiing my children around while trying to make sure that everyone has something decent to eat too. An almost impossible task when you have such a large family, but, nine times out of ten, I manage it, if only by the skin of my teeth.

When time allows, fresh gnocchi are a true blessing and if I decide to make the filled ones, then even better. Making gnocchi is a Sunday dinner job for me as, while they aren't too complicated to make, they do take a bit of time.

Gnudi are my ultimate pasta, especially the most basic variety. Give me a bowl of spinach and ricotta gnudi with a little nutmeg, boiled or poached in salted water and spooned onto a bed of tomato sauce, and I would be one happy lady. This simple filling is my favourite, but the key is ensuring the filling can be formed into small balls or quenelles. If the filling is too wet, you have a mess on your hands. Remember to squeeze out your blanched spinach and drain your ricotta overnight for full satisfaction. These pillows swell so slightly and become almost tender in texture with a welcoming bite.

Asparagus gnocchi (*Gnocchi agli asparagi*)

In the height of asparagus season this dish highlights these glorious medieval-looking spears in a simple yet sublime manner. Baked gnocchi are not your average pillow gnocchi. They have a wonderful soft and sponge-like centre with a firm, golden outer crust. Did I mention they are totally addictive too?

Preparation time: 30 minutes to prepare plus 10 minutes resting of gnocchi dough
Cooking time: 10 minutes
Serves: 4

750ml/26fl oz milk
200g/7oz semolina
750g/1lb 10oz asparagus spears
100g/3½oz butter
50g/1½oz Parmigiano Reggiano, grated
150g/5oz prosciutto cotto, sliced (cooked Italian ham)
Salt and pepper to season

1. Warm the milk slowly and when simmering, slowly pour in the semolina and stir with a wooden spoon.
2. Cook through, this may take approximately 25–30 minutes.
3. Prepare the asparagus spears by removing the woody base.
4. Steam the asparagus until tender (include the woody discards too).
5. Add the woody discards to a small food processor and blitz until smooth.
6. Add the asparagus purée to the semolina mixture and stir. Season with a pinch of salt and a light grinding of black pepper.
7. Add 40g/1½oz of the butter, proscioutto cotto and half the Parmigiana Reggiano to the semola mixture and stir. Spread the mixture onto a lined tray and rest for 30 minutes in the fridge.
8. Preheat the oven to 210°C/190°C fan-assisted/Gas 6.
9. Take a large bakeware dish and cut circles of the semolina, 6cm/2½in in diameter to roughly 1cm/½in in depth (give or take).
10. Lay the cut discs into the dish and top with the steamed asparagus tops.
11. Splodge on the remaining butter and sprinkle over the rest of the grated Parmigiano Reggiano cheese.
12. Bake in the oven for 15 minutes.

Chickpea gnudi with dressed tomatoes
(*Ceci gnudi al pomodoro*)

The chickpea flour adds an almost nutty flavour, subtle yet with a perfect presence. No potato in sight; just a naked pasta filling and a little flour, dressed in wonderfully juicy room temperature tomatoes with a little honey. Room temperature and ambient is key here; refrigerated cold tomatoes will never do, and in all fairness they should never be cooked directly from the fridge.

Preparation time: 15 minutes plus 15 minutes resting
Cooking time: 10 minutes
Serves: 4

500g/1lb 1½oz ricotta (drained overnight)
1 egg yolk
Salt and pepper, to season
250g/9oz semola di grano duro rimacinata, plus extra for dusting
140g/5oz chickpea flour
450g/1lb tomatoes
2 garlic cloves, peeled, minced
3 tbsp extra virgin olive oil
Small bunch of basil, torn
1 tbsp celery leaves, finely sliced
40g/1½oz Pecorino Romano, grated

1. Place the ricotta and egg yolk into a large bowl. Stir well.
2. Season with a little salt and pepper and add the semola and chickpea flour. Stir with a wooden spoon and combine until it forms a soft workable dough. Cover and rest for 15 minutes at room temperature.
3. Dust two trays with a little semola.
4. Dust your hands with a little semola, to prevent sticking. Pinch walnut-sized amounts of the gnudi and roll into small rounds.
5. Lay each rolled gnudi onto the semola-dusted trays.

6. Place a large pan of water on to boil. Once boiling, salt well.
7. Quarter your tomatoes and place them into a large bowl.
8. Add the minced garlic and extra virgin olive oil and season generously with salt and pepper.
9. Scatter in the basil and celery leaves and stir well.
10. Cook the gnudi until *al dente*.
11. Scoop them out with a slotted spoon and place them into the dressed tomatoes.
12. Toss to combine and dress with the grated Pecorino Romano. Serve.

Grape-stuffed potato gnocchi (*Gnocchi di uva*)

Grape-filled gnocchi with a sweet and savoury flavour. This may
sound a little odd, but it works incredibly well. The use of grapes in
savoury cooking takes the dish to another level in terms of bite and
balance of flavour. Boiled and served with a simple butter sauce
they are scrumptious, but you can also pan-fry them, so they
develop a sweet, golden top and bottom, and eat them as a frankly
awesome potato snack.

Preparation time: 30 minutes
Cooking time: 10 minutes
Serves: 4

1kg/2lb 4oz potatoes
30g/1oz butter
70g/2½oz Parmigiano Reggiano, grated
1 egg
280g/10oz 00 flour
Bunch of grapes, seedless ideally however not essential
Salt and pepper, to season
80g/3oz butter
8 sage leaves

1. Place the potatoes with their skins on into a large pan of boiling
   water. Salt well and boil until fork tender.
2. Once tender, drain the potatoes and allow them to cool until you
   can handle them easily. Peel the potatoes and rice them with a
   potato ricer, then place them into a bowl. A standard potato
   masher will also do, just ensure they are lump-free.
3. Add the butter, grated Parmigiano Reggiano and egg. Stir.
4. Spoon the flour into the potatoes and season with a little salt and
   pepper.
5. Form the gnocchi mixture into a ball of dough. Please do not
   overwork the dough as it will become glutinous and heavy;
   2 minutes of kneading would be enough. You are looking for a
   soft, not sticky dough.

6. Cut the grapes in half and set aside in a bowl until required, also slice a small handful of grapes for the dressing.
7. Divide the dough into four portions. Roll each portion into long sausages to the thickness of approximately 2cm/1in.
8. Cut the sausages into 3cm/1¼in pieces. Flatten the potato gnocchi into your palm of your hand, add a halved grape and fold the potato gnocchi around the grape. Repeat with the remaining dough.
9. Cook the gnocchi in a large pan of salted, boiling water.
10. When the gnocchi bounce to the top, stir gently, and allow the gnocchi to cook for an additional 2 minutes.
11. Melt the butter in a small pan until just browned, add the sage and a handful of sliced grapes with a pinch of salt.
12. Drain and serve the gnocchi with the browned butter grapes and sage.

Naked pasta filling, rolled and served with a cherry tomato sauce
(*Gnudi con sugo di pomodorini*)

A lighter option to filled pasta with so many possibilities. Gnudi (naked) is the recognised name but these delicate morsels are also known as malfatti and ndunderi. They are rolled and served classically in a butter dressing or tomato sauce as below. The important point to try and control here is the moisture of all the ingredients, as gnudi may be delicious and effortless but they also tend to split and break up easily. Patience may be required.

Preparation time: 15 minutes plus 10 minutes resting
Cooking time: 5 minutes
Serves: 4 (as a starter)

250g/9oz ricotta (drained overnight in a sieve or butter muslin)
500g/1lb 1½oz spinach, blanched
¼ tsp freshly grated nutmeg
70g/2½oz Parmigiano Reggiano, grated, plus a little extra to serve
50g/1½oz semola di grano duro rimachinata, plus a little more for dusting
Salt and pepper, to season
2 tbsp extra virgin olive oil
1 shallot, peeled, finely cubed
2 garlic cloves, peeled, finely sliced
400g/14oz cherry tomatoes (fresh or tinned)
4 basil leaves

1. If you have time and the inclination, I recommend that you drain the ricotta over a sieve or a piece of muslin overnight in the fridge to remove excess liquid. If overnight is not an option, then an hour or so will suffice.
2. Take the blanched spinach and drain it very well. I tend to squeeze it in a clean tea towel and wring it. A little rough, I must admit, but this is a necessity.
3. Chop the spinach.
4. Tip the ricotta and spinach into a bowl and mix well with a wooden spoon.

5. Sprinkle in the nutmeg, grated Parmigiano Reggiano, semola and a pinch of salt and pepper. Mix.
6. Dust a tray with a little semola to prevent sticking. Form the mixture into small balls approximately 3cm/1¼in in diameter.
7. Place on the tray and use up the remaining filling. Dust with a little more flour and place in the fridge to firm up while you prepare the sauce.
8. In a large sauté pan that will be large enough to accommodate the gnudi, fry off the shallot in a little olive oil for 5 minutes, until just softened.
9. Add the garlic and tumble in the cherry tomatoes. Season with salt and pepper and add the basil leaves. Cook for 15 minutes.
10. Place a large pan of water on to boil for the gnudi. Once boiling, salt well.
11. Cook the gnudi for a few minutes until they bounce and bob to the top.
12. Spoon a layer of the tomato sauce onto each plate. Scoop the gnudi out (with a slotted spoon) and nestle equal amounts onto the tomato sauce.
13. Top with a little extra Parmigiano Reggiano and serve.

CARMELA'S TIP:

- I prefer to use semola flour as opposed to 00 flour as the semola is firmer in texture and holds the naked balls together very well. However, for gluten-free options you could also use chickpea or chestnut flour.

Polenta gnocchi with meat sauce (*Gnocchi di farina gialla con ragu di carne*)

Polenta is the gluten-free grain that just keeps on giving, yet this versatile grain is still very much underused in the UK. I think many are still unsure of how to cook it well. Over the years I have written about my love of this diverse grain, and the key to cooking it: polenta loves and requires flavour; without it, it is incredibly bland and unsatisfying, similar to gruel with nobody asking for more please, sir. These polenta gnocchi also work incredibly well with the famous white polenta from Veneto. Here I have paired them with a decadent and slow-cooked meat ragu.

Preparation time: 20 minutes
Cooking time: 3 hours
Serves: 4–6

Ragu

25g/1oz dried porcini
3 tbsp extra virgin olive oil
1 shallot, peeled, finely cubed
1 stick celery, finely cubed
1 carrot, peeled, finely cubed
Small bunch of parsley, including stalks, finely chopped
500g/1lb 1½oz stewing steak, chopped into 2cm/1in cubes
150ml/5½fl oz red wine
350g/12½oz ripe tomatoes, chopped (or passata in the height of winter)
1 bay leaf
300ml/11fl oz beef stock (page 80)
Small bunch of basil leaves, torn
Salt and pepper, to season

Polenta

2 litres/3½ pints vegetable stock or salted water
600g/1lb 5oz polenta (yellow or white)
60g/2oz butter
80g/3oz Parmigiano Reggiano, grated
Salt and pepper, as required

1. Place the porcini into a small heatproof bowl and cover with boiling water so that the porcini are fully immersed. Push the porcini down with a spoon and allow them to bathe in the boiling water for around 15 minutes until hydrated and plump.

2. Heat the extra virgin olive oil in a large pan and add the chopped shallot, celery and carrot. Cook over a medium heat for 10 minutes until tender and translucent.

3. Add the parsley stalks and beef, stir well and sear all over for 5 minutes.

4. Pour in the red wine and stir with a wooden spoon. Allow the alcohol to evaporate, which should take 5 minutes or so, then add the tomatoes and bay leaf.

5. Drain the porcini through a piece of kitchen paper and reserve the liquid. The kitchen paper will pick up any unnecessary and unwanted sediment.

6. Chop the porcini and add them to the tomatoes along with the strained porcini liquid and the bay leaf. Stir well.

7. Season with salt and pepper, and cook for an hour. Add half the beef stock and stir. Cook for a further 2 hours, until the sauce has thickened, and add the stock as required; go steady as you may not need to use all of the stock. Check for a final seasoning and remove the bay leaf before serving.

8. Half an hour or so before the sauce is ready, prepare the polenta gnocchi.

9. Bring the vegetable stock (or salted water) to the boil; my preference is always stock.

10. Sprinkle the polenta into the stock in a slow yet steady stream, while using a balloon whisk to incorporate; the whisk will eliminate any lumps.

11. After 3 minutes of whisking, change to a wooden spoon and beat the polenta until cooked through. Add the butter and half the Parmigiano Reggiano, and season with salt and pepper to taste.

12. Using two tablespoons, make quenelles of the polenta and lay them across a large warm platter, spoon over some ragu and top with the remaining Parmigiano Reggiano. Top with the basil leaves and serve.

Potato gnocchi with a Parmigiano Reggiano, speck and cream sauce

(Gnocchi di patate al Parmigiano Reggiano, speck e crema)

Potato gnocchi are comforting, filling, and the perfect base for many seasonal sauces. These elongated gnocchi are a little opulent and offer some warmth, especially through the cooler months. Equally, in warmer weather dress them with a light sauce and they make an early-evening garden supper a little more special. They are simple, inexpensive and speedy to make as well.

It can be difficult to provide you with a foolproof potato gnocchi recipe that effectively works every time because of many factors, including the type of potatoes used (I use King Edward or Maris Piper) and how much moisture is in them. That said, here is my recipe. I have opted to boil the potatoes here with their skins on, but you can also bake or even steam them in their entirety if preferred.

Preparation time: 40 minutes
Cooking time: 20 minutes
Serves: 4

Potato gnocchi
400g/14oz potatoes
1 egg (optional but preferable)
Salt and pepper, to season
150g/5oz–180g/6½oz 00 flour

Parmigiano Reggiano cream
80g/3oz butter plus an additional teaspoon for the sage dressing
1 tbsp extra virgin olive oil
1 large shallot, peeled, finely sliced
1 garlic clove, peeled, finely sliced
600ml/1 pint/20fl oz double cream
250g/9oz Parmigiano Reggiano, grated, plus extra to serve
¼ tsp freshly grated nutmeg
4 slices speck, sliced thinly
8 fresh sage leaves
Salt and pepper, to season

1. Peel the potatoes and cook in a large pan of boiling water for 20 minutes or until tender. Drain and allow to cool then, using a potato ricer or grater, press or grate potatoes into a large bowl. Add the egg, if using, add the egg and season with salt and pepper. Combine fully with a wooden spoon.
2. Gradually add the flour until you have a pliable potato dough. You may not need all the flour, then again you may need a little more. Your dough should be smooth, workable and not sticky.
3. Knead the potato dough for 2 minutes. Be careful when working the dough because overworking will lead to a heavy, glutinous dough.
4. Portion the dough into six pieces. Roll each portion into a long sausage and cut off 1.5cm/^{5}/8in nuggets.
5. Flour your hands and roll each gnocchi in between your palms. I like to form them a little thinner than most, as they do in the northern regions of Italy. If you prefer you can simply roll a piece of potato dough down the prongs of a fork or use a wooden gnocchi board.
6. Place each rolled gnocchi onto a clean tea towel or tray dusted with a little semola flour.
7. Put the butter and extra virgin olive oil into a medium, heavy-based saucepan over a medium heat.
8. Tumble in the chopped shallot and fry gently for 5 minutes to soften.
9. Add the sliced garlic and fry for 1 minute before pouring in the double cream. Reduce the heat so that you do not scorch the cream.
10. Season with salt and pepper to your specific taste and add a little freshly grated nutmeg.
11. Sprinkle in the grated Parmigiano Reggiano and stir. Simmer the sauce for 10 minutes.
12. Into a dry frying pan, place the sliced speck and fry until crispy. This will take 4–5 minutes or so.
13. When you have 1 minute left to cook the speck, add the sage leaves and an additional teaspoon of butter. Stir to melt the butter and coat the sage leaves.
14. Boil the gnocchi in a large pan of salted boiling water. When the gnocchi bob to the top of the water, give the gnocchi a further 2 minutes.
15. Using a slotted spoon or spider, place the gnocchi into the Parmigiano Reggiano cream sauce. Stir carefully to coat the gnocchi.

16. Spoon the gnocchi onto warmed plates and scatter over a little pan-fried speck, crispy sage and a generous scattering of Parmigiano Reggiano.

CARMELA'S TIP:
- To freeze gnocchi, place them onto a tray (a single layer only) lined with greaseproof or parchment paper and pop into the freezer. After 2 hours the gnocchi will be perfectly frozen. Place them into an airtight container and freeze for up to 6 months. Cook directly from the freezer.

Potato gnocchi with spinach and provolone cream (*Gnocchi di patate, spinachi e provolone fonduta*)

A verdant little potato parcel dressed in a silky snow-like sauce. This sounds like the beginning of a food lover's fairy tale, but it is this evening's dinner. Feel free to use a combination of soft green tender herbs with or instead of the spinach. Give the dish your own signature – a spritz of lemon zest, chilli flakes, or a combination of cheeses within the cream will add a welcome interest.

Preparation time: 20 minutes
Cooking time: 30 minutes
Serve: 4

450g/1lb potatoes, skin on
120g/4oz spinach
200g/7oz semola di grano duro rimacinata, plus extra for dusting
225g/8oz ricotta (drained overnight)
2 eggs
¼ tsp fresh nutmeg, grated
250g/9oz provolone piccante
250ml/9fl oz double cream
¼ tsp freshly grated nutmeg
130g/4½oz peas
Salt and pepper, to season

1. Place the potatoes with their skins on in a saucepan with cold water.
2. Boil for 15 minutes until knife tender. Drain and cool.
3. Peel and put the potato flesh in a bowl. Mash well with a potato masher or ideally a potato ricer, removing any lumps and bumps as you go.
4. Place spinach in boiling water and blanch for 30-40 seconds until it turns bright green. Drain and squeeze out excess water from the blanched spinach and finely chop. Add the spinach to the potato and combine.
5. Add the semola, ricotta, eggs, nutmeg and a twist of salt and pepper, and combine into a ball of dough. Place on a lightly floured surface and knead for a couple of minutes. Do not overwork otherwise the dough will become heavy and glutinous.
6. Cover and rest at room temperature for 15 minutes.
7. Roll ropes of the gnocchi dough to the thickness of your little finger and cut 2.5cm/1in pieces.
8. Flour your gnocchi board and use your thumb to roll each piece down the board; repeat until all the gnocchi dough has been used up. Place the spinach gnocchi on a semola-dusted tray and set aside. An alternative if you do not have a gnocchi board could be a sushi mat, or a flat cheese grater.
9. Chop the provolone up into small pieces.
10. Warm the double cream and add the provolone, stir to combine and add the grated nutmeg and a twist of salt and pepper.
11. Add the peas to the cream mixture. Cook over a low heat for 10 minutes.
12. Bring a large pan of water to the boil. Once boiling, salt well. Cook the gnocchi until they rise to the top of the pan, then cook for a further minute and drain.
13. Dress the gnocchi with the provolone cream and simply get stuck in.

CARMELA'S TIP:
- Make sure the gnocchi do not touch each other on the tray as they tend to stick together.

Pumpkin gnocchi with sausage

(Gnocchi di zucca con verza e salsiccia)

The morning after Halloween, children normally awake still a little excited from all their sweet treats from the night before, while parents wake to compost or bin their decorative pumpkins. I like to save and use up the flesh from mine (I always carve four pumpkins) in a few different ways. I always make a pumpkin soup, a pasta filling with amaretti biscotti and mostarda di frutta, a pumpkin and nutmeg pie, or this golden nugget-studded gnocchi recipe. As with many wet vegetables you need to make sure that you remove and drain as much of the moisture away as possible prior to making and forming these pumpkin gnocchi.

Preparation time: 40 minutes to prepare plus 15 minutes resting at room temperature
Cooking time: 25 minutes
Serves: 4

600g/1lb 5oz pumpkin, flesh chopped
150g/5oz 00 flour
150g/5oz semola, plus extra for dusting
1 egg
3 tbsp extra virgin olive oil
200g/7oz sausage, de-skinned, chopped
50ml/1½fl oz white wine (or vermouth)
400g/14oz cabbage, finely sliced
100ml/3½fl oz chicken stock (page 81)
2 shallots, peeled, halved, finely sliced
Salt and pepper, to season
50g/1½oz Parmigiano Reggiano, grated
80g/3oz fontina

1. Preheat the oven to 200°C/180°C fan-assisted/Gas 6. Season and place the pumpkin on a baking tray, then roast in the oven for 30-35 minutes until soft and lightly browned at the edges. Allow to cool and mash. Mix the mashed pumpkin, 00 and semola flours and egg together. Stir with a wooden spoon and form a dough.
2. Cover and rest the dough for 15 minutes or so.
3. Dust some semola over the pumpkin dough. Portion the dough and roll long sausages to the thickness of your forefinger. Cut into 3cm/1in nuggets. Dust with semola and set aside.
4. Pour the extra virgin olive oil into a large shallow pan, tumble in the sausage pieces and gently fry for 10 minutes.
5. Pour in the vermouth and cook for 2–3 minutes.
6. In the meantime boil the cabbage in the chicken stock for 5 minutes. Drain and set aside.
7. Add the sliced shallots to the browned sausage and soften for 5 minutes.
8. Use a slotted spoon to scoop out the cabbage and add it to the sausage mixture. Season with salt and pepper.
9. Place a large pan of water on to boil. Once boiling, salt well.
10. Cook the gnocchi for 3 minutes until they bob to the top, then cook for a further minute or so.
11. Drain the gnocchi and add them gently to the sausage and cabbage pan. Stir to incorporate and add the Parmigiano Reggiano. Stir once again.
12. Spoon onto a warmed serving platter and tear small pieces of the fontina, nestling the soft cheese over and in between the gnocchi.

Semolina gnocchi with lentils and clams

(*Gnocchi di semolina con lenticchie e vongole*)

The gnocchi here are plump and wonderful, but I truly believe the textured lentils and salty clams are the star of this dish. They pair perfectly together and add wonderful balance, flavour and a tender bite. The gnocchi could easily be replaced with fregola pasta or another short pasta shape of your choosing.

Preparation time: 15 minutes plus 1 hour resting at room temperature
Cooking time: 15 minutes
Serves: 4

Semolina gnocchi
Pinch of salt
650ml/23fl oz milk
200g/7oz semolina

Sauce
20ml/4 tsp extra virgin olive oil
1 shallot, peeled, finely sliced
1 celery stick, finely chopped
1 garlic clove, peeled, finely sliced
Small bunch of parsley, including stalks, finely chopped
150g/5oz cherry tomatoes, halved
200g/7oz tin of lentils, drained (see note below)
300ml/11fl oz vegetable stock (page 84)
1kg/2 lb 3oz clams
200g/7oz prawns
2 tbsp celery leaves, finely chopped
Salt and pepper, to season

1. Add a pinch of salt to the milk. Warm the milk gently and when simmering, slowly pour in the semolina and stir with a wooden spoon.
2. Cook through until thickened and glossy, this may take approximately 25–30 minutes.

3. Spread the mixture onto a lined tray. Chill until the golden mixture has set.
4. Preheat the oven to 200°C/180°C fan-assisted/Gas 6.
5. Press out circles around 4cm/1½in in diameter, 1cm/½in in depth. Lay the discs on a lined and buttered baking dish.
6. Bake for 20 minutes while you prepare the sauce.
7. Add the extra virgin olive oil to a medium sauté pan and fry the shallots and celery for 15 minutes until softened. Add the garlic and chopped parsley stalks, and cook over a low heat for a further 2 minutes.
8. Tumble in the tiny button lentils and halved cherry tomatoes. Stir and cook for 15 minutes. Season with salt and pepper.
9. Pour in the stock, clams and prawns. Scatter in the celery leaves and clamp on a lid.
10. Cook for 5 minutes. Discard any clams that remain closed. Check the seasoning, then top the baked semolina gnocchi with the lentil sauce and serve.

CARMELA'S TIP:
• If preferred you can soak some dried lentils overnight. Just bathe them in water with a stalk of chopped celery, then cover and leave until you're ready to cook. Drain and cook for an additional 45 minutes until tender.

Spelt gnocchi (*Gnocchi di farro*)

I have a love affair with farro. I call it the good grain because it offers a resounding sense of comfort and pleasure on the palate. These gnocchi are made with farro flour, known in the UK as spelt. Spelt is milled from an ancient Italian grain that is similar in taste to barley. Paired with a wonderful curried sauce, spring onions and dill, these gnocchi are taken out of their traditional Italian realm and given a sauce with a difference.

Preparation time: 35 minutes to prepare plus 10 minutes resting
Cooking time: 10 minutes
Serves: 4

100g/3½oz farro flour (spelt), plus extra for dusting
200g/7oz breadcrumbs (slightly stale)
1 tbsp chives, finely chopped
1 tbsp parsley, finely chopped
250ml/9fl oz vegetable stock (page 84)
250ml/9fl oz milk
¼ tsp freshly grated nutmeg
½ tsp curry powder
2 spring onions, peeled, finely sliced lengthways
1 garlic clove, peeled, minced
2 tbsp 00 flour
Small sprig dill, finely chopped
Salt and pepper, to season

1. Tip the farro flour and breadcrumbs into a bowl. Stir to combine.
2. Add the chopped chives and parsley to the farro mix. Stir with a wooden spoon and slowly add a little of the vegetable stock until a ball of dough is produced. You may not need all the stock so please approach with caution.
3. Knead the dough for a couple of minutes, cover and rest at room temperature for 10 minutes.
4. Form the gnocchi mixture into small balls; using two teaspoons may be best when forming.
5. Sit them on a lightly dusted tray until required.

6. Pour the milk into a shallow sauté pan and gently warm.
7. Add the grated nutmeg, curry powder, finely sliced spring onions and sliced garlic. Cook over a medium heat for 10 minutes, stirring intermittently so the base of the pan does not catch.
8. Sprinkle the flour into the milk and stir, to thicken the sauce. Season with salt and pepper and cook for a further 5 minutes.
9. Place a large pan of water on to boil. Once boiling, season well and cook the gnocchi until they bob to the top of the pan. Allow them to cook for a further minute, then using a slotted spoon lift the gnocchi and add them to the thickened sauce.
10. Stir and sprinkle with the prepared dill. Serve.

Sweet potato gnocchi with prosciutto and crushed pistachio (*Patate dolce con prosciutto e pistacchio*)

As far as vegetables go, these sunset-coloured potatoes with their textured outer bodies are very high on my list. Growing up I never had the pleasure of encountering them, but these days I tend to overeat them along with my daughter Natalia. Roasted, baked and mashed sweet potatoes are a sweet pleasure, but in this recipe I have chosen to pair them with a little savoury, salty prosciutto and emerald pistachio slivers, which take them to another level.

Preparation time: 20 minutes
Cooking time: 45 minutes
Serves: 4

450g/1lb sweet potatoes, skins on
2 tbsp extra virgin olive oil
185g/6½oz Parmigiano Reggiano, grated
250g/9oz ricotta (drained in a sieve or muslin overnight)
150g/5oz 00 flour
100g/3½oz semola
Salt and pepper, to season
150g/5oz prosciutto, sliced
125g/4½oz butter
1 tbsp fresh thyme, finely chopped
40g/1½oz pistachio nuts, shelled, skins removed, roughly chopped
50g/1½oz Parmigiano Reggiano, grated

1. Preheat the oven to 210°C/190°C fan-assisted/Gas 6.
2. Cut the potatoes in half lengthways and place cut side down on a lined baking tray. Drizzle with a little extra virgin olive oil and bake until knife tender (until the knife pierces the skin easily).
3. Remove from the oven. Scoop out the vibrant flesh and pop into a bowl along with the Parmigiano Reggiano, drained ricotta, 00 and semola flour and stir well to incorporate. Season with salt and pepper.

4. Combine and knead the dough lightly for 2 minutes. Cover and rest the dough for 30 minutes at room temperature.
5. Lightly dust a tray with semola and portion the dough in half. Cut a section off and roll to form a sausage 2.5cm/1in in width. Cut pieces of the gnocchi dough to 2.5cm/1in in length.
6. Using a gnocchi board, a fork or a sushi mat, roll each piece of sweet potato gnocchi until small grooves have been made.
7. Place on a tray dusted with semola and continue to form gnocchi using the remaining dough.
8. Tumble the prosciutto slices into a dry frying pan and fry over a medium heat until lightly coloured on both sides.
9. Place a large pan of water on to boil. Once boiling, salt well. Boil the gnocchi until they bob to the top, cook for a further minute, and drain.
10. Spoon the butter and thyme into a sauté pan and allow the butter to brown lightly and go slightly nutty.
11. Add the gnocchi to the butter and toss.
12. Spoon in the golden prosciutto along with any excess juices.
13. Stir and add the chopped pistachio nuts.
14. Top with the grated Parmigiano Reggiano and serve.

Filled pasta

Choose your filling and off you go. Sometimes I start with the intention of making a specific shape, but then when I begin I might opt for something a little easier and quicker, like mezzalune. Some of my most adored filled pasta shapes are: tortellini floating innocently like little, plump buttons in fresh brodo (stock); filled cappelletti in browned butter; and pumpkin cappellacci in browned butter, topped with a crowning glory of amaretti crumble.

I have a delicious hack when it comes to filled pasta if you are searching for comfort food that doesn't require lots of precision. I like to make spinach and ricotta ravioli, slightly over-sized, boil them for two minutes and drain. Mix them with your chosen sauce and layer the pasta in a bakeware dish with a little grated Parmigiano Reggiano and freshly torn mozzarella. Bake until bubbly. Any filled pasta would work, though obviously the filling would change based on the sauce that you choose to make.

Freshly made pasta is my preferred pasta to freeze as it keeps and freezes incredibly well and can be cooked directly from frozen, dressed with browned butter and a grating of Pecorino Romano. If you are not eating your filled pasta on the day you make them, I would suggest you place them onto a tray lined with parchment paper and pop the tray into the freezer for an hour. Once frozen, tumble the pasta into food-safe bags or lidded containers. Cook from frozen and just adjust the cooking time by adding a couple of minutes.

Casoncelli parcels (*Casoncelli alla Bergamasca*)

These delicate half-moon parcels with indented tummies from Bergamo are also known as 'casonsei' in the local Bergamasco dialect. Simple to master and, what's more, they freeze incredibly well. Here, they are served with an uncomplicated dressing and a filling that you can interchange with other filled pasta shapes too.

Preparation time: 30 minutes plus 30 minutes to rest the casonsei
Cooking time: 15 minutes
Serves: 4–6

Filling
100g/3½oz stale breadcrumbs
3 tbsp milk
300g/10½oz soft Italian sausage
125g/4½oz mortadella
1 garlic clove, peeled, minced
1 large egg
1 tbsp fresh parsley, including stalks
Salt and pepper, to season

Pasta
400g/14oz fresh egg pasta dough, rolled into thin lasagne sheets
(as per page 36)

Sauce
1 tbsp olive oil
80g/3oz butter
300g/10½oz guanciale, small cubes
1 garlic clove, peeled, crushed
6 sage leaves
60g/2oz Grana Padano, grated
Small bunch of parsley, chopped, to finish

1. Soak the stale breadcrumbs in milk in a small bowl for 20 minutes. Into a food processor place the ingredients for the filling, ensuring the sausages have been skinned first. Blitz for 30 seconds to a textured paste and set aside.

2. Place the lasagne sheets onto a lightly floured surface. Using a 6cm/2^1/2in pastry cutter, press and cut circles of dough using all the lasagne sheets.
3. Add a tablespoon amount of the mixture onto each circle of dough. Fold and form into a half-moon (mezzaluna) and seal with a little water if required. Take the half-moons and gently press the curved centre in a little, almost denting the pasta.
4. Place the prepared casoncelli on a tray dusted with a little semola; this will eliminate sticking.
5. Rest the casoncelli for a minimum of 30 minutes before cooking.
6. Place a large pan of water on to boil. Once boiling, salt well.
7. Put the olive oil and butter into a sauté pan. Cook the guanciale over a medium heat for 5 minutes, until golden in colour.
8. Add the garlic and sage leaves. Cook over a low heat for 2 minutes.
9. Cook the casoncelli in the boiling water; these should take approximately 7 minutes. Drain and add them with care to the sauté pan. Coat the casoncelli gently with the butter and serve with a generous dusting of Grana Padano and chopped parsley leaves.

Chestnut ravioli with rabbit and thyme

(Ravioli di castagne con ripieno di Coniglio)

Chestnut pasta transports me to my favourite season: autumn, with its blue skies, crisp chill in the air and crunchy leaves. The aromas that surround this season are what I long for throughout the year. This wonderful dish as it stands is a pure joy to behold, but it can also take on more if you so wish (see note below). What I will say, though, is that preparing the filling in advance will not only save you time, it will also add flavour by allowing the rabbit to rest in the fridge overnight.

Preparation time: 45 minutes plus 30 minutes to rest the dough at room temperature
Cooking time: 1 hour 20 minutes
Serves: 4

Pasta
100g/3½oz 00 flour, plus extra for kneading and dusting
100g/3½oz chestnut flour
2 eggs
Semola, as required for kneading and dusting

Filling
5 tbsp extra virgin olive oil
400g/14oz rabbit
1 shallot, peeled, finely cubed
1 carrot, peeled, finely cubed
1 stick celery, finely cubed
2 garlic cloves, peeled, sliced
80ml/3fl oz white wine
200ml/7fl oz vegetable stock (page 84)
1 egg
65g/2oz Grana Padano, grated, plus extra for finishing
Small bunch of parsley
100g/3½oz spinach
stale breadcrumbs, if needed

Dressing
100g/3½oz butter
Salt and pepper, to season
Small bunch of thyme, chopped (stems removed)
Zest of 1 small orange (optional)

1. Combine the 00 flour and chestnut flour. Tip onto a wooden board and make a well in the centre.
2. Crack in the eggs and work the flour with the eggs to form a dough. Knead for 7 minutes until smooth and elastic.
3. Cover with a tea towel and set aside for a minimum of 30 minutes while you prepare the filling.
4. Pour 3 tbsp olive oil into a sauté pan over a medium heat and add the rabbit pieces. Sear until lightly golden in colour, for approximately 10 minutes.
5. Remove the rabbit from the pan and add another 2 tbsp olive oil along with the shallot, carrot and celery. Cook over a medium heat for 10 minutes.
6. Add the garlic to the pan along with the seared rabbit and white wine. Allow the white wine to evaporate and add the vegetable stock.
7. Season with salt and pepper. Cook for 45 minutes without a lid.
8. Remove the pan from the hob. In a separate pan place spinach in boiling water and blanch for 30–40 seconds until it turns bright green. Drain and squeeze.
9. Remove the rabbit from the bone and add the meat to a food processor along with the egg and Grana Padano, parsley and spinach. Blitz, taste and season as required. If you find the mixture is a little loose, add a small handful of stale breadcrumbs. Set the filling aside.
10. Take the rested pasta and roll it out with your pasta machine or rolling pin to a 2mm/^{1}/$_{16}$in thickness.
11. Spoon tablespoon amounts of the filling along the long side of the pasta sheet, leaving a 3cm/1in gap between mounds.
12. Fold the sheet over and secure the chestnut pasta around each mound, always trying to dispel any air as you go.
13. Use a knife or fluted pasta wheel and cut around the mounds to form ravioli; alternatively you can stamp them with a decorative cutter, such as a triangle, star or heart.

14. Lay the ravioli on a tray dusted with semola and continue as required.
15. Place a large pan of water on to boil; once boiling, salt well.
16. Cook the ravioli for 3 minutes or until *al dente*. Drain, reserving a ladleful of pasta water.
17. Put the butter in a large sauté pan and add a twist of salt and pepper.
18. Allow the butter to melt and become a light shade of nutty brown. Add the thyme and orange zest.
19. Using a slotted spoon add the ravioli to the butter pan and toss; you can also add a little pasta water as this will emulsify the sauce.
20. Serve on warm plates with a little extra Grana Padano.

CARMELA'S TIP:

- You can add a little chestnut purée to the rabbit filling if you so desire.

Crab and saffron ravioli
(*Ravioli di granchio e zaffarano*)

These pillows of delicate crab meat are simply divine: light, aromatic and wonderful served in a bowl of piping hot stock. I have opted for vegetable stock as I prefer a neutral-tasting stock, but this stock has the benefit of a pinch of golden saffron as its crowning glory.

Preparation time: 45 minutes
Cooking time: 8 minutes
Serves: 4

500g/1lb 1½oz white crab meat
100g/3½oz brown crab meat
1 tbsp fennel tops, finely chopped
Zest of 1 small lemon (optional)
Salt and pepper, to season
Saffron pasta dough (page 16)
1 litre/1¾ pints vegetable stock (page 84) or good-quality shop-bought stock
Small pinch of saffron
Small bunch of chives, finely chopped
Pepper, to season

1. In a bowl, put the white and brown crab meat along with the fennel tops, lemon zest (if using) and a twist of salt and pepper, Stir, taste and adjust the seasoning as required.
2. Roll the pasta through a pasta machine starting at the widest setting first. Fold the pasta six times on the widest setting, then pass the pasta sheet through every consecutive setting twice without folding. Then roll to setting 6 of your pasta machine, or 2mm/^{1}/$_{16}$in in thickness. You should be able to see your hand through the pasta sheet if you were to hold it up to the window.
3. To make the ravioli, cut the pasta sheet into 50cm/20in lengths: you will need two lengths at a time for the base and top sheets.
4. Place small teaspoon amounts of the mixture in two rows with a 10cm/4in gap in between the mounds.

5. Take another pasta sheet of the same size and gently cover the filling mounds on the base sheet. If required, stretch the dough a little over to meet the edges of the base sheet.
6. Secure the pasta around each mound of filling with your palms and apply pressure.
7. Using a 7cm/3in cutter, press out each mound into ravioli.
8. Place the ravioli onto a tray dusted with semola.
1. Repeat the process as required.
10. Warm the stock and add a pinch of saffron for a hit of colour.
11. Place a large pan of water on to boil. Once boiling, salt well and cook the pasta until *al dente*, around 5 minutes or so.
12. Drain the pasta and plate up into warm bowls, topping with a ladle of the saffron stock, chopped chives and a twist of pepper.

Culurgiones with a simple tomato sauce
(*Culurgiones al pomodoro*)

Culurgiones come from the island of Sardinia. The fillings vary across the island from the addition of saffron to meat fillings, steamed chard or mint.

This is one of the most technical pasta shapes you will ever encounter – the perfect pleating will have you on your knees. That said they are an absolute joy to eat, so they are well worth the effort. The first culurgiones I made resembled small plump Cornish pasties. So, if I can make them, then there's hope for us all.

Preparation time: 1 hour plus 30 minutes resting of the dough
Cooking time: 30 minutes
Serves: 4

Pasta
400g/14oz semola di grano duro rimacinata
200g/7oz warm water

Filling
1kg potatoes, peeled, mashed
200g/7oz Pecorino Sardo, grated, plus extra to serve
2 tbsp extra virgin olive oil
4 tbsp fresh mint, finely sliced
Salt and pepper, to season

Tomato sauce
3 tbsp extra virgin olive oil
1 shallot, peeled, diced
1 litre/1¾ pints passata
Salt and pepper, to season
12 basil leaves

1. To make the pasta dough, tip the semola onto a wooden board and make a well in the centre. Add the water a little at a time and incorporate to form a dough.
2. Knead for 7–10 minutes until elastic and smooth.

3. Cover and leave at room temperature while you prepare the filling.
4. To make the filling, spoon the mashed potato into a bowl, add the Pecorino Sardo along with the extra virgin olive oil and stir.
5. Add the fresh mint and season generously with salt and pepper. Cover and pop in the fridge for an hour or until required.
6. For the tomato sauce, pour the olive oil into a saucepan and fry off the shallot over a medium heat for 7 minutes until softened and translucent.
7. Add the passata and season with salt and pepper. Cook for 30 minutes.
8. Roll the pasta dough out to a thickness of 2mm/^{1}/$_{16}$in. Use an 8cm/3^1/$_4$in circular cutter and cut out as many discs as you can.
9. Add walnut-sized balls of filling to each circle.
10. Here comes the tricky bit. Pick up a disc and place it on your left palm. Pinch the seam from one side to the other until you have a closed parcel that has a decoratively pinched seam across the top. Have a look at my Instagram IGTV videos for a how-to video guide (@carmelaskitchen).
11. Repeat. Place all the culurgiones onto a tray dusted with semola.
12. Place a large pan of water on to boil. Once boiling, salt well.
13. Cook the culurgiones for about 5 minutes. Spoon them out of the pan and place on warm plates. Top with the tomato sauce and sprinkle over a little extra Pecorino Sardo for good measure. Top with the basil leaves.

CARMELA'S TIP:
- You can also add saffron to the filling. Infuse the saffron in 2 tbsp warm stock for 5 minutes and add to the potato filling.

Dirty pasta stamps (*Pasta lorda*)

I was sold on the name alone in all honesty – I mean, who wouldn't be? Referred to as dirty pasta solely because of the thin layer of filling used, pasta lorda is one of my go-to filled pasta dishes because of how quickly you can make, roll, layer and cut the filled pasta sheets into perfectly presentable stamps known in Italian as 'Francoboli'. Try and cut the sheet into smaller squares rather than larger ones; however, when you're hungry, I know that's easier said than done. I can feed my hungry family of six on a Sunday incredibly quickly. Choose your preferred stock and enjoy.

Presentation: 1 hour plus 30 minutes resting of pasta dough at room temperature
Cooking time: 5 minutes
Serves: 4–6

400g/14oz egg pasta dough (page 6)
2 litres/3½ pints fresh chicken stock (page 81)

Filling
250g/9oz ricotta, drained overnight
150g/5oz asiago, grated
75g/2½oz Parmigiano Reggiano, grated, plus extra for serving
½ tsp freshly grated nutmeg
1 egg
2 tbsp celery leaves, finely sliced
Salt and pepper, to season

1. In a bowl mix together the ricotta, asiago and Parmigiano Reggiano.
2. Stir well and add the nutmeg, egg, celery leaves, and a pinch of salt and a generous grinding of black pepper.
3. Mix the filling together and chill in the fridge while you roll out the pasta.
4. Roll out the prepared dough with a rolling pin or broom handle on a large wooden board or table top that has been dusted with semola.

5. [see step 4] Roll the pasta sheet out into as much of an even circle as you can. Aim for a relatively see-through dough, about 2mm/^{1}/16in thick.
6. Fold the dough in half and make a gentle fold or crease in the middle to help you gauge where to spread the filling.Unfold the pasta back out into a circle.
7. Using a flexible spatula or the back of a spoon, spread the filling over half the sheet, making sure you leave a 2cm/1in gap all the way around.
8. Fold over and press to secure with your palms.
9. Using the prongs of a fork, secure the edges of the circle by indenting the seam of the sheet carefully. You should now have a large semi-circle that is filled and secured.
10. Take a fluted pasta wheel and cut strips of dough, lengthways and then widthways, to the shape of a traditional-sized stamp.
11. Dust two trays or clean tea towels with semola and lay the francoboli onto them.
12. Dry the pasta for 30 minutes.
13. Warm the stock and tumble in the pasta. Cook for 3 minutes and ladle into warmed bowls with a little extra Parmigiano Reggiano.

CARMELA'S TIP:
- Feel free to substitute the asiago with taleggio or robiola, all amazing cheeses.

Filled parcels with rabbit, veal and pork

(Faggotini con coniglio, vitello e maiale)

Faggotini are little parcels, a gift, a perfectly formed square of pasta dough that is filled and enclosed by pulling up each corner and forming a four-sided pyramid. Formed and filled, it is served with browned butter and a flurry of Parmigiano Reggiano. I adore the filling and can happily eat it straight from the pan so I always suggest making a little more and also making the filling a day in advance, if time allows, as it benefits no end from being chilled; the flavour seems to intensify overnight.

Preparation time: 1 hour
Cooking time: 2 hours
Serves: 4

300g/10½oz egg pasta dough (page 6)

Filling
30g/1oz butter
3 tbsp extra virgin olive oil
1 stick celery, chopped into small cubes
2 small carrots, peeled, chopped into small cubes
1 shallot, peeled, chopped into small cubes
2 garlic cloves, peeled, finely sliced
150g/5oz rabbit, roughly chopped, bones removed
250g/9oz loin of veal, chopped into small pieces
200g/7oz boned shoulder pork, chopped into small pieces
1 tbsp tomato purée
125ml/4fl oz red wine
800ml/1⅓ pints vegetable stock
250g/9oz spinach
80g/3oz Parmigiano Reggiano, grated, plus extra to serve
¼ tsp freshly grated nutmeg
2 egg yolks (freeze the whites for a mallow meringue)
Salt and pepper, to season

Sauce
40g/1½oz butter
4 sage leaves
50ml/1½fl oz cooking juices

1. Put the butter and extra virgin olive oil into a large shallow pan.
2. Tumble in the celery, carrot, shallot and garlic and cook over a low heat for 15 minutes until softened and tender.
3. Add the rabbit, veal and pork, and stir. Cook and sear the meat all over, around 10 minutes.
4. Add the tomato purée, red wine and vegetable stock. Season with salt and pepper. Cover and cook over a medium heat for 1 hour 30 minutes. Check every 20 minutes for seasoning.
5. Once the meat is cooked, drain the cooking juices and retain them to serve.
6. Add all of the contents of the pan into a food processor and blitz gently.
7. Place the spinach in boiling water and blanch for 30–40 seconds until it turns bright green. Drain and squeeze, then add to the food processor with the Parmigiano Reggiano, nutmeg and egg yolks. Blitz for 30 seconds.
8. Stir, taste and check for seasoning.
9. Spoon into a bowl, cover and chill. Making this a day ahead will save time and allow flavours to develop.
10. Roll the pasta dough out into long lasagne sheets, level 6 with a pasta machine or 3mm/^{1}/sin if rolling by hand. Cut the dough with a fluted pasta wheel into 6cm/2^1/2in squares.
11. Pinch a piece of the filling and roll it into a ball the size of a grape. Place the meaty ball onto the centre of each square.
12. Fold the pasta along each of the long edges, turning up the edges and corners so that they meet. It is difficult to explain but imagine a 4-sided pyramid. Use all the pasta dough and filling, and place the fagottini onto a lightly dusted tray.
13. Place a large pan of water on to boil. Once boiling, salt well and cook the fagottini until cooked through and *al dente* (4 minutes).
14. Put the butter into a sauté pan along with the sage leaves and add 50ml/1^1/2fl oz of the cooking juices that were reserved. Cook for 5 minutes.
15. Drain the fagottini and use a slotted spoon to place them into the sauce.
16. Spoon into warm bowls with extra Parmigiano Reggiano.

Filled pasta parcel shoes with browned butter and fresh peas

(Scarpinocc con burro e pinoli e piseli)

The filling for these characterful scarpinocc is fresh, light, and versatile. As its Italian name states, the final pasta shape resembles a rustic shoe. Once you are confident at forming these scarpinocc, they will soon become a firm favourite when filled pasta is called for at mealtimes.

Preparation time: 45 minutes
Cooking time: 15 minutes
Serves: 4

300g/10½oz egg pasta dough (page 6)

Filling
250g/9oz peas
250g/9oz mascarpone
100g/3½oz Parmigiano Reggiano, grated
¼ tsp freshly grated nutmeg
Zest and juice of 1 small lemon
1 tbsp fresh marjoram leaves
Salt and pepper, to season

Sauce
2 tbsp extra virgin olive oil
80g/3oz butter
50g/1½oz pine nuts
50g/1½oz peas
Salt and pepper, to season
Lemon juice (leftover from the filling)
40g/1½oz Parmigiano Reggiano, grated, to serve

1. Prepare the filling. In a small food processor blitz the blanched peas, mascarpone, grated Parmigiano Reggiano, nutmeg, lemon zest, half the lemon juice and marjoram leaves, until fully incorporated, approximately 30 seconds. Stir with a spatula and taste. Season with a little pinch of salt and twist of black pepper.
2. Spoon the mixture into a clean bowl and cover. Place in the fridge until required.
3. Take your egg pasta dough and roll it to setting 6 of your pasta machine. If rolling with a rolling pin take the dough to 3mm/^{1}/$_8$in.
4. Cut out 6–8cm/2^1/$_2$–3in discs of dough and spoon teaspoon amounts of the filling into the centre of each disc. Fold the disc over to form a half-moon (mezzaluna).
5. To finish forming the mezzaluna into scarpinocc, hold the mezzaluna flat side up and roll it onto its curve, then apply an indent into the top using your finger. The pasta should resemble a rustic shoe.
6. If you are struggiling with the scarpinocc, you could form the pasta into a caramelle as per page 57 and then indent the top, forming a deep dent.
7. Repeat with the remaining pasta and filling. Dust a tray with a little semola flour and place the pasta on it to prevent sticking.
8. Place a large pan of water on to boil. Once boiling, salt well.
9. Cook the pasta until *al dente*, around 4 minutes or so.
10. Into a large shallow sauté pan, put the extra virgin olive oil and butter. Bring the fats to a gentle melting heat and add the pine nuts and peas. Cook for 3 minutes.
11. Stir and season with salt and pepper.
12. Spritz in the reserved lemon juice and stir. Check for additional seasoning.
13. Using a slotted spoon, lift out the *al dente* pasta and add them gently into the sauce to coat them.
14. Plate up your pasta as required. Spoon over a little of the sauce and a sprinkle of Parmigiano Reggiano.

CARMELA'S TIP:
- For ease you can use a piping bag to pipe the filling.

Filled skirtless ravioli coins with stock
(*Anolini in brodo*)

A festive celebration of pasta and stock, with two of the very best in one hearty bowl: fresh anolini floating in a bowl of freshly made stock. Plump and full of filling, these anolini are as light as they look and beyond delicious. Anolini are a stuffed, small circular pasta from Parma that can be enjoyed any day of the year, but throughout the festive season if you were to walk around the region of Emilia Romagna, you'd smell a heavy scent of brodo and hear the gentle toss of anolini as they hit each bubbling pan.

Preparation time: 45 minutes plus 30 minutes drying the dough at room temperature
Cooking time: 1 hour
Serves: 4–6

50g/1½oz butter
1 garlic clove, peeled, finely minced
450g/1lb ground beef (I prefer 5 per cent fat)
70g/2½oz stale breadcrumbs
1 egg yolk
½ tsp dried basil
100g/3½oz Parmigiano Reggiano, grated, plus extra to finish
300g/10½oz egg pasta dough (page 6)
Chicken or beef stock, shop-bought or see page 80
25g/1oz parsley, chopped
Salt and pepper, to season

1. Put the butter in a sauté pan and over a medium heat fry off the garlic and beef until seared all over; this should take about 5 minutes.
2. Drain off excess fat and place the beef into a clean bowl.
3. Allow the beef to cool for about 15 minutes, then add the stale breadcrumbs, egg yolk, dried basil and grated Parmigiano Reggiano.
4. Stir with a wooden spoon and season with salt and pepper. Cover and place the filling in the fridge.

5. Roll out your pasta dough with a pasta machine to level 6 or to 2mm/^{1}/₁₆in in thickness with a rolling pin.
6. Cut the sheets into 30cm/12in lengths.
7. Add half-teaspoon amounts of the filling along the entire length of the pasta sheet in two rows, leaving 5cm/2in between each half-teaspoon amount.
8. Lay a sheet directly on top of the filling and secure each mound with the side of your hand, trying to remove any air pockets before you stamp them out.
9. Use a circular cutter 2.5cm/1in in diameter and push firmly over each mound.
10. Pick up each anolini and place it on a semola-dusted tray.
11. Fill the remaining pasta dough with filling. Allow the anolini to air dry for 30 minutes before simmering them in the stock.
12. Warm your chosen stock and check for seasoning.
13. Add the anolini to the stock and boil for 3–4 minutes.
14. Ladle into bowls and top with a sprinkle of Parmigiano Reggiano and a little parsley garnish.

CARMELA'S TIP:
• These freeze like a dream and can be cooked directly from frozen.

Green ravioli parcels with burrata and pine nuts (*Ravioli verdi con burrata*)

Spinach pasta dough adds a certain sense of richness, opulence and 'va va voom' to this simple dish. It has a unique sophistication that wills me to go back to Puglia, the regional home of burrata. Burrata is a cheese that is full of curds and needs nothing more to accompany it than a pinch of salt and a little extra virgin olive oil. In all honesty cooking, heating, warming, or messing with burrata is, in my opinion, sacrilege. Which makes me a hypocrite, I know, but I enjoyed the most exquisite burrata ravioli in Sorrento a few years back, so here is my simple take on this dish.

Preparation time: 45 minutes
Cooking time: 10 minutes
Serves: 4

300g/10½oz spinach pasta dough (page 11)
600g/1lb 5oz burrata
80g/3oz butter
40g/1½oz pine nuts (Italian ones preferably)
1 small sprig rosemary
70g/2½oz Parmigiano Reggiano, grated
Salt and pepper, to season

1. Roll out the spinach pasta dough into an even sheet to level 6 (approx. 2mm in thickness) using a pasta machine.
2. Roll two long sheets of pasta dough, one for the base and one for the top.
3. Cut the burrata into 16 pieces.
4. Place pieces of burrata along one side of a pasta sheet, leaving gaps of 2mm/^{1}/16in in between the burrata mounds.
5. Dampen in between each piece of burrata and lay a pasta sheet on top. Secure around each mound, removing any air, and cut using a fluted pasta wheel.
6. Place each ravioli onto a lightly floured tray.
7. Bring a large pan of water to the boil. Once boiling, salt well.

8. Brown the butter in a shallow sauté pan and tumble in the pine nuts and the rosemary sprig. Season with salt and pepper.
9. Cook the ravioli until *al dente*.
10. Using a slotted spoon, place the ravioli onto a pre-warmed serving platter.
11. Drizzle with the browned butter and slightly bronzed nuts.
12. Top with lots of Parmigiano Reggiano and enjoy.

Half-moons of pasta filled with grouper and spinach (*Mezzalune di cernia e spinaci*)

Using fish as a filling adds a lighter feel to pasta. If you would prefer to not add Parmigiano Reggiano to the filling, then please just omit it; I just love the salty balance that the cheese offers.

Preparation time: 1 hour plus 30 minutes resting of the pasta dough at room temperature
Cooking time: 30 minutes
Serves: 4

400g/14oz grouper, filleted (seabass makes for a great substitute)
350g/12½oz spinach, blanched
80g/3oz Parmigiano Reggiano, grated
1 egg
Small bunch of parsley, finely chopped
150g/5oz ricotta, drained overnight
¼ tsp freshly grated nutmeg
Salt and pepper, to season
300g/10½oz saffron pasta dough (page 16)
80g/3oz butter
100ml/3½fl oz double cream
2 tbsp chives, chopped

1. Preheat the oven to 200°C/180°C fan-assisted/Gas 6. Place the fish fillets onto a lined baking tray with a little seasoning and bake for 10 minutes.
2. Allow the fish to cool slightly, then pop the well-drained spinach into a food processor along with the grouper fillets (remove any skin and bones), 50g/1¹/₂oz Parmigiano Reggiano, the egg and parsley. Pulse and blitz for 30 seconds.
3. Scrape into a clean bowl and stir.
4. Add the ricotta and freshly grated nutmeg. Stir and season with salt and pepper.
5. Place the mixture into a piping bag for ease or just cover and refrigerate until required.

6. Take the pasta dough, halve it and roll out one section (covering the other half until required).
7. Roll out with your pasta machine to level 6. If using a rolling pin, roll to 3mm/^{1}/₈in in thickness. The shapes I have chosen to form are mezzalune half-moons. Press out circles of dough 6cm/2^1/₂in in diameter and add a teaspoon amount of mixture onto the centre. Dampen the edges of the pasta dough if required and seal to secure into a half-moon shape.
8. Set the pasta aside onto lightly floured trays and use up the remaining half of dough.
9. Warm the butter in a sauté pan over a low heat, gently pour in the cream and season with salt and pepper.
10. Fill a large pan with water and once boiling, salt well. Cook the pasta until *al dente*, approximately 4 minutes.
11. Remove the mezzalune with a slotted spoon and bathe them in the cream sauce. Stir, add the remaining Parmigiano Reggiano, and serve with a scattering of chopped chives.

Milk pasta with beetroot and ricotta

(Agnolotti col plin con barbabietole e' ricotta)

Roasted fresh beetroot drizzled with olive oil, a pinch of salt and pepper and tender thyme leaves is one of my favourite sides imaginable, spritzed with a little lemon zest just before serving. Here I have chosen to roast and blitz the beetroot and mix it with ricotta, then add it to my most wonderful agnolotti col plin. A famous filled pasta from Piedmont that would normally be made with a meat filling, it is brought to life here with a little colour and freshness.

Preparation time: 1 hour, plus 30 minutes resting of pasta dough
Cooking time: 5 minutes
Serves: 4

200g/7oz semola flour
200g/7oz 00 flour
200ml/7fl oz full fat milk, tepid
500g/1lb 1½oz fresh beetroot
olive oil, to drizzle
1 tbsp fresh thyme leaves
500g/1lb 1½oz ricotta
¼ tsp freshly grated nutmeg
80g/3oz Parmigiano Reggiano, grated, plus extra to serve
Salt and pepper, to season
90g/3oz salted butter
8 small sage leaves

1. Make the pasta dough. Tip the semola and 00 flours onto a board. Make a well in the centre and add the tepid milk. Combine and knead until smooth and elastic. Cover and allow the dough to rest for 30 minutes at room temperature.
2. Preheat the oven to 200°C/180°C fan-assisted/Gas 6. Peel and slice the beetroot. Tumble into a bakeware dish with a drizzle of olive oil, salt and pepper. Stir well and cover with foil. Roast for 30 minutes or until knife tender throughout.

3. Allow the beetroot to cool for 15 minutes. Pop the ruby gems into a food processor and blitz until smooth. Scatter in the thyme leaves and blitz.

4. Scrape the beetroot purée into a clean bowl and spoon in the ricotta. Stir to combine with a spatula.

5. Add the grated nutmeg, additional salt, pepper and Parmigiano Reggiano. Taste and check for any additional seasoning, adjusting to suit your palate. Spoon the mixture into a small piping bag and place into the fridge until required. Using a piping bag makes the filling easier to handle.

6. Cut the pasta dough in half and flour well. Re-cover one half the dough so that it does not dry out. Push the dough down into a flat disc using your palms and pass it through the pasta machine on the first setting. Envelope the dough, flour and repeat six times on the first setting.

7. Pass the pasta sheet through each setting twice until you reach level 6, without folding.

8. Cut your pasta sheets into workable lengths; I like to work with 90cm/30in lengths.

9. Pipe large bite-size amounts of filling along one side of each pasta sheet, approximately 2.5cm/1in in from the edge, leaving a 2.5cm/1in gap between each amount of filling.

10. Roll the pasta sheet and secure each piece of filling.

11. Pinch the filling in between each mound. Using a fluted pasta wheel, roll across each pinch. This will create the final shape.

12. Repeat with the remaining pasta and set each agnolotto onto a tray dusted with semola. Repeat as required.

13. Place a large pan of water on to boil. Once boiling, salt well.

14. Cook the agnolotti for approximately 3–4 minutes until the edge of the pasta that has been pinched feels tender.

15. Put the butter into a shallow skillet, with a pinch of salt and the sage leaves. Warm gently until just browned.

16. Using a slotted spoon lift the agnolotti, and plate up with a drizzle of browned butter and a generous grating of Parmigiano Reggiano.

CARMELA'S TIP:
- The filling can be made a day in advance to save time.

Open mushroom raviolo
(*Raviolo aperto con funghi*)

Dare I even use the term deconstructed raviolo? Yes, I do, and with a smile on my face. This is such a quick pasta dish to prepare. There is not any methodical sealing, it is simple and easy. What would finish this off, in my opinion, would be a beautifully cured egg yolk, that, once touched, oozes over the dish. I give you the perfect deconstructed raviolo.

Preparation time: 1 hour plus 30 minutes resting of pasta dough at room temperature
Cooking time: 20 minutes
Serves: 4

200g/7oz herb-laminated egg pasta (page 31)
2 tbsp parsley, Greek basil or fresh thyme leaves
25g/1oz dried porcini, soaked in boiling water for 15 minutes
60ml/2fl oz extra virgin olive oil
30g/1oz butter
2 garlic cloves, peeled, finely sliced
500g/1lb 1½oz mixed mushrooms, sliced
1 tbsp thyme, stems removed, finely chopped
Small bunch of parsley, including stalks, finely chopped
Salt and pepper, to season
100g/3½oz butter
120g/4oz Parmigiano Reggiano, grated

1. I have upped the beauty of this dish by laminating the pasta sheets with a few Greek basil leaves. You can simply omit this step for speed if you prefer. Roll the dough into a sheet to level 4 with a pasta machine and lay the fresh herb leaves over one side. Fold the sheet over the herbs and secure with a few light finger pushes. Dust with semola and roll the sheet once through level 4 and then through level 5. Cut the sheets into 12cm/5in squares.

2. If you are making ordinary pasta sheets without the Greek basil, roll the dough in a sheet to level 5. Cut the sheets into 12cm/5in squares. Cover with a clean tea towel while you prepare the filling.
3. Drain the porcini through a sieve lined with kitchen paper, reserving the liquid.
4. Finely chop the porcini.
5. Heat the extra virgin olive oil, butter and sliced garlic in a wide, shallow sauté pan over a low heat. Gently fry off the garlic, soften but do not colour.
6. Tumble in the sliced mushrooms and stir, cooking for 10 minutes.
7. Add the chopped porcini along with the thyme. Stir and season with salt and pepper. Sprinkle in the parsley leaves and stalks.
8. Boil the pasta sheets for 2 minutes in salted boiling water.
9. Brown the butter in a small pan with a touch of salt and some freshly ground black pepper.
10. Add a sprinkle of Parmigiano Reggiano over each plate to act as a base.
11. Top with a laminated pasta sheet, then a generous spoonful of mushrooms and a sprinkle of Parmigiano Reggiano.
12. Add a pasta sheet to the top of the mushrooms and finish with a drizzle of browned butter and a generous handful of Parmigiano Reggiano.

Pea, mascarpone, ham and lemon cappellacci (*Cappellacci con piseli, limone, prosciutto cotto e mascarpone*)

Cappellacci must be my favourite pasta shape. Two folds lead you to perfection. Across my main Instagram account @carmelaskitchen you will find an array of pure unadulterated cappellacci pleasure. You can use any dough blend and filling; however, below I am sharing with you one of my treasured summer fillings.

Preparation time: 45 minutes, plus 30 minutes resting of pasta dough at room temperature
Cooking time: 10 minutes
Serves: 4

Pasta
300g/10½oz 00 flour, plus extra for kneading and dusting
3 eggs

Filling
350g/12½oz peas, blanched
250g/9oz mascarpone
Zest of 1 small lemon
70g/2½oz Parmigiano Reggiano, grated
¼ tsp nutmeg, grated
Small bunch of chopped basil
150g/5oz proscuitto cotto, chopped into tiny pieces
50g/1½oz provolone piccante, grated
Salt and pepper, to season

Sauce
100g/3½oz butter
2 tbsp extra virgin olive oil
Juice of 1 small lemon
40g/1½oz pine nuts
25g flaked almonds
100g/3½oz peas
Salt and pepper, to season
50g/1½oz Parmigiano Reggiano, grated

1. Tip the flour onto a wooden board and make a well in the centre.
2. Crack the eggs into the centre and slowly incorporate them to form a dough.
3. Knead until smooth and elastic. Cover and rest at room temperature for 30 minutes.
4. Prepare the filling by blitzing the peas in a food processor and adding the mascarpone, lemon zest, Parmigiano Reggiano, nutmeg, chopped basil and a twist of salt and pepper.
5. Scrape the filling into a bowl and add the prosciutto cotto and provolone piccante. Taste. Adjust the seasoning as required.
6. Take the pasta dough and cut it in half. Work with one portion at a time, covering the portion you are not using to prevent it drying out.
7. Pass the dough through the widest setting six times, enveloping every time, leaving you with a smooth starter dough.
8. Continue to roll out the dough with your pasta machine to $2mm/^1/_{16}in$ in thickness (setting 6).
9. Using a circular cutter, $6cm/2^1/_2in$ in diameter, cut out discs. Place a large teaspoon amount of the filling on each disc.
10. Fold and seal each disc making a mezzaluna, a half-moon shape.
11. Then take each corner, pull them together and attach them, open and fold the back out to form the finished shape.
12. Repeat as required on the remaining discs. Place the finished pasta onto a tray dusted with semola and allow to dry for 30 minutes before cooking.
13. Place a large pan of water on to boil. Once boiling, salt well and cook the pasta until *al dente*.
14. In a large sauté pan melt the butter and oil over a medium heat for 2 minutes.
15. Add a spritz of lemon juice, along with the pine nuts, flaked almonds and peas.
16. Season with salt and pepper.
17. Use a slotted spoon or spider and drain the pasta. Gently tumble the cappellacci into the butter and toss.
18. Spoon onto plates and dress with the remaining Parmigiano Reggiano.

Potato-filled tortelli parcels
(*Tortelli di patate*)

The Italians seem to embrace, with love, dishes that are carb on carb with no hesitation or apology, and I accept this with pure joy and a forever hungry belly. The ricotta lightens the filling while these pasta parcels also are a great vessel to carry leftover mashed potato. Add caramelised onions to the filling for added texture and bite.

Preparation time: 1 hour plus 30 minutes resting of the pasta dough at room temperature
Cooking time: 7 minutes
Serves: 4

400g/14oz egg pasta dough (page 6)
400g/14oz mashed potato
100g/3½oz ricotta, drained overnight
180g/6½oz Parmigiano Reggiano, grated
1 tbsp extra virgin olive oil
80g/3oz pancetta, finely sliced
1 shallot, peeled, finely chopped
1 garlic clove, peeled, minced
1 egg yolk
1 tbsp parsley, finely chopped
Salt and pepper, to season
¼ tsp freshly grated nutmeg
100g/3½oz butter

1. Mix the mashed potato, ricotta and half the Parmigiano Reggiano together in a bowl.
2. In a frying pan heat 1 tbsp extra virgin olive oil and lightly colour the pancetta and shallot. Fry for 5–7 minutes and allow the pancetta to release its natural fat.
3. Stir in the garlic and incorporate off the heat. Cool for 10 minutes.
4. Add the pancetta mixture (retaining any fat juices for later) to the mashed potato and stir.

5. Add a yolk to the mash and stir. Sprinkle in the freshly chopped parsley.

6. Taste the filling and season with salt, pepper and a pinch of freshly grated nutmeg.

7. Roll out the pasta dough using a pasta machine (setting 6) or to the thickness of 3mm/⅛in with a rolling pin. Cut the pasta sheets into 30cm/12in lengths.

8. Spoon small tablespoon amounts of the filling across a sheet, leaving a two-finger gap as you go.

9. Dampen with a little water around each mound and cover with a top sheet.

10. Remove any trapped air as you lay down the top sheet, cupping the mounds with the sides of your hands.

11. Using a fluted cutter, cut small parcels of dough, 6cm x 6cm/2½in x 2½in squares. Place each square onto a tray dusted with semola. Repeat as necessary with the other pasta sheets.

12. Place a large pan of water on to boil; once boiling, salt well and cook the tortelli until *al dente*.

3. Warm the butter in a sauté pan until just golden. Season with salt and pepper.

14. Using a slotted spoon, add the tortelli to the butter and lightly toss.

15. Spoon onto plates with the remaining Parmigiano Reggiano.

CARMELA'S TIP:
• Retain the egg white to make sweet meringues, amaretti biscuits or an egg white omelette. The egg whites freeze well.

Pumpkin and amaretti tortelli,
Mantova-style (*Tortelli di zucca e amaretti*)

Food pairings are a key element of cooking we pick up as our love of
food expands and our repertoire becomes a little more confident.
When I think about my most loved pairings, my mind sometimes
veers off onto undiscovered paths. Pumpkins would be my
preference here but any squash, including butternut squash, would
be more than acceptable. The sweetness of pumpkin is paired with
mostarda di frutta (mustard fruit, which can be found in any well-
stocked Italian deli) and crushed amaretti.

Preparation time: 1 hour
Cooking time: 45 minutes
Serves: 4

400g/14oz egg pasta dough (page 6)

Filling
1kg/2 lb 3oz pumpkin, unpeeeled, de-seeded and cut into wedges
90g/3oz hard amaretti, crushed
150g/5oz Grana Padano, grated
60g/2oz mostarda di frutta, finely chopped in tiny pieces
20ml/½fl oz mostarda di frutta syrup
¼ tsp freshly grated nutmeg
Zest of 1 small lemon
Salt and pepper, to season

Sauce
1 tbsp olive oil
90g/3oz butter, unsalted
sage leaves
70g/2½oz Grana Padano, grated
30g/1oz hard amaretti, crushed

1. Preheat the oven to 210°C/190°C fan-assisted/Gas 6 and start
   by roasting the prepared pumpkin for 30 minutes until tender.

2. Remove the pumpkin from the oven and cool at room temperature for 15 minutes.
3. Skin and blitz the pumpkin in a food processor.
4. Pass the pumpkin through a sieve.
5. Mix the pumpkin purée with the crushed amaretti biscuits, Grana Padano, mostarda di frutta, syrup, nutmeg and lemon zest. Taste and season with salt and pepper.
6. Cover the mixture and set aside.
7. Roll the dough out, either with a rolling pin or using your pasta machine, to 2mm/^{1}/₁₆in. I normally roll the dough out into manageable portions using my pasta machine and form lasagne sheets.
8. Place the lasagne sheets onto a lightly floured surface. Cut the sheets into squares measuring approximately 4cm/1^1/₂in on a side.
9. Place a teaspoon amount of the mixture onto each square. Using a little water, dampen the corners of the dough and fold each square into a triangle, gently squeezing out any air.
10. Hold the triangle with the point facing upwards, and join the two lower corners together to form a perfect tortello. Repeat with the remaining dough and filling.
11. Set each tortello to rest on a tray dusted with semola.
12. Bring a large pan of water to the boil. Once boiling, salt well. Cook the pasta for 4 minutes until *al dente*.
13. Pour the oil into a frying pan and add the butter along with the sage leaves. Brown for 3 minutes.
14. Drain the pasta and spoon into warmed bowls. Add a delicate drizzle of the browned butter.
15. Add a final sprinkle of Grana Padano and a crowning glory of amaretti crumbled on top to finish the dish. Seriously sensational.

Baked pasta

I could eat my way through this entire chapter and not look back with guilt; I would simply flick my way back to the first dish and experience Groundhog Day all over again with comfort, greed and willingness. Baked pasta fills my heart with joy and the house with an aroma that would immediately remind you that it's Sunday pasta day (even if it is not!).

There is no roast dinner on a Sunday at Casa Sereno. I am a little embarrassed to say this out loud, but I never grew up eating roast dinners so am happy to go without. Roast dinner was eaten on Christmas Day, but I've always loved Boxing Day lasagne much more. I remember as a child going to the Northampton cattle market and choosing our turkey. More often than not, Dad would choose an absolute whopper and Mum would need to wrestle with it like Rocky and Apollo Creed to fit it in the Aga! I shop with simpler tendencies and tend to make a fuss-free mid-week roast chicken. I always roast two birds and serve them with a large leafy salad, garlic green beans with softened tomatoes and rosemary potatoes; that is as close as my poor husband and eldest son Rocco get to a classic roast dinner.

Natalia, Santino, Chiara and I count down sleeps for Sunday baked pasta instead. Even as a child I did this, and today I continue the tradition as a pot-bellied woman. So now I pass on the gauntlet and ask you to join me in the occasional Sunday pasta.

Anelletti pasta pie (*Timballo di anelletti*)

When the moon hits your eye like a big 'pasta pie', yes, that most certainly is *amore*. Anelletti are small hoop earring shapes. They are delicious in soups, but here they are embraced with a rich tomato and pea sauce then baked. This dish is said to come from the province of Palermo and has a very special place at our family table. It is one of those dishes that everyone enjoys, a real crowd-pleaser and show-stopper with its slightly burnished outer body and soft gooey centre.

Preparation time: 25 minutes
Cooking time: 2 hours 30 minutes
Serves: 4

3 tbsp extra virgin olive oil
1 shallot, peeled, finely chopped
1 carrot, peeled, finely chopped
1 stick celery, finely chopped
2 garlic cloves, peeled, minced
200g/7oz beef mince
200g/7oz veal mince
200g/7oz pork mince
1 tbsp tomato purée
200ml/7fl oz red wine
670ml/23fl oz passata
400g/14oz tomato polpa (I use Mutti)
Parmigiano Reggiano rind (optional)
Small bunch of celery leaves, finely chopped
1 bay leaf
1 tbsp marjoram leaves, chopped, stems removed
10 basil leaves
Salt and pepper, to season
500g/1lb 1½oz anelletti pasta, dried
1 tbsp butter
3 tbsp breadcrumbs, lightly toasted
200g/7oz peas
200g/7oz caciocavallo cheese, grated
250g/9oz mozzarella, grated

4 eggs, boiled, peeled, chopped
60g/2oz Parmigiano Reggiano or Pecorino Romano, grated

1. Into a large saucepan pour the olive oil and add the shallot, carrot and celery. Cook gently over a medium heat until softened, for around 15 minutes.
2. Scrape in the minced garlic and stir.
3. Add the beef, veal and pork mince to the pan and colour completely, for approximately 10 minutes.
4. Squeeze the tomato purée into the red wine and stir.
5. Add the red wine to the mince, stir and allow the wine to evaporate fully; this will take about 5 minutes or so.
6. Pour the passata and tomato polpa into the mince along with the Parmigiano Reggiano rind (if using), celery leaves, bay, marjoram and basil. Stir and season with salt and pepper.
7. Allow the *sugo* to cook over a medium to low heat for 2 hours 30 minutes, stirring occasionally and checking intermittently for additional seasoning.
8. Boil a large pan of water. Once boiling, salt well and cook the anelletti as per packet instructions, less 4 minutes as you will be baking this dish.
9. Preheat the oven to 200°C/180°C fan-assisted/Gas 6.
10. Butter a medium bakeware dish or spring-form cake tin (23cm/9in in diameter).
11. Sprinkle the toasted breadcrumbs into the buttered dish, covering the base and sides of the tin.
12. Remove the bay leaf and rind from the sauce, tumble in the peas (I use frozen peas straight from the freezer) and stir.
13. Drain the pasta. Tumble the pasta back into the saucepan and add 2 ladles of the *sugo*. Stir. Ladle a layer of pasta into the dish, sprinkle over a mixture a third of the cheese and chopped eggs and add another ladle of sauce.
14. Repeat the layering until the dish is full and you have used up all the sauce. Finish the top with sauce and cheese.
15. Bake in a preheated oven for 30–40 minutes and serve. If you have baked the pasta pie in a bakeware dish then simply serve, but if you have used a spring-form tin you should be able to turn it out gently.

Baked lasagne with radicchio

(Lasagne al radicchio)

Lasagne must be one of the most versatile baked pasta dishes available, and I will say with a very loose tongue that anything goes, within reason. This radicchio lasagne is light, fragrant and a pure joy to eat. To speed up the process you can use pre-made fresh pasta sheets or dried pasta. Bagsie the crispy and slightly burnt bits please!

Preparation time: 30 minutes
Cooking time: 30 minutes
Serves: 4–6

450g/1lb radicchio
30g/1oz butter
2 tbsp extra virgin olive oil
1 garlic clove, peeled, minced
Salt and pepper, to season
600ml/1 pint/20fl oz béchamel (page 100)
Small handful of parsley, finely chopped
200g/7oz egg pasta (page 6)
30g/1oz butter
120g/4oz provolone piccante, grated
250g/9oz mozzarella, finely chopped
70g/2½oz Parmigiano Reggiano, grated
6 tbsp breadcrumbs, slightly stale

1. Cut the radicchio in half and remove any wilted outer leaves.
2. Slice the radicchio into thin slices, wash and dry thoroughly.
3. Heat the butter and oil in a medium sauté pan.
4. Add the radicchio and sauté over a medium heat for 5 minutes.
5. Add the garlic and season as required. Cover and cook for 15 minutes until softened. When ready, remove from the heat and set aside.
6. Add 500ml/18fl oz of the béchamel to the radicchio along with the parsley and stir, reserving the remaining amount for the topping.
7. Roll your pasta out to lasagne sheets as per page 36.

8. Blanch the pasta sheets in a pan of boiling salted water for 1 minute then carefully place each pasta sheet onto a clean tea towel to dry a little. Repeat as required.
9. Preheat the oven to 210°C/190°C fan-assisted/Gas 6.
10. Take a 30cm x 20cm/12in x 8in bakeware dish and add a couple of tablespoons of the warm béchamel sauce to the base, using the back of a spoon to evenly cover.
11. Lay lasagne sheets over the base; slightly overlapping is fine.
12. Spoon over some of the radicchio and béchamel mixture, followed by a scattering of the provolone piccante, mozzarella, Parmigiano Reggiano and a twist of black pepper.
13. Repeat once again with the lasagne sheets and layers. I always aim for three layers; any more is a bonus.
14. Finish with grated cheese and béchamel and top with the stale breadcrumbs.
15. Bake for 25–30 minutes, until bubbling and golden.

CARMELA'S TIP:
- When you spoon on the radicchio I also like to add prosciutto cotto for added flavour. A great addition in my opinion. You would need about eight slices.

Baked pancake pasta with radicchio and béchamel

(Crespelle gratinate con radicchio e besciamella)

Crespelle are a light pancake, filled, rolled, topped with sauce and baked. Delicious as they are, I am the worst pancake maker you will ever meet, my husband and children would wholeheartedly agree. So, for this recipe I employ my husband James to methodically, carefully make the crespelle for me, then I take over and usher him back out of the kitchen. The crespelle pancakes are key and the star of the recipe in terms of flavour and how thin you can make them. Nobody in their right mind would want one of my irregular-shaped chunky pancakes.

Preparation time: 1 hour plus 30 minutes chilling of batter
Cooking time: 25 minutes
Serves: 4

Crespelle
3 eggs
500ml/18fl oz milk
250g/9oz 00 flour
Salt and pepper, to season
40g/1½oz butter

Filling
40g/1½oz butter
2 tbsp extra virgin olive oil
1 small head radicchio, finely sliced
100g/3½oz prosciutto cotto (cooked Italian ham)
250g/9oz ricotta, drained overnight
60g/2oz Parmigiano Reggiano, grated
2 tbsp parsley, chopped
Salt and pepper, to season
½ quantity béchamel sauce (page 100 – you can make the full quantity and freeze the remainder for another day)

1. To make the crespelle, crack the eggs into a bowl and add the milk, then whisk to incorporate.
2. Slowly spoon in the flour a little at a time and whisk. Season with salt and pepper.
3. Place the batter into the fridge for 30 minutes to chill or until required.
4. Now for the filling. Put the butter into a sauté pan along with the olive oil and fry off the sliced radicchio over a medium heat for approximately 10 minutes.
5. Chop the prosciutto cotto into small pieces and mix with the ricotta.
6. Add the grated Parmigiano Reggiano, chopped parsley and radicchio to the ricotta and season to taste with salt and pepper.
7. Wipe a frying pan with a little olive oil, using a piece of kitchen paper.
8. Add a small ladle of batter into the frying pan and cook for 1 minute, then flip and cook for a further 30 seconds. Repeat until all the batter has been used up. Set the pancakes to one side.
9. Preheat the oven to 200°C/180°C fan-assisted/Gas 6.
10. Take a medium baking dish and add a thin layer of béchamel. Spread the filling mixture evenly over each pancake and roll.
11. Lay the crespelle into the dish and top with the béchamel.
12. Bake for 30 minutes or until golden.

CARMELA'S TIP:
- Crespelle are also known as manicotti.

Baked tagliatelle lattice pie with béchamel and porcini

(Tagliatelle in crosta con besciamella ai funghi)

As I write this recipe, I am smiling because I have a pasta lattice pie in my cookbook. I feel complete, my work is done. This is my mic drop moment. Light pastry with a lump-free béchamel and fresh egg pasta: all I can say is, welcome to your ultimate baked pasta pie.

Preparation time: 1 hour plus 1 hour chilling of the pastry
Cooking time: 45 minutes
Serves: 4–6

Pastry
200g/7oz 00 flour, plus extra for dusting
1 egg
1 yolk
70g/2½oz butter, cubed

40g/1½oz dried porcini
300ml/11fl oz béchamel sauce (see page 100)
300g/10½oz tagliatelle
1 garlic clove, peeled, minced
Small bunch of parsley, finely chopped
50g/1½oz butter, plus extra for greasing
50g/1½oz Grana Padano, grated
Salt and pepper, to season
1 egg, for glazing

1. Into a food processor put the flour, whole egg, yolk and cold cubed butter. Pulse to form a dough, adding a tablespoon or two of cold water if required.
2. Tumble out and form the dough into a flat disc. Cover and chill for an hour.
3. Pop the porcini into a bowl and add 50ml/1¹/₂fl oz boiling water. Let them bathe and rehydrate for 15 minutes.
4. Cook the tagliatelle in a pan of salted boiling water, until *al dente*.

5. Chop and drain the porcini mushrooms and mix well with the garlic and parsley. Add to the béchamel and stir. Taste for additional seasoning.
6. Drain the pasta and return it to the pan. Add the butter and Grana Padano and stir.
7. Grease a (24cm/10in) spring-form cake tin and use three-quarters of the pastry to line the base and sides.
8. Stir the béchamel into the tagliatelle.
9. Preheat the oven to 210°C/190°C fan-assisted/Gas 6.
10. Spoon the mixture into the prepared cake tin.
11. Roll out the remaining pastry and cut strips of pastry to form a lattice or weave.
12. Brush a little egg wash around the rim of the lattice pie and attach the pastry strips as required across the top.
13. Brush the strips with the egg wash. Place the pie on a hot baking tray and bake for 40 minutes.

CARMELA'S TIP:

- Add a combination of pan-fried mushrooms to the béchamel with tender thyme leaves; some boiled eggs would be scrumptious too.

Buckwheat pizzocheri with potatoes and cavolo nero (*Pizzocheri alla Valtellinese*)

Pizzocheri are short, flat, textured pasta strips made with a combination of buckwheat flour, 00 flour and tepid water. Pizzocheri are a speciality of the Valtellina valley in Lombardia, served with the local Valtellina Casera cheese, cubed potatoes and greens. I have chosen to use cavolo nero because I simply adore the prehistoric structure of the leaf with its firm yet forgiving tender bite. You could also use kale, spinach or escarole if preferred.

Preparation time: 1 hour plus 30 minutes resting of the pasta at room temperature
Cooking time: 45 minutes
Serves: 4

400g/14oz buckwheat flour
100g/3½oz 00 flour
250ml/9fl oz warm water
Semola, for kneading and dusting
250g/9oz cavolo nero leaves
1.5 litres/2¾ pints vegetable stock (page 84, or a stock cube will suffice)
250g/9oz red potatoes, peeled, cubed
85g/3oz butter
1 tbsp olive oil
1 garlic clove, peeled, left whole
4 sage leaves
250g/9oz Valtellina Casera DOP, pinched into pieces
(fontina and taleggio work well too)
125g/4½oz Grana Padano, grated
Salt and pepper, to season

1. Tumble the buckwheat flour and 00 flour onto a wooden board. Combine the flours and make a well in the centre.
2. Slowly add the water into the centre of the well. Gently combine and form into a dough, kneading until smooth and pliable. Cover and allow the dough to rest for a minimum of 30 minutes at room temperature.

3. Lightly flour your surface and roll the dough out with a rolling pin to a thickness of 3mm/$\frac{1}{8}$in. Cut strips of dough to 10cm/4in in length and to a width of just over 1 cm/$\frac{1}{2}$in. Place the pasta onto a tea towel dusted with a touch of semola and set aside.
4. Prepare the cavolo nero by running your knife along the central stem of each leaf, each side. Discard the stems.
5. Take a large pan of vegetable stock and bring to the boil. Tumble in the potatoes and cavolo nero. Cook for 10 minutes. Cavolo nero is a hardy leaf that doesn't mind being overcooked.
6. Add the pizzocheri to the potatoes and cavolo nero and cook for a further 10 minutes.
7. In the meantime, melt the butter in a small frying pan with the olive oil, clove of garlic and sage leaves. Brown the butter.
8. Preheat the oven to 210°C/190°C fan-assisted/Gas 6.
9. Once the pizzocheri are cooked, drain them. Layer half the pizzocheri, potatoes and cavolo nero in a warmed baking dish. Sprinkle generously with the Casera cheese and then layer the remaining pizzocheri and vegetables over the top, sprinkling over the leftover cheese.
10. Remove the garlic clove from the browned butter and discard. Drizzle the browned butter over the pizzocheri, and add a twist of black pepper and the Grana Padano cheese.
11. Bake for 20 minutes until bubbling ferociously and serve.

CARMELA'S TIP:
- If you are unable to find Valtellina Casera cheese, use delicious fontina or taleggio instead.

Cannelloni with Gorgonzola

(*Cannelloni al Gorgonzola*)

As I'm sure you're aware by now, I adore pasta, but especially filled and baked pasta. The oozing tubes, the many layers and the moment the aroma wafts through the house, it all reminds me of when my mother would make filled pasta and say to me as I walked into the kitchen, 'Melly the pasta needs to rest.' The 15-minute resting time felt like forever. I would sit on the cold tiled kitchen floor and watch the tray of bubbling pasta rest with the door left slightly ajar. Mum would say, 'Get up off the floor, you'll get piles!' I personally only rest lasagne, so as soon as these joyful cannelloni are ready, you can eat immediately but with caution – don't scald your lips!

Preparation time: 30 minutes
Cooking time: 40 minutes
Serves: 4

200g/7oz Gorgonzola, rind removed
Small bunch of parsley, finely chopped
500g/1lb 1½oz ricotta (drained overnight)
Pinch of nutmeg, grated
60g/2oz Parmigiano Reggiano, grated
Salt and pepper, to season
1.5 litres/2¾ pints béchamel (page 100)
1 box cannelloni tubes

1. Preheat the oven to 210°C/190°C fan-assisted/Gas 6.
2. Take a large bowl and prepare the filling for the cannelloni by adding the Gorgonzola, parsley, ricotta, nutmeg and 40g/1^{1}/₂oz of the Parmigiano Reggiano. Stir to combine with a wooden spoon. Season with salt and pepper.
3. Warm the béchamel sauce.
4. Take a bakeware dish that will fit your pasta tubes and add a ladle of the béchamel to the base. Use the bottom of the ladle to spread the béchamel around.
5. Use teaspoons to fill the cannelloni shells or scoop the filling mixture into a piping bag. I prefer the piping bag method;

however, my lovely mamma still uses two teaspoons and her fingertips to fill the shells.

6. Fill each cannelloni and lay them onto the béchamel. Top with the remaining béchamel and sprinkle over the reserved Parmigiano Reggiano.

7. Bake for 40 minutes until golden.

CARMELA'S TIP:

- You can substitute the Gorgonzola with a milder Dolcelatte cheese if you prefer and you can make your own fresh pasta. Use the egg dough on page 6, roll out the pasta dough (in portions) with a pasta machine to setting number 5 and cut the pasta sheets into 10cm x 12cm/4in x 5in squares. Allow the squares to dry for 10 minutes then simply pipe a little filling into the centre and roll, then place seam down onto the béchamel. If you prefer to you can blanch each sheet and dry them before filling; however, I feel that life is too short, so I never bother with the blanching.

Celebration lasagne (*Sagne Chime*)

Be prepared to fall in love with the ultimate lasagne. Filled and layered pasta is the staple of a classic Italian Sunday lunch and this one originates from the region of Calabria and takes a while to prepare. We would always say that Sunday lunch was the highlight of our week. I hope my children feel the same. Lasagne in each region of Italy will vary tremendously. This version from Calabria does remind me a little of my mum Solidea's version from Molise, however this 'Sagne Chime' is packed with even more time-consuming yet reassuringly pleasing delights.

Preparation time: 90 minutes
Cooking time: 1 hour 30 minutes
Serves: 6–8

Meatballs
225g/8oz pork mince
225g/8oz beef mince
225g/8oz veal mince
2 garlic cloves, peeled, crushed
1 egg
100g/3½oz dried breadcrumbs
40g/1½oz Pecorino Crotonese, grated, or Pecorino Romano
Small bunch of parsley, including stalks, finely chopped
1 tsp dried oregano
½ tsp dried chilli
Salt and pepper, to season
Olive oil, as required, for frying

Sauce
3 tbsp extra virgin olive oil
1 shallot, peeled, finely cubed
1 small carrot, peeled, finely cubed
1 celery stick, finely cubed
2 garlic cloves, peeled, crushed
1.2 litres/2 pints passata
200ml/7fl oz mozzarella water (from the fresh mozzarella below)
1 tbsp tomato purée

Salt and pepper, to season
Bunch of fresh basil, torn
Parmigiano Reggiano rind (optional)

Filling
600g/1lb 5oz lasagne sheets, fresh (page 36) or dried
6 boiled eggs, peeled, thinly sliced
300g/10½oz peas (from the freezer)
300g/10½oz chestnut mushrooms, thinly sliced
500g/1lb 1½oz mozzarella, torn into small pieces
200g/7oz Pecorino Crotonese, grated, or Pecorino Romano

1. Start by making the meatballs. These can be made in advance and frozen to save time. Place the pork, beef and veal mince into a large bowl and break up using a wooden spoon. Add the garlic and egg, and stir.
2. Tumble in the dried breadcrumbs, grated pecorino, parsley, oregano, chilli, salt and pepper. Incorporate the mixture fully.
3. Form the meatballs. You need to roll the meat into tiny meatballs, just a little bigger than a marble. These will take time and patience.
4. Once the meatballs are ready, fry them off in batches with a little olive oil. Once coloured all over, allow them to drain on kitchen paper until required. Alternatively bake them in the oven for 15 minutes.
5. To prepare the sauce, pour the olive oil into a large pan and over a medium heat fry off the shallot, carrot and celery for 15 minutes until softened. Add the garlic and stir for a further minute.
6. Pour in the passata and mozzarella water. Stir well, squeeze in the tomato purée and add the basil. Season with salt and pepper.
7. Gently drop the bronzed meatballs into the sauce and cook for 2 hours over a medium heat. I like to add a Parmigiano Reggiano rind in for added flavour, but this is optional and only if you have one knocking about in the fridge. Be sure to remove the rind before constructing the lasagne – this is the chef's perk!
8. Preheat the oven to 200°C/180°C fan-assisted/Gas 6.

9. Blanch the fresh lasagne sheets for 1 minute each and place onto a clean tea towel. Repeat with all the fresh pasta sheets. If you opted for the dried pasta sheets, just start assembling the dish.
10. To layer the lasagne, take a large bakeware dish, roughly 40cm x 30cm/16in x 12in with a good depth to it. Alternatively, you could make two smaller dishes, one for now and one for the freezer.
11. Ladle in some tomato sauce and ensure the base has a light blanket covering.
12. Take the lasagne sheets and cover the base and sides of the bakeware dish. Do not overlap the pasta, just ensure there are no big gaps.
13. Cover the base layer of pasta with a ladle of the meatball sauce, followed by a sprinkle of sliced boiled eggs, a handful of peas, mushrooms, mozzarella and a dusting of pecorino. Spoon over a tiny amount of sauce.
14. Repeat with the filling so you have at least three layers.
15. For the final layer, if there are any sheets hanging over from the base layer, fold them over and top with lasagne sheets, sauce and a sprinkle of pecorino and mozzarella.
16. Cover with foil and bake for an hour, then remove the foil and bake with no covering for a further 30 minutes.
17. Once cooked, cover and allow to rest before slicing.

Earring encased pasta pie
(*Pasticcio di anelletti*)

A pie filled with pasta: No, this is not a fairy-tale. Welcome to heaven. Pastry filled with meat, pasta earrings and peas. I'm not sure I could love carbs any more than I do already but, dear me, this pie has me falling to my knees every single time. When baked, transfer the pasta pie to a large platter because when you come to slice it the tiny hoops and peas cascade everywhere in perfect madness.

Preparation time: 30 minutes plus 1 hour chilling of pastry dough
Cooking time: 2 hours
Serves: 4–6

Pastry
300g/10½oz 00 flour
150g/5oz butter
20g/½oz sugar
1 egg
1 yolk
1 tbsp cold water
Salt, to season

Filling
2 tbsp extra virgin olive oil
1 shallot, peeled, cubed
1 carrot, peeled, cubed
1 celery stalk, cubed
250g/9oz pork mince
250g/9oz beef mince
125ml/4½fl oz red wine
1 tbsp tomato purée
1 litre/1¾ pints passata
500g/1lb 1½oz anelletti pasta (dried tiny rings)
200g/7oz peas (I use frozen)
70g/2½oz caciocavallo, tiny cubes
70g/2½oz Parmigiano Reggiano, grated
Salt and pepper, to season
1 egg, whisked

1. Prepare the pastry. Into a food processor place the flour, cubed butter, sugar, the egg and yolk and the water along with a pinch of salt. Blitz.
2. Tip the pastry onto a board and form a ball. Flatten the ball to a circular disc, cover, and chill for 1 hour.
3. Pour the olive oil into a saucepan and over a medium heat add the shallot, carrot and celery. Cook for 15 minutes.
4. Tumble the pork and beef mince into the pan and sear all over for 5–10 minutes.
5. Add the red wine and cook until almost evaporated. Squeeze in the tomato purée and stir.
6. Pour in the passata, stir and season with salt and pepper. Cook over a medium heat for an hour, stirring intermittently.
7. Place a large pan of water on to boil. Once boiling, salt well and cook the anelletti until *al dente*.
8. Drain the pasta and mix with the pasta sauce, frozen peas, cubed caciocavallo and Parmigiano Reggiano cheese.
9. Preheat the oven to 180°C /160°C fan-assisted/Gas 4.
10. Roll out three-quartersof the pastry to a thickness of 5mm/^{1}/$_4$in and line the base and sides of a 26cm/10in spring-form cake tin.
11. Spoon the filling into the centre.
12. I adore vintage retro, so I always pop my little pie bird in the centre to rid my pie of excess steam. Roll out the reserved pastry disc to cover the pasta pie.
13. Beat the egg. Add a little whisked egg to the edge of the pie.
14. Secure the lid and pinch all the way around. Decorate if you have any scraps left.
15. Brush the top of the pasta pie with the remaining egg and bake for 1 hour. Remove the pie from the oven and rest for 10 minutes before slicing.

Lasagne with spinach and pesto

(*Lasagne con pesto*)

Lasagne has developed over the years. Each region, province and village has its own take on this classic baked pasta dish. This version is speedy and being vegetarian can feed my entire family easily, even though Rocco, my eldest son, will always try to search out the non-existent meat and sigh with disapproval and a little annoyance. This wonderful family dish can be made in advance and pulled out of the fridge when you are pushed for time.

Preparation time: 20 minutes
Cooking time: 40 minutes
Serves: 4

750g/1lb 10oz spinach, washed
40g/1½oz butter
Salt and pepper, to season
Zest and juice of 1 small lemon
200g/7oz Grana Padano
80g/3oz basil pesto
400ml/¾ pint/14fl oz béchamel sauce (page 100)
400g/14oz lasagne sheets (dried or fresh, page 36)

1. Blanch the spinach in a little salted water for a couple of minutes. Drain and squeeze out any excess water. Wrap the spinach tightly in a clean tea towel.
2. Put the butter and spinach into a sauté pan. Add a pinch of and salt and pepper and stir. Cook for 4 minutes over a medium heat.
3. Pour in the juice and zest of a lemon and 40g/1^{1}/$_{2}$oz of the Grana Padano and stir. Take off the heat and set aside.
4. Make the béchamel: in a small saucepan melt the butter, sprinkle in the flour and stir vigorously with a wooden spoon until you have incorporated all the flour.
5. In another pan warm the milk. Slowly pour the milk, while whisking, into the butter and flour mixture. Cook for 10 minutes until the mixture has become gloriously thick. Add a little salt and pepper along with a little grated nutmeg to taste.

6. Stir the pesto into the béchamel and check for seasoning.
7. Preheat the oven to 210°C/190°C fan-assisted/Gas 6.
8. Add a ladle of béchamel to the base of your oven dish. Top with lasagne sheets.
9. Lay spinach all over the lasagne sheets along with a sprinkle of Grana Padano and a spoon of béchamel. Repeat with another layer of pasta, spinach and béchamel.
10. Top with another lasagne sheet and a spoon of béchamel. If there is any Grana Padano cheese left, sprinkle it on top of the béchamel and bake the dish for 40 minutes until golden.

Mamma's baked pasta shells

(Conchiglioni ripieno sotto forno)

A favourite dish from my childhood. My heart aches with happiness when I think about this dish; when I eat it, well, that is a different matter altogether. Nothing else seems to matter, my worries vanish and all I can think of is filling my tummy with simple, soulful home-cooked food. This recipe is one of my mum Solidea's most sought after, one that I request as frequently as possible if and when I'm asked what she should cook for Sunday dinner. No roast dinner in sight: I will always ask for baked pasta till I just can't take it anymore.

Preparation time: 25 minutes
Cooking time: 60 minutes
Serves: 6

500g/1lb 1½oz minced pork
500g/1lb 1½oz conchiglioni shells
500g/1lb 1½oz mozzarella, grated or chopped
500g/1lb 1½oz ricotta, drained overnight
100g/3½oz Parmigiano Reggiano, grated
3 garlic cloves, peeled, crushed
Salt and pepper, to season
2 large eggs
4 tbsp parsley, chopped
600ml/1 pint/20fl oz tomato sauce (page 99)

1. Brown off the minced pork (with no oil) in a frying pan, and when coloured remove any excess fat.
2. Place a large pan of water on to boil for the pasta shells. Once bubbling, salt well and cook the conchiglioni shells for 9–10 minutes (or 3 minutes less than the packet instructions specify).
3. For the filling, combine the mozzarella, ricotta, Parmigiano Reggiano, garlic, salt and pepper, and mix well. Add the eggs and stir.

4. Spoon in the drained pork mince. Scatter in the chopped parsley and stir.
5. Add a ladle of the tomato sauce to the filling. Stir to combine.
6. Preheat the oven to 210°C/190°C fan-assisted/Gas 6.
7. Spoon a small ladle of sauce into the base of a 30cm x 30cm/12in x 12in ovenproof dish for the shells to sit on once filled.
8. Drain and fill each conchiglioni shell with the filling and place into the dish. Once the whole dish is bursting with shells, pour over a couple of ladles of sauce and place in the oven to bake.
9. Cover the pasta with foil and bake for 45 minutes, then remove the foil and bake for a further 15 minutes.
10. Rest the pasta for 10 minutes and serve.

CARMELA'S TIP:

- This is hardly a tip, but these are sensational, dare I say even better, the day after, when warmed up in a microwave. I've lost track of how often I have leftover pasta for breakfast on a cold winter's day.

Penne baked in paper

(Penne allo zafferano in cartoccio)

I feel a sense of celebration and excitement when I make a dish that is presented to my guests in individual portions at the dinner table. In essence this is a tightly gifted bag of pasta with a crowning glory of sweet clams. The diners are left to their own devices to open the gift. As they gently rip the bag open, the aroma hits them, as does the steam. I like to think they are immediately transported to a small costal town on the Mediterranean.

Preparation time: 10 minutes
Cooking time: 20 minutes
Serves: 4

350g/12½oz penne
150g/5oz pancetta, cubed
70g/2½oz guanciale, cubed
200ml/7fl oz double cream
Pinch of saffron
Salt and pepper, to season
120g/4oz Parmigiano Reggiano, grated
20 clams

1. Preheat the oven to 210°C/190°C fan-assisted/Gas 6.
2. Cook the penne in a pan of salted boiling water for 3 minutes less than the packet instructions advise.
3. In a dry frying pan, fry off the cubed pancetta and guanciale until golden, 10 minutes or so.
4. Remove the pancetta and guanciale from the heat and drain on kitchen paper. Retain the fat and use it in another dish for flavour: store the excess fat in a ramekin and pop in the fridge.
5. Drain the pasta and set aside.
6. Warm the cream in a shallow saucepan and add the saffron.
7. Introduce the drained pancetta and guanciale to the cream mixture and season as required with salt and pepper.
8. Mix the pasta in with the cream sauce, add the grated Parmigiano Reggiano and stir.

9. Cut four rectangles of parchment paper, 30cm x 20cm/12in x 8in. Spoon the pasta and sauce onto the centre of each piece of parchment paper.
10. Top each parcel with five clams, roll and secure.
11. Place the parcels onto a baking tray and bake for 5–7 minutes.

CARMELA'S TIP:
- Serve in the scorched paper on warm plates with an optional bowl of finely chopped parsley in the centre of the table.

Rigatoni and aubergine cake
(*Torta di rigatoni e melanzana*)

A pasta cake formed and dressed in decorated lengths of aubergine with a centrepiece of pasta and cheese. Takes a little effort and time, but you can take away some of the preparation by using dried pasta, which I prefer for baked dishes, and skip the salting of the aubergines. I still salt my aubergines to take away excess moisture and bitterness, but it's more out of a love of tradition than out of need. The rigatoni can also be changed to penne, casarecce or fusilli.

Preparation time: 50 minutes
Cooking time: 25 minutes
Serves: 4

500g/1lb 1½oz aubergines
Olive oil, for frying, as required
450g/1lb rigatoni
1 quantity tomato sauce (page 99)
60g/2oz butter
300g/10½oz mozzarella, chopped into tiny pieces
70g/2½oz Parmigiano Reggiano, grated
100g/3½oz asiago cheese, grated
½ tsp oregano, dried
Pinch of dried chilli
Salt and pepper, to season
4 tbsp stale breadcrumbs

1. Peel and slice the aubergines into 6m/¼in slices lengthways. Place the aubergine lengths into a colander and sprinkle with salt.
2. Leave the aubergine to sit over a sink for at least an hour. Place a weight on top of the aubergines to help them on their way. I use a couple of tins wrapped in a little cling film.
3. Brush the salt off the aubergine slices and pat dry.

4. Fry the aubergine slices in a little olive oil and fry off until coloured; do this in batches. Place the aubergines onto a few sheets of kitchen paper and set aside until required.

5. Place a large pan of water onto boil; once boiling, salt well and cook the rigatoni pasta (4 minutes short of the packet instructions).

6. Drain the pasta and pop it back into its pan.

7. Dress the pasta with the tomato sauce and stir in the butter (reserving a little butter to grease the cake tin).

8. Add the mozzarella, Parmigiano Reggiano and asiago to the rigatoni and stir well to incorporate. Add the dried oregano, chilli and a twist of black pepper.

9. Preheat the oven to 210°C/190°C fan-assisted/Gas 6.

10. Grease a 20cm/8in spring-form cake tin with a little of the reserved butter.

11. Line the tin with the sliced aubergine along the base and sides, cutting any pieces and patching if required. If you have any excess, double layer the base for maximum security.

12. Tumble the pasta into the cake tin, pushing down firmly. Top with the stale breadcrumbs and bake for 25 minutes, until bubbling and golden.

CARMELA'S TIP:

- Allow the pasta cake to sit for 15 minutes before unclipping it and helping it out with a palette knife.

Solidea's egg layered lasagne

(*Lasagne Molisana*)

This recipe reigns supreme over every single recipe I have ever written, my desert island dish. It would be impossible for me to write a book on fresh pasta and not include my mum Solidea's recipe for egg layered lasagne. This recipe is from Molise, Campobasso, where my mum was born and raised. Laced with chopped boiled eggs, slow-cooked mincemeat *sugo* and lots of freshly torn mozzarella and grated Parmigiano Reggiano.

Preparation time: 40 minutes
Cooking time: 4 hours 30 minutes
Serves: 10–12

Sauce (*sugo*)
2 tbsp extra virgin olive oil
400g/14oz pork mince
400g/14oz beef mince
500g/1lb 1½oz veal mince
3 garlic cloves, peeled, crushed
2 tbsp tomato purée
1.2 litres/2 pints passata
300ml/11fl oz mozzarella water (from the fresh mozzarella, below)
Handful of basil, torn
Salt and pepper, to season

Lasagne
8 eggs, boiled
600g/1lb 5oz fresh lasagne sheets (page 36)
750g/1lb 10oz mozzarella, grated or chopped
2 eggs, beaten
150g/5oz Parmigiano Reggiano, grated

1. Start by making the *sugo*. Fry the mince in the extra virgin olive oil, in a large saucepan for approximately 10 minutes, until browned. Remove any excess cooking fat and place back on the heat.

2. Add the garlic and tomato purée and stir.
3. Pour in the passata along with the mozzarella water and stir again, then season with salt and pepper. Scatter over the basil and simmer for 2 hours 30 minutes.
4. When the *sugo* is ready, preheat the oven to 190°C/170°C fan-assisted/Gas 5 and start to assemble the lasagne. You will need a large ovenproof dish, 30cm x 40cm/12in x 16in.
5. Peel and chop the boiled eggs.
6. Ladle 3 spoonfuls of passata mince into the ovenproof dish, covering the base of the dish, and place a layer of lasagne pasta sheets on top, covering the base.
7. Sprinkle over some mozzarella, chopped egg and a ladle of the meat sauce.
8. Using a fork, drizzle over some of the beaten egg to bind the filling.
9. Repeat this process layer by layer. Finish the lasagne with a layer of mince sauce and a grating of mozzarella. Sprinkle over the Parmigiano Reggiano.
10. Cover with foil and bake for 1 hour 15 minutes. Remove the foil and cook for a further 15 minutes to allow the lasagne to brown.
11. Switch off the oven and rest the lasagne for 15 minutes before slicing; the best way to do this is to leave the lasagne in the oven but with the door held slightly ajar.
12. Slice and serve.

CARMELA'S TIP:
- You can cut down the cooking time considerably if you make the *sugo* a day or so in advance. Lasagne freezes well too, so cook in batches and freeze.

Spaghetti frittata with aubergines

(*Spaghetti alla Norma*)

My love affair with aubergines continues. I tend to chip and bake them, pan fry them with far too much salt, add them to a variety of pasta dishes, and fill and bake them within an inch of their plump lives. So, here is my spaghetti alla Norma, a leftover dish that offers so many possibilities. Roasting the vegetables adds an intensity and removes excess liquid and moisture. This dish makes for a great lunch and, for extra carby goodness, sliced and squashed in between two slices of bread it takes you to a sense of total euphoria.

Preparation time: 10 minutes
Cooking time: 45 minutes (this includes roasting the vegetables)
Serves: 4–6

1 medium aubergine
600g/1lb 5oz cherry tomatoes (or use a tin of cherry tomatoes)
4 garlic cloves, squashed, skins on
60ml/2fl oz extra virgin olive oil
2 eggs
½ tsp chilli flakes
2 tbsp tomato purée
2 tbsp capers, drained, rinsed, finely chopped
Salt and pepper, to season
10 basil leaves, roughly torn
1 tbsp celery leaves, chopped
400g/14oz spaghetti

1. Preheat the oven to 200°C/180°C fan-assisted/Gas 6. Peel the aubergine and cut into 2cm/1in cubes.
2. Halve the cherry tomatoes.
3. Place the aubergines, tomatoes, squashed garlic cloves and 30ml of the extra virgin olive oil onto a baking tray.
4. Stir to incorporate and bake for 20 minutes.
5. Crack the eggs into a bowl along with the chilli flakes and tomato purée. Stir.
6. Add the capers, torn basil leaves and chopped celery leaves. Stir.

7. Cook the spaghetti until *al dente* in a pan of salted water.
8. Remove the roasted vegetables from the oven. Peel the garlic and chop it well.
9. Drain the spaghetti and tumble back into the saucepan.
10. Spoon the vegetables into the spaghetti, along with any juices, and stir.
11. Season with salt and pepper.
12. Scrape the tomato purée mixture into the pan and stir.
13. Pour the remaining olive oil into a large frying pan. Bring to a medium heat and tumble in the spaghetti mixture.
14. Push the ingredients down and cook until the base has a crust, about 4 minutes.
15. Place a large plate over the spaghetti pie and turn it out carefully.
16. Slip it back into the frying pan and finish the cooking for a further 5 minutes.
17. Remove from the pan, cool slightly and slice.

CARMELA'S TIP:
- Any pasta works here; use your leftovers and alter the ingredients as required. This spaghetti pie can also be oven baked. Start it off in the frying pan (that must have a metal not plastic handle) then finish it off by baking it at 210°C/190°C fan-assisted/Gas 6 for 15 minutes.

Spinach, prosciutto cotto and ricotta roll (*Rotolo di spinachi, cotto e ricotta*)

Filled pasta has always been a Sunday family treat. My rotolo is a dish that I teach as part of my cookery classes because it gives the students the opportunity to practise a variety of skills.

Preparation time: 1 hour
Cooking time: 45 minutes
Serves: 6

500g/1lb 1½oz fresh egg pasta dough (page 6)

Pasta filling
500g/1lb 1½oz ricotta, drained overnight in a sieve
600g/1lb 5oz spinach, blanched
125g/4½oz Grana Padano, grated
80g/3oz peas
1 egg yolk
½ tsp freshly grated nutmeg
Small bunch of basil, roughly torn
Salt and pepper, to season
8 slices prosciutto cotto (cooked Italian ham)

Sauce (*sugo*)
2 tbsp extra virgin olive oil
1 garlic clove, peeled, finely minced
600ml/1 pint/20fl oz passata
150ml/5½fl oz water
Salt and pepper, to season
Bunch of basil leaves, roughly torn
½ tsp dried oregano

1. Put the ricotta into a large bowl and use a wooden spoon to break it up a little.
2. Ensure the blanched spinach has been squeezed very well to eliminate too much moisture. I tend to find wrapping it in a clean tea towel and squeezing it is the best way.

3. Chop the spinach well and combine with the ricotta.
4. Add the Grana Padano cheese, peas, egg yolk, nutmeg and basil to the ricotta mixture, season with salt and pepper and stir well. Cover with cling film and chill whilst you prepare the pasta dough.
5. Roll out the pasta dough with a rolling pin to a rectangle with a thickness of 3mm/$\frac{1}{8}$in, approximately 40cm x 25cm/16in x 10in.
6. Place the pasta sheet on a piece of cling film that is lying on a piece of muslin or a large clean tea towel. Ensure the muslin is slightly bigger than the pasta sheet.
7. Spread the ricotta mixture all over the pasta dough sheet, leaving a 1cm/$\frac{1}{2}$in gap all the way round.
8. Lay the prosciutto cotto along the pasta sheet in a single layer.
9. Lift the cling film at one side and use it to help roll the pasta into a sausage, similar to a Swiss roll.
10. Roll the cling film tightly around the rotolo. Secure and twist the ends like a giant sweetie.
11. Now roll the muslin around the cling-filmed rotolo and secure firmly with string.
12. Place a large pan of water on to boil (or use a fish kettle). Once boiling, salt well. Lay the rotolo in the pan and gently boil the pasta for 30 minutes.
13. Put the olive oil and garlic in a small saucepan pan, add the passata and water, basil and oregano. Stir and cook for 25 minutes over a medium heat. Season with salt and pepper.
14. Preheat the oven to 210°C/190°C fan-assisted/Gas 6.
15. Remove the pasta from the pan, being careful to not bend it. Cool for 15 minutes and unwrap. Spoon half the sauce into the base of the ovenware dish. Slice the rotolo into 3cm/1in discs and place each piece flat onto the sauce.
16. Spoon the remaining tomato sauce on top of the rotolo and sprinkle over some freshly grated Grana Padano. Bake for 20 minutes.
17. Serve on warmed plates.

CARMELA'S TIP:

- Retain and freeze the egg white (for up to 3 months) to use in sweet treats.

Stuffed pasta shells with mushroom and ricotta (*Conchiglioni ripieno con funghi e ricotta*)

Conchiglioni come in a variety of sizes, from tiny ones used in soups to large shells. They are a wonderful shape; my children always refer to them as pasta boats. When parboiled they can be filled with whatever takes your fancy and baked. This is one of the dried pasta shapes I would always recommend for you to have in your larder cupboard because they can add a little something special to any midweek meal.

Preparation time: 20 minutes
Cooking time: 30 minutes
Serves: 4–6

3 tbsp extra virgin olive oil
400g/14oz mushrooms, sliced into small cubes (I use a combination of porcini and chestnut)
500g/1lb 1½oz conchiglioni
400g/14oz ricotta, drained overnight
¼ tsp freshly grated nutmeg
200g/7oz Grana Padano, grated
300g/10½oz spinach, blanched, squeezed of water
Salt and pepper, to season
Butter, melted, to coat the bakeware dish
Olive oil, to drizzle

1. Pour the extra virgin olive oil into a shallow sauté pan and over a medium heat fry the mushrooms for 10 minutes or until touched with a little colour. Remember, if you overcrowd the pan, the mushrooms will not brown.
2. Place a large pan of water on to boil. Once boiling, salt well and cook the pasta shells as per the packet instructions, less 3 minutes.
3. Drain the shells and set aside.
4. In a bowl mix the ricotta, nutmeg and 150g/5oz Grana Padano cheese. Stir well.

5. Drain the mushrooms of any liquid and add them to the ricotta mixture.
6. Chop the blanched spinach and add it to the mushrooms.
7. Season well and taste, adjusting as required.
8. Preheat the oven to 210°C/190°C fan-assisted/Gas 6.
9. Take a bakeware dish and coat it with a little melted butter.
10. Add a spoonful of the filling to each pasta shell and pop into the buttered dish. Repeat as required.
11. Sprinkle over the remaining Grana Padano cheese along with a drizzle of olive oil.
12. Bake for 30 minutes.

CARMELA'S TIP:
- You could make half the quantity of béchamel sauce from page 100 to spoon into the base and drizzle on top of the dish.

Tiny baked tagliolini fritattas
(*Frittatine di tagliolini*)

Ideally these delicately baked nests would work perfectly for those of us that always seem to cook far too much pasta at mealtimes. That said, I seem to always manage the pasta cooking very well – unlike my rice cooking. That I have no control over at all, it would seem. These nests are wonderful, but you can always add more to the basic mixture to pep it up a bit if preferred, from some sliced and pan-fried mushrooms, to roasted peppers or even a kiss of n'duja spreadable salami for added heat.

Preparation time: 15 minutes
Cooking time: 20 minutes
Serves: 6

125g/4½oz prosciutto cotto (cooked ham)
2 tbsp extra virgin olive oil
1 shallot, peeled, finely sliced
90g/3oz peas
170g/6oz tagliolini (page 176 or dried)
4 eggs (or 300g/10½oz in weight)
80ml (3fl oz) milk
¼ tsp freshly grated nutmeg
100g/3½oz provolone piccante, tiny cubes
40g/1½oz Grana Padano, grated
20g/½oz Parmigiano Reggiano, grated
1 tbsp celery leaves (optional)
1 tbsp marjoram or oregano leaves
Salt and pepper, to season
20g/½oz butter, for greasing

1. Preheat the oven to 210°C/190°C fan-assisted/Gas 6.
2. Finely cube the prosciutto cotto and place it into a sauté pan with two tablespoons of extra virgin olive oil.
3. Fry over a medium heat and add the sliced shallot; cook for 5 minutes.

4. Tumble in the peas and cook for a further 2 minutes. Season with salt and pepper.
5. Scrape the ingredients from the pan into a bowl to cool a little.
6. Place a large pan of water on to boil. Once boiling, salt well. Cook the pasta until *al dente* and drain.
7. Into the prosciutto bowl, add the eggs and milk and stir to incorporate, followed by the nutmeg, cubed provolone, Grana Padano and Parmigiano Reggiano. Stir.
8. Add the chopped celery leaves and marjoram. Season as required. You could add a sprinkle of chilli if you fancy a kick of warmth.
9. Tumble in the *al dente* pasta and stir.
10. Grease six ramekins on the base and sides with a little butter.
11. Spoon the mixture equally into the ramekins and bake for 25 minutes, or until golden and set.

CARMELA'S TIP:
- Enjoy as a starter, a light lunch or snack. It is wonderful warm, but equally delicious at room temperature.

Vincigrassi lasagne (*Vincigrassi*)

If time is precious, then this lasagne is not for you. It is a celebration
centrepiece dish that requires time and a table full of people to
enjoy it. Baked pasta does not come any richer than the signature
pasta dish 'Vincigrassi'. A typical lasagne dish from Le Marche
featuring no tomatoes but layers of pasta filled with mushrooms,
chicken, chicken livers and truffle, wrapped up with an indulgent
béchamel sauce. Get ready to fall in love with Marsala pasta dough.

Preparation time: 1 hour plus 30 minutes chilling pasta dough
Cooking time: 60 minutes
Serves: 6

Pasta
150g/5oz semola flour
300g/10½oz 00 flour
30g/1oz butter, softened
3 eggs
3 tbsp Marsala wine

Vincigrassi (filling)
80g/3oz butter, unsalted, plus extra for greasing
1 shallot, peeled, finely sliced
220g/7½oz prosciutto, sliced
125g/4½oz chestnut mushrooms, sliced
1 small truffle (jarred), drained, finely sliced
950g/2 lb 2oz chicken breast, finely sliced, thickness of your little finger
300g/10½oz chicken livers, sinew removed, roughly chopped
100g/3½oz sweetbreads, cleaned, sliced
4 tbsp Madeira
100ml/3½fl oz chicken stock (page 81)
Salt and pepper, to season
Small bunch of parsley, finely chopped
800ml/1⅓ pints béchamel sauce (page 100)
100g/3½oz Parmigiano Reggiano, grated
50g/1½oz Pecorino Romano, grated

1. Make the pasta as described on page 6. Just add the butter and Marsala into the eggs. Combine, knead and rest in the fridge for a minimum of 30 minutes.
2. Once the dough is rested and ready, roll it through your pasta machine (setting 4) into sheets approximately 10cm x 15cm/4in x 6in. If rolling with a rolling pin, roll to 4mm/^{1}/8in in thickness.
3. Into a large shallow pan put half the butter and scatter in the shallots. Fry gently over a medium heat for a couple of minutes.
4. Tumble in the prosciutto and sliced mushrooms, fry for 5 minutes until the mushrooms have softened and the pancetta has gained a little colour, then add the thinly sliced truffle.
5. Add the chicken breast slices and fry for 4 minutes on each side.
6. Tumble in the chicken livers and sweetbreads, and cook for 5 minutes.
7. Pour in the Madeira and allow to evaporate for 3 minutes.
8. Pour in the chicken stock, season with salt and pepper and stir.
9. Sprinkle in the parsley then pour in 400ml/14fl oz of the prepared béchamel sauce and stir into the filling.
10. Blanch the lasagne sheets in a large pan of salted boiling water. Place on tea towels to dry out.
11. Butter an ovenproof dish and lay a base of pasta sheets. Sprinkle over a little Parmigiano Reggiano and Pecorino Romano.
12. Ladle over some of the filling and cover the pasta.
13. Lay pasta sheets on top of the filling, sprinkle with Parmigiano Reggiano and Pecorino Romano and repeat, finishing with a layer of pasta.
14. Lay the remaining butter on the top layer of pasta.
15. Allow to cool, cover and chill overnight or for a few hours.
16. Preheat the oven to 200°C/180°C fan-assisted/Gas 6.
17. Top with the remaining 400ml/^{3}/4 pint/14fl oz béchamel and bake for 30 minutes covered in foil, then remove the foil for the last 30 minutes. Once baked, cover and allow to rest for 15 minutes. Slice and serve.

CARMELA'S TIP:
- This dish benefits from being made a day ahead up to step 15 as it will slice with ease if it has time to settle. Bring to room temperature, pour over the béchamel, cover and bake.

Sweet and celebration pasta

The moment you realise pasta can be served as a sweet, your life will, through the power of carbs, be totally and utterly changed. I lose track of how often Chiara, my youngest daughter, asks me if I can make 'Chiacchiere', which are deep-fried pasta biscuits, for her to take to school, or some raspberry jam-filled vanilla ravioli as an after-school treat.

Chiara, however, prefers Nonna Solidea's chiacchiere, and so do I. What is it with your mum's cooking? No matter how I try to recreate her recipe, it is delicious but never fully hits the mark. There is always a difference and it's never a small, insignificant difference, it's noticeable. My children always question my meatballs (I know, how dare they?); they prefer my mum's pork-only version, but I prefer mine as I combine beef, pork and veal. I, on the other hand, would sell my soul to make our family lasagne as good as mum's and she knows it too. Mum, your lasagne is the best and it is my desert island dish, and always will be. I suppose we are always learning, and for that reason I am happy with my failures just as much as my successes.

From being fried to baked and boiled, sweet pasta can be a wonderful treat or end-of-dinner sweet. Some may think that sweet pasta may be a little heavy, but it really is not. I would most definitely suggest that you try as many of these as your waistline will allow. The chocolate pasta is wonderful and is not overly sweet, but the chickpea-filled and baked ravioli are my absolute favourite, a marvel in fact.

The fregula budino is my take on a pasta pudding, and you can change the fruit to whatever you'd prefer. The baked garganelli are eaten like I would a packet of malted milk biscuits – so good. The first time sweet pasta crossed my lips was years ago in Bologna. I remember buying a small tart that was topped with deep-fried spaghetti and dusted with vanilla icing sugar. I always go on about the beauty of this tart but am yet to recreate what I tasted, so I will have to be visiting Bologna again very soon.

Angel hair pasta twists (*Pasta fritta alla Siracusa*)

Easy, quick and a joy to eat. These are a quick, go-to sweet treat and perfect for using up leftover pasta. Everyone overestimates the amount of pasta they need to cook, is that due to carelessness or a subconscious desire for leftovers? Mine is most definitely the latter. I always cook enough for my family with the hope of leftovers, so I cook a portion or two for the pot to make this a happen as a reality.

Preparation time: 15 minutes
Cooking time: 10 minutes
Serves: 6

150g/5oz angel hair pasta
60g/2oz honey
1 tbsp candied orange peel, finely chopped
¼ tsp ground cinnamon
Zest and juice of 1 small orange
Olive oil, as required for frying
30g/1oz pistachio nuts, blitzed to a textured powder
Vanilla icing sugar, to dust

1. Cook the pasta in salted boiling water as per the packet instructions until *al dente*, then drain.
2. Twist small tablespoons of pasta into little nests and set aside until required.
3. Combine the honey, orange peel, cinnamon and orange juice and warm.
4. Pour the oil into a sauté pan to a depth of 4cm/1½in.
5. Heat the oil until hot but not to a smoking heat.
6. Prepare a tray and line it with kitchen paper to absorb excess oil.
7. With care and in batches, fry the nests off for 2 minutes on each side until lightly golden.
8. Lay the cooked nests onto the kitchen paper to drain for 2 minutes.
9. Place the nests onto a plate dusted with vanilla icing sugar.
10. Mix the pistachio nuts and orange zest together.
11. Drizzle the warmed honey over the nests and top with the pistachio and orange dust.

Baked chocolate, lemon and Strega garganelli tubes

(Garganelli ai cioccolato, limone e strega)

Garganelli are a favourite pasta of mine to make, possibly because of the diversity of shape and size. They are great for housing and clinging onto sauce with their delicate grooves and pointed vole-like noses. Garganelli are from the rich region of Emilia Romagna and are said to resemble the gullet of a chicken. I can see the likeness a little, but I try to not think too much about this … This dish, however, takes garganelli to a whole new level.

Preparation time: 1 hour plus 30 minutes resting of the pasta dough at room temperature
Cooking time: 8 minutes
Serves: 6

300g/10½oz 00 flour, plus extra for kneading
2 tbsp icing sugar
2 eggs, plus an extra yolk
1–2 tbsp Strega liqueur
Zest of ½ lemon
Semola, for kneading and dusting
Chocolate and Frangelico pasta dough (page 289)

Chocolate sauce
150g/5oz dark chocolate
100ml/3½fl oz double cream
Zest and juice of 1 clementine
Vanilla icing sugar, for dusting

1. Put the 00 flour and icing sugar into a bowl and stir.
2. Make a well in the centre and add the eggs, yolk, Strega and lemon zest. Combine and knead for 7 minutes until smooth.
3. Cover and rest the dough for 30 minutes at room temperature.
4. Take the chocolate pasta and roll it through the widest setting of the pasta machine. Fold and roll the pasta through the widest setting six times to create a smooth and elastic sheet. Continue to roll to the 4th setting of your pasta machine. Cover and set aside.

5. Take the Strega dough and, as above, roll the dough through the widest setting of the pasta machine, folding six times. Then roll the pasta (without folding) to the 4th setting of your pasta machine, just as above.
6. Dust the chocolate sheet and cut tagliatelle strands through your pasta machine, 40cm/16in in length.
7. Cut the Strega dough to 30cm/12in in length.
8. Lay the chocolate strands over the Strega pasta sheet, leaving a 1cm/^{1}/$_2$in gap between each piece.
9. Press down each chocolate ribbon, starting from the top left-hand corner, pressing along each length until the chocolate pasta has adhered to the base sheet.
10. Trim both ends with a knife and dust with semola.
11. Take the sheet and roll it through the 4th, 5th and 6th settings on the pasta machine. Cover the dough and repeat the lamination process with the remaining pasta dough.
12. Turn the pasta sheets over so that the decorative side is face down. Cut the pasta sheets into small squares measuring approximately 5cm x 5cm/2in x 2in. Allow the squares to dry for 5–7 minutes before forming and rolling.
13. Take your gnocchi board, or use a sushi mat or butter pat, and dust it with a little semola flour.
14. Take a square of pasta, decorative side facing down, and place a small dowel, the thickness of a pencil, on top, from corner to corner.
15. Roll the square around the pin, pushing down to form ridges from the board. Behold, your first laminated garganelli. Repeat as required.
16. Place the garganelli on a lightly floured tray until you are ready to bake.
17. Preheat the oven to 200°C/180°C fan-assisted/Gas 6.
18. Line two baking trays with parchment paper and place the garganelli onto the trays.
19. Bake for 8 minutes.
20. Finely chop the dark chocolate. Pour the cream into a small saucepan and add the chocolate.
21. Over a low heat, allow the chocolate to melt. Once melted, remove from the heat and add the clementine zest and juice. Pour into a small bowl.
22. Place the firm baked garganelli onto a serving platter with the chocolate pot in the centre, dust with icing sugar and tuck in.

Chickpea oven-baked ravioli

(Ravioli con ceci)

As a lover of chickpeas in any form, I find these sweet baked raviolis are a pleasure beyond my wildest imagination. Change the jam to suit your taste. I adore peach, apricot and cherry jam, but for these morsels I opt for some of my plump fig and vanilla jam, which I enjoy making each summer.

Preparation time: 45 minutes plus 30 minutes resting of pasta dough at room temperature
Cooking time: 25 minutes
Makes: around 30

Pasta dough
450g/1lb 00 flour, plus extra for kneading and dusting
100g/3½oz caster sugar
2 tbsp olive oil
120ml/4fl oz white wine or vermouth
60ml/2fl oz tepid water, or as required

Filling
240g/8½oz chickpeas (drained weight)
240g/8½oz apricot jam (or your chosen flavour)
2 tbsp amaretto
Zest of ½ lemon
1 tbsp honey (optional)
½ tsp cinnamon
1 egg

1. To make the pasta dough, tumble the flour and sugar onto a board and combine.
2. Form a well in the centre and add the olive oil and white wine. Begin to incorporate the flour and add a little tepid water as required.
3. Form a ball of dough and knead until soft and elastic.
4. Cover and rest the pasta dough for 30 minutes at room temperature.

5. To make the filling, blitz the chickpeas and pass them through a food mill (mouli) or coarse sieve until you get a thick chickpea purée.
6. Place the purée into a bowl and add the jam, amaretto, zest, honey and cinnamon. Stir and taste, adjusting the sweetness if required.
7. Add the egg and stir.
8. Cut the dough in half as it is easier to work with smaller batches.
9. Roll the dough out to the 3rd setting of the pasta machine.
10. Repeat with the other half of pasta dough.
11. Spoon tablespoon amounts of the filling across each side of the sheet, leaving 4cm/1½in gaps in between. You should have two rows of filling along the length of the sheet.
12. If required, add a little water around each tablespoon of the filling with your fingertip and lay the top sheet on top.
13. Press the top layer of dough around the filling. Using a ravioli cutter, a square or decorative shape, press over each mound.
14. Repeat as required.
15. Preheat the oven to 200°C/180°C fan-assisted/Gas 6.
16. Place the ravioli onto parchment-lined baking trays and bake for 25 minutes until lightly golden.
17. Serve with a dusting of vanilla sugar.

CARMELA'S TIP:
- If you have any pasta dough left over, roll it out and cut strips of dough. Bake in the oven until golden. Perfect to have alongside your morning espresso.

Chocolate ribbons with hazelnuts and amaretto (*Fettuccine di cioccolato*)

I enjoyed a bowl of chocolate pasta with a rich and very deep venison ragu in Tuscany which was just sublime. However, here the chocolate ribbons are a joy with a sweet take on them. I make fettuccine for a change; they are the same width as tagliatelle but are generally slightly thicker. For a lighter take on this dish, make the pasta lovely and thin.

Preparation time: 1 hour
Cooking time: 15 minutes
Serves: 4

200g/7oz chocolate and Frangelico pasta dough (page 289)
50g/1½oz butter
40g/1½oz hazelnuts, shelled, roughly chopped
40g/1½oz pine nuts
½ tsp cinnamon
40g/1½oz golden caster sugar
50g/1½oz stale breadcrumbs
1 tbsp amaretto liquor
25g/1oz icing sugar
4 hard amaretti biscuits
pinch of salt

1. Roll out the chocolate pasta dough to a thickness of 3mm/^{1}/$_8$in. Dust with a little icing sugar as you go to prevent sticking.
2. Cut the chocolate pasta into 25cm/10in lengths and pass it through your tagliatelle cutter, or cut ribbons by hand to the width of 5mm/^{1}/$_4$in.
3. Place the fettuccine on a tray until required.
4. Heat the butter in a saucepan along with the nuts and cinnamon. Stir.
5. Sprinkle in the golden caster sugar and stale breadcrumbs.
6. Pour in the amaretto. Stir and cook for 5–7 minutes until golden and aromatic.

7. Place a large pan of water on to boil; once boiling, add a small pinch of salt.
8. Cook the pasta for 3 minutes until *al dente*.
9. Drain and add the pasta to the butter sauce. Toss lightly.
10. Serve on warm plates with a fine dusting of icing sugar and a crumbled amaretti biscuit over each plate.

Decorative fried pasta roses
(Cartellate, carteddate)

This pasta shape – a decorative circular crown – is said to depict the baby Jesus's halo, while some say it depicts the thorn-embossed crown that was placed on Jesus's head at crucifixion. I concur with the halo option wholeheartedly. A festive period in the south of Italy will always be finished with these stunning vintage-styled cartellate pasta roses, fried and dressed with a little honey, mosto cotto or simply a sprinkle of sugar. I enjoy the making them just as much as the eating in all honesty. They don't come much prettier than these southern fried roses.

Preparation time: 1 hour plus 30 minutes resting of the pasta dough at room temperature
Cooking time: 20 minutes (batch cooking)
Resting: 2–8 hours to allow the finished cartellate to dry out prior to frying
Makes: around 20

270g/9½oz 00 flour, plus extra for kneading and dusting
1 tbsp caster sugar
1 sachet vanilla pane degli angeli or 1 tsp vanilla extract
80ml/3fl oz white wine or vermouth
1 egg
2 tbsp extra virgin olive oil
Olive oil, for frying, as required
Drizzle of mosto cotto or honey (optional or as required)
Vanilla icing sugar, to finish, as required

1. Put the flour in a bowl along with the sugar and vanilla sachet/extract. Stir to combine.
2. Make a well in the centre and add the white wine, egg and extra virgin olive oil.
3. Begin to incorporate the ingredients together in the bowl. When a ball of dough comes together, tumble it onto a wooden board.
4. Knead the dough for 5–8 minutes until soft, elastic and pliable.
5. Push the dough into a disc with the palm of your hands, cover and rest for 30 minutes at room temperature.

6. Cut the dough into six portions. Working with one portion at a time, cover the other five until required.
7. Roll the dough through the widest setting of the pasta machine. Fold and roll it through the widest setting again. Repeat this process six times.
8. Then run the pasta sheet through each setting twice (without folding) to setting 6 of the pasta machine.
9. Cut the dough with a fluted cutter into 30cm x 12cm/12in x 5in rectangles. Each rectangle will make three cartellate roses.
10. Cut the pasta sheet lengthways with a fluted cutter into 4cm/1½in strips. (You should have three rectangular strips, 30cm x 44cm/12in x 18in.)
11. Pull up the two sides as if you were folding the dough in half lengthways. Starting 2.5cm/1in in, pinch the dough at every 2.5cm/1in point. Pinch along the entire length.
12. Both ends should remain open and you should have six tiny pockets along the length of dough.
13. Roll the length of pasta into a coil and pinch the pockets together at the widest point. You should have a circular, coiled rose with lots of small pinched pockets. Repeat with the remaining dough.
14. Set the cartellate onto a tea towel or a tray dusted with a little semola.
15. Allow the cartellate to sit uncovered for 2 to 8 hours, or overnight if time allows.
16. Prepare a tray or two with kitchen paper. Heat 5cm/2in of oil in a wide sauté pan to 180°C.
17. Carefully place two or three roses in the oil. Cook for 3 minutes until golden; you may need to use a slotted spoon to keep pushing down the bobbing up roses.
18. Drain and place the pasta onto the kitchen paper. Repeat until all the pasta has been cooked.
19. To dress, warm the honey or mosto cotto. Sit the cartellate in the warm liquid and bathe for 30 seconds.
20. Drain and place on a platter. Serve at room temperature.

CARMELA'S TIP:
- Retain all the scraps of discarded pasta dough and cut them into maltagliati pieces and bake or fry until golden. I also prefer to have my cartellate naked, with no warm dressing and just a sprinkle of vanilla icing sugar.

Fregola with milk and blackberries

(Budino di fregola e more)

Fregola is a small pasta from Sardinia which comes in different sizes: fine, medium, and large. This pasta is one that you can make as per page 5, but I would suggest purchasing a dried bag from your local Italian deli. If you love rice pudding, then you will most definitely fall heart first into this dish. It pairs beautifully with seasonal berries, but my absolute favourite is with a baked pear or apple. However, I am currently ankle deep in my dad Rocco's blackberry harvest so blackberries it is – thanks Papa.

Preparation time: 5 minutes
Cooking time: 45 minutes
Serves: 6

500ml/18fl oz double cream
500ml/18fl oz milk
200g/7oz fregola pasta
3 tbsp borage honey
300g/10½oz blackberries
60g/2oz caster sugar
Zest and juice of 1 clementine

1. Pour the cream and milk into a saucepan and place over a medium heat. When simmering, pour in the fregola pasta.
2. Stir gently and cook the pasta for 25 minutes until the pasta and milk become a little creamy. Remove from the heat and add the honey and clementine zest.
3. Wash the blackberries and remove any woody tops. Pop them into a small saucepan with the caster sugar and clementine juice.
4. Stir until the blackberries have broken down a little and the sauce has become a little jammy.
5. Spoon the pasta into small ramekins and top with a generous spoonful of fruit.

CARMELA'S TIP:
- A great breakfast alternative too as a treat.

Gossip biscuits (*Chiacchiere*)

Every day is a festival or celebration day when you deep-fry pasta. This dough can be made into simple wide strips or, for a little interest, slice each strip in the centre making a slit and pass each end of dough through the slit. Chiacchiere means to chit-chat or gossip. Make, fry, drain on kitchen paper, and dust with icing sugar. My daughter Chiara absolutely loves these and asks most days if it is a festival day! Dust with vanilla icing sugar and enjoy with your espresso.

Preparation time: 45 minutes plus 30 minutes resting and chilling of pasta dough
Cooking time: 20 minutes
Makes: around 40

60g/2oz softened butter
60g/2oz caster sugar
1 egg
1 sachet pane degli angeli or 1 tsp vanilla extract
80ml/3fl oz white wine
2 tbsp Strega or grappa liqueur
340g/12oz 00 flour, plus extra for kneading and dusting
Pinch of salt (optional, I prefer to not add it as my butter is salted)
1 litre/1¾ pints vegetable oil, for deep frying
Vanilla icing sugar, for dusting

1. I prefer to use a food processor to make chiacchiere; however, you can also make them traditionally on a wooden board in the style of a volcano. Add the butter, caster sugar, egg, pane degli angeli, white wine and Strega to a food processor. Blitz to fully incorporate.
2. Slowly add the flour and blitz until a dough is formed.
3. Tip the mixture onto a wooden board, add a little more flour if required and knead the dough until smooth and elastic. I would suggest only a couple of minutes as the dough will be softer than a standard pasta dough.
4. Cover and chill the chiacchiere dough for at least 30 minutes in the fridge as you will need the dough to firm up.

5. Portion the dough for ease and work with one half, covering the other portion until required.
6. Form the dough with your hands into a flat disc and pass it through each setting on your pasta machine twice, making the fourth setting your last thickness.
7. Using a pastry wheel, cut into 13cm x 3cm/5in x 1in lengths.
8. Fry in vegetable oil at 170°C until puffy and golden.
9. Drain on kitchen paper and dust with vanilla icing sugar.

CARMELA'S TIP:
• These can also be made without frying! Instead of dropping the dough shapes into hot oil, boil them for 2 minutes, then drain and lay onto a lined baking tray. Sprinkle with sugar and bake at 200°C/180°C fan-assisted/Gas 6 until golden.

Hazelnut, chocolate and Frangelico
pasta (*Pasta al gianuiotti*)

Pasta may be perceived to be the speedy go-to in terms of lunch or dinner, but when my sister Daniela and I were young, we were also offered a tiny bowl of pasta (normally ditalini) served with warm butter and a sprinkle of cinnamon sugar. I remember my dad Rocco telling me that he would often have sugared bread for breakfast and my mum Solidea said that pasta with sugar was a real treat when she was a little girl. Suddenly pasta was seen in a different manner altogether.

Preparation time: 10 minutes
Cooking time: 15 minutes
Serves: 4

200g/7oz vermicelli pasta (or any other long pasta you would prefer)
4 tbsp hazelnut chocolate spread
8 Gianduiotti or Baci chocolates
30g/1oz butter
¼ tsp ground cinnamon
2 tbsp Frangelico liqueur
30g/1oz dark chocolate, grated
30g/1oz hazelnuts, finely chopped

1. Cook your chosen pasta until *al dente*.
2. Take four glasses or ramekins and spoon a tablespoon of the chocolate spread into the base of each.
3. Unwrap the individual chocolates and chop them up.
4. Melt the butter, add the cinnamon and stir.
5. Dress the drained pasta with the warm butter and cinnamon.
6. Tong the pasta into loose nests and place a nest into each glass.
7. Drizzle a teaspoon of Frangelico over each nest and add a sprinkle of the chopped chocolates, grated dark chocolate and hazelnuts.

CARMELA'S TIP:
- I buy my Gianduiotti hazelnut chocolates from my local Italian deli 'The Italian Shop', but roughly chopped Baci or Ferrero Rocher chocolates are just as delightful.

Jam-filled and baked ravioli
(*Ravioli ripieno di marmellata*)

Time to share one of my most cherished recipes, baked jam-filled
pastas. Sweet, yet firm and portable. I use the term portable with a
smile on my face because these are one of my children's favourite
lunchbox treats. That said, they are wonderful with a mid-morning
espresso, as an after-dinner sweet or just because you're worth it.
Please beware that when they come out of the oven the jam centre
will be molten to the touch, so watch your lips because they are hard
to resist.

Preparation time: 45 minutes plus 30 minutes resting of pasta
dough in the fridge
Cooking time: 15 minutes
Serves: 6

> 250g/9oz 00 flour, plus extra for dusting
> 2 tbsp vanilla icing sugar, plus extra for dusting
> 2 eggs
> 1 yolk
> 25g/1oz butter, softened
> 150g/5oz jam (I adore fig, raspberry or peach)
> Semola, for dusting, as required

1. Put the flour and icing sugar into a food processor and blitz for
   10 seconds.
2. Crack in the whole eggs, yolk and butter. Blitz to form a dough.
3. Knead for 3 minutes, using a little more flour if needed. Cover
   and chill in the fridge for 30 minutes.
4. Preheat the oven to 200°C/180°C fan-assisted/Gas 6.
5. Roll the chilled pasta out with a pasta machine or rolling pin to
   2mm/^{1}/$_{16}$in in thickness.
6. Cut the pasta sheets into 50cm/20in lengths.
7. Spoon teaspoon amounts of jam along the length of the pasta
   dough, 2cm/1in from the edge, also leaving a 2cm/1in gap in
   between the jam teaspoons.

8. Fold the pasta sheet over and, using your palm, secure the pasta around each mound.

9. Use a pastry cutter or stamp and cut out each ravioli, approximately 5cm x 5cm/2in x 2in.

10. Place the ravioli on a tray or tea towel dusted with semola and repeat until you have an array of filled pasta squares.

11. Place the ravioli on a tray lined with baking parchment and bake for 14–18 minutes.

12. Dust with icing sugar and enjoy.

CARMELA'S TIP:

- You can also deep fry the ravioli in vegetable oil for 2 minutes or until slightly puffy and golden in colour.

Pasta cake (*Torta di pasta*)

If I knew you were coming, I'd have baked a cake – a pasta cake. Quirky and different with a sense of celebration about it. You can adjust the sweetness as required by using honey in place of the sugar and also by adding a variety of soaked fruit, nuts or chocolate to make it your own, but I just adore this original combination. Soaking the raisins in Marsala overnight, or a little in advance, adds a delicate flavour. I would recommend the angel hair pasta to be dried and from your local deli as the texture and density is vital.

Preparation time: 15 minutes
Cooking time: 50 minutes
Serves: 8

220g/7½oz angel hair pasta, preferably dried
salt
250ml/9fl oz milk
50ml/1½fl oz single cream
60g/2oz golden caster sugar
2 tbsp butter, to prepare the cake tin
3 tbsp 00 flour, to prepare the cake tin
4 eggs
60g/2oz walnuts, chopped
60g/2oz pine nuts
40g/1½oz raisins (soaked for 30 minutes in 2 tablespoons of Marsala)
½ tsp ground cinnamon
Vanilla icing sugar, as required

1. Preheat the oven to 200°C/180°C fan-assisted/Gas 6.
2. Cook the pasta in a pan of salted boiling water for 3 minutes.
3. Warm the milk and cream in a saucepan large enough to take the pasta.
4. Sprinkle the sugar into the milk and stir.
5. Drain the pasta and add it to the warmed milk. Cook until the pasta has absorbed the milk. This will take about 5 minutes.
6. Allow the pasta to cool.

7. Butter and flour a 23cm/9in spring-form cake tin. Line the base with parchment paper.
8. Whisk the eggs together in a large bowl for 1 minute and add the walnuts, pine nuts, raisins, any residual Marsala liquid and the cinnamon.
9. Add the pasta and any liquid into the whisked eggs and combine. Stir well and pour into the cake tin.
10. Bake for 30–35 minutes until the cake is set in the middle and has slightly caught edges.

Spaghetti tart (*Torta di spaghetti*)

I remember clasping firmly an individual spaghetti tart while away in one of my favourite cities, Bologna; there was no chance I was sharing. I sat in the square and was mesmerised at the beauty of this layered spaghetti encased in a delicately balanced sweet pastry. This was five years ago, and if I close my eyes tightly, I can imagine being transported back to this memory that thankfully never seems to fade.

Preparation time: 1 hour plus 30 minutes resting of the pastry dough
Cooking time: 45 minutes
Serves: 8

Pasta
200g/7oz egg pasta dough (page 6)
Semola, for dusting

Pastry
240g/8½oz 00 flour
150g/5oz caster sugar
115g/4oz butter, cold, cubed
2 eggs
2 yolks
Zest of 1 lemon
1 sachet of vanilla pane deli angeli or 1 tsp vanilla extract
Pinch of salt

Filling
230g/8oz almonds, blanched
150g/5oz caster sugar
40g/1½oz candied peel, finely chopped
2 tbsp cocoa powder
80g/3oz jam (optional)
80g/3oz butter, tiny cubes
6 tbsp Frangelico or rum
Vanilla sugar, as required

1. Take the pasta dough and roll to 2–3mm/$^1/_{16}$–$^1/_{18}$in thickness with a pasta machine or rolling pin.
2. Cut the pasta sheets into 30cm/12in lengths and allow them to dry for 20 minutes.
3. Roll the sheets through the spaghetti attachment of the pasta machine or roll the sheets into sausages and cut by hand into thin 2–3mm/$^1/_{16}$–$^1/_{18}$in strips.
4. Set the cut pasta aside onto semola-dusted trays until required. Split the pasta up into three portions; this will help with layering.
5. For the pastry, put the flour, caster sugar and cubed butter into a food processor and pulse to form breadcrumbs. Add the eggs, yolks, lemon zest, vanilla and salt, and pulse to form a dough.
6. Bring the pastry together and use your palms to push the dough into a flat disc. Cover and chill for 30 minutes.
7. For the filling, blitz the almonds and caster sugar together then add the candied peel and cocoa powder.
8. Preheat the oven to 200°C/180°C fan-assisted/Gas 6.
9. Roll out the pastry and line a 25cm/10in spring-form baking tin.
10. Spread the jam across the base of the pastry in an even layer.
11. Now to layer the cake tin. Add a layer of spaghetti followed by a layer of the almond filling and a few butter cubes dotted about.
12. Repeat with another layer of spaghetti, some almond crumb, and more butter, then finish with a final layer of pasta.
13. Cover with foil and bake. After 25 minutes, remove the foil and bake for a further 20 minutes.
14. Remove the spaghetti pie from the oven and place on a baking tray. Drizzle over the liqueur and cool.
15. Dust with vanilla icing sugar and slice.

CARMELA'S TIP:
- The best candied peel I can find comes from a deli in Soho called Lina Stores.

Sweet half-moons filled with ricotta, hazelnuts and chocolate (*Mezzalune dolci ripiene di ricotta con nocciole e cioccolato*)

Now that I have your attention, I would most definitely suggest that you double this recipe, because it is known to produce greed. I tend to eat two while I am frying them so the serving suggestion may need altering too. What's more is they are delicious as a snack with coffee or as a pick-me-up. Feel free to add 30g/1oz cocoa powder to the pasta dough for a more indulgent taste; you may also need to add a touch of water to bring the dough together.

Preparation time: 30 minutes plus 30 minutes chilling of the pasta dough
Cooking time: 15 minutes
Serves: 4

250g/9oz 00 flour, plus extra for dusting as required
2 tbsp caster sugar
Pinch of ground cinnamon
2 eggs
1 yolk
50g/1½oz butter, slightly softened
250g/9oz ricotta, drained overnight
Zest and juice of 1 clementine
45g/1½oz hazelnuts, finely chopped
45g/1½oz dark chocolate (I use tiny buttons)
1 tsp caster sugar
Olive oil for frying, as required
4 tbsp honey, orange blossom would work beautifully
Vanilla icing sugar, to dust

1. Combine the flour and sugar and add the cinnamon.
2. Whisk the eggs together.
3. Tip the flour onto a wooden surface and make a well in the centre to take the wet ingredients. Alternatively, you can work the ingredients in a large bowl with a wooden spoon.

4. Pour the eggs, yolk and softened butter into the flour and incorporate, mixing well into a dough.
5. Knead for 5 minutes, until smooth. Cover and rest in the fridge (as butter is present in the dough) for 30 minutes.
6. Into a bowl combine the ricotta, clementine zest, hazlenuts, chocolate buttons and caster sugar. Mix well.
7. Roll out the pasta dough with a pasta machine or rolling pin to 2mm/^{1}/16in in thickness and cut 12 discs 10cm/4in in diameter.
7. Add a spoonful of the ricotta filling to the centre of each disc.
8. Dampen the edges of the discs with a little water (only if they seem too dry to seal) and fold, removing any trapped air and sealing to form a half-moon.
10. Use a fork and seal the raw edge, giving additional pressure and a decorative finish.
11. Pour the olive oil into a sauté pan to a depth of 5–7cm/2–3in. Warm over a high heat.
12. Test the oil by dropping in a tiny piece of pasta dough: if the oil bubbles and the dough colours you are ready to rock.
13. Prepare a tray and line it with kitchen paper to drain excess oil.
14. Cook the pasta in batches for 2 minutes on each side, or until golden.
15. Remove with a slotted spoon and place onto the kitchen paper.
16. Warm the honey and add the clementine juice.
17. Plate up the mezzalune with a drizzle of honey and dusting of vanilla sugar.

CARMELA'S TIP:
- Use up any leftover pasta by cutting it into strips and frying for 2 minutes or until golden. The perfect sweet treat with your morning espresso.

Sweet Sardinian ravioli with orange blossom honey (*Sebadas, gnocco fritto*)

The first time I ate an authentic sebadas was when I visited the island of Sardinia for my fortieth birthday. It is the most memorable dessert with an intense sweetness and a perfectly paired savoury offering. The sebadas was circular and filled with pecorino fresco; it was so big that it almost covered my entire plate, and was drizzled with the most sensational orange honey I had ever tasted. I am longing to go back to the island, as you can imagine, but for now I'll leave you with a taste of my recipe made using pecorino from my friend Mario Olianas.

Preparation time: 30 minutes plus 30 minutes chilling of the pasta dough
Cooking time: 15 minutes
Serves: 4

200g/7oz 00 flour
60g/2oz caster sugar
2 eggs
2 tbsp Marsala wine
125g/4½oz fresh Pecorino Sardo
Olive oil for frying
120g/4oz orange blossom honey
Zest and juice of 1 clementine
2 tbsp vanilla icing sugar

1. Combine the flour and sugar in a bowl or on a wooden board, then form a well in the centre.
2. Crack the eggs into the well and add the Marsala wine.
3. Incorporate into a dough and knead until smooth and elastic. The dough will be a little soft due to the added liquid so wrap and pop in the fridge until required.
4. Cut the pecorino into four portions, creating discs of around 8cm/3¼in in diameter.
5. Roll out the pasta dough with a machine or rolling pin to a thickness of 2mm/¹⁄₁₆in.

6. Cut eight large circles, 15cm/6in in diameter.
7. Place pieces of pecorino onto four discs. Dampen the edges and cover with another circle of pasta dough, sealing and securing all the way round.
8. Place the sebadas onto a lightly dusted tray while you wait for your oil to come to temperature, 170°C.
9. Fry the sebadas until golden.
10. Warm the honey over a bowl of hot water to loosen it and allow the aromas to be released further. Add the clementine zest and juice to the honey.
11. Scoop out the sebadas with a slotted spoon, shaking off any excess oil, and plate up with a drizzle of warmed honey and a dusting of vanilla icing sugar.

CARMELA'S TIP:

- If you have scraps of pasta dough left after you've made the sebadas, cut them into irregular shapes similar to malfatti or maltagliati and fry them off for 2 minutes. Dust them with icing sugar and enjoy. The perfect pasta biscuits

Index

agnolotti 58
Agnolotti col plin con barbatietole e'ricotta 228–229
almond flour 23, 24
almonds
  Almond, Basil and Tomato Pesto 102–103
  Spaghetti Tart 294–295
anchovies
  Linguine with Anchovy and Grapes 160–161
  Pici with Cauliflower, Leaves and Breadcrumbs 164–165
  Polenta Quadretti [squares] with a Bean and Anchovy Sauce 150–151
Anelletti Pasta Pie 239–240
Angel Hair Pasta Twists 277
anolini 56
Anolini in brodo 222–223
aquafaba 25
asparagus
  Asparagus Gnocchi 185
  Asparagus Pesto 104–105
  Farfalle Pasta Bows with Asparagus Pesto and Spears 120–121
aubergines
  Pasta with Aubergine 146–147
  Rigatoni and Aubergine Cake 262–263
  Spaghetti Frittata with Aubergines 266–267
autumn leaves (pasta shapes) 45
Avocado Pasta Dough 13

Basil Pesto 105
beans
  Bread Pasta Dumplings and
  Borlotti Beans 114–115
  Pasta and Bean Soup 142–143
  Polenta Quadretti [squares] with a Bean and Anchovy Sauce 150–151
beef
  Anelletti Pasta Pie 239–240
  Beef Stock 80
  Bolognese Ragu 86–87
  Celebration Lasagne 251–253
  Earring Encased Pasta Pie 254–255
  Filled Skirtless Ravioli Coins with Stock 222–223
  Polenta Gnocchi with Meat Sauce 192–193
  Rich Rib Ragu 96–97
  Solidea's Egg Layered Lasagne 264–265
beetroot
  Beetroot Pasta Dough 15
  Milk Pasta with Beetroot and Ricotta 228–229
bell peppers: Scialatelli with Yellow Bell Peppers, Cherry Tomatoes and Walnuts 168–169
Besciamella 100
Bigoli con l'anara 180–181
Biscuit Soup 112–113
black chickpea flour 24
blackberries: Fregola with Milk and Blackberries 286
Blutnudeln (pasta dough using pig's blood) 22
Bolognese ragu 86–87
Bolognese sugo 88–89
breadcrumbs
  Bread Pasta Dumplings and Borlotti Beans 114–115

Bread Pasta in Stock 116–117
Breadcrumb Pasta Filling 64
Breadcrumb Textured Pesto 106
making 76
Pici with Cauliflower, Leaves and
Breadcrumbs 164–165
Poor Man's Parmesan
(Breadcrumb Topping) 109
broad beans: Little Hats wit Broad
Beans, Summer Peas and
Pistachio 132–133
Brodo di carne 80
Brodo di pesce 82–83
Brodo di pollo 81
Brodo vegetale 84–85
Brown Rice Gluten-Free Pasta 27
Bucatini alla salsa di noci 154
Bucatini with a Spicy Ragu and
Whipped Ricotta 152–153
Bucatini with Walnut Sauce 154
buckwheat flour 24
Buckwheat Pizzocheri with Potatoes
and Cavolo Nero 247–248
Budino di fregola e more 286
burrata: Green Ravioli Parcels with
Burrata and Pine Nuts 224–225
busiate 47

cabbage: Pumpkin Gnocchi with
Sausage 198–199
Cannelloni al Gorgonzola 249–250
capers
Garden Tomatoes and Honeyed
Ricotta 92–93
Pici with Cauliflower, Leaves
and Breadcrumbs 164–165
Spaghetti Frittata with
Aubergines 266–267
*Cappellacci con piseli, limone,
prosciutto cotto e mascarpone*
232–233
cappellacci/cappelletti 59
Cappelli con piseli e pistacchio 132–
133

caramelle 57
Carmela's Bolognese Sauce 88–89
Cartellate, carteddate 284–295
Casconcelli alla Bergamasca 207–
208
Casoncelli Parcels 207–208
cauliflower
Pici with Cauliflower, Leaves and
Breadcrumbs 164–165
Pici with Gorgonzola and
Romanesco 166–167
Cavatelli con funghi e salsicce
119–120
Cavatelli, Mushrooms and Sausage
119–120
cavatelli/cazzarille/-
cecatidde/cecatielle 44
cavolo nero
Buckwheat Pizzocheri with
Potatoes and Cavolo Nero
247–248
Cavolo Nero Pesto 107
Ceci gnudi al pomodoro 186
cheese 74
see also Gorgonzola; mascarpone;
mozzarella; ricotta
chestnut flour 23, 24
Chestnut Ravioli with Rabbit and
Thyme 209–211
Chiacchiere 287–288
chicken
Chicken Stock 81
Square-cut Pasta Ribbons with
Chicken Dumplings in Stock
172–173
Tortellini Filling 61
Vincigrassi Lasagne 274–275
chickpea flour 23, 24
chickpeas
Chickpea Gnudi with Dressed
Tomatoes 186–187
Chickpea Oven-baked Ravioli
280–281
Orecchiette with Chickpeas,

Smoked Pancetta and Celery
Leaves 136–137
Polenta Quadretti [squares] with
a Bean and Anchovy Sauce
150–151
chocolate
Baked Chocolate, Lemon and
Strega Garganelli Tubes 278–279
Chocolate and Frangelico Pasta
Dough 19
Chocolate Ribbons with Hazelnuts
and Amaretto 282–283
Hazelnut, Chocolate and
Frangelico Pasta 289
Sweet Half-moons Filled with
Ricotta, Hazelnuts and
Chocolate 296–297
Sweet Ricotta Pasta Filling 65
cicatelli/capunti 43
clams
Fregola with Fish Stock and
Clams 122
Semolina Gnocchi with Lentils
and Clams 200–201
coloured and flavoured pasta 8–22
Avocado Pasta Dough 13
Beetroot Pasta Dough 15
Blutnudeln (pasta dough using
pig's blood) 22
Chocolate and Frangelico Pasta
Dough 19
Cuttlefish/Squid Ink Pasta Dough
17
Grano Arso Pasta (Burnt Wheat
Pasta) 20
Hemp Pasta 21
Pea Pasta Dough 14
Red Wine Pasta Dough 18
Saffron Pasta Dough 16
Spinach Pasta Dough 11
striping pasta 32–33
Tomato Pasta Dough 12
vegetable and fruit powders 9–10
Conchiglioni ripieno con funghi e

ricotta 270–271
Conchiglioni ripieno sotto forno 258–
259
cookery tips 76–78
cooking pasta 66–67, 76
al dente 66
dried pasta 66
oil 67
portion size 66–67
reserving pasta water 67, 76
cornflour 24
corzetti 34, 71
Corzetti con miele 145–146
Crab and Saffron Ravioli 212–213
*Crespelle gratinate con radicchio e
besciamella* 243–244
Culurgiones al pomodoro 214–215
Culurgiones with a Simple Tomato
Sauce 214–215
Cuttlefish/Squid Ink Pasta Dough
17

Decorative Fried Pasta Roses 284–
285
Dirty Pasta Stamps 216–217
duck: Wholewheat Spaghetti with
Duck Offal Ragu 180–181

egg whites, freezing 76
eggs 77
Celebration Lasagne 251–253
Egg Pasta Dough 6
Enriched Egg Yolk Pasta Dough 7
Fresh Egg Yolk Raviolo 54
Solidea's Egg Layered Lasagne
264–265
Spaghetti Carbonara 170
Tagliarini with Spring Nettles
and Egg Yolk 176–177
see also frittatas
equipment 69–71
care of 69
extruders 3, 31, 71

Faggotini con coniglio, vitello e maiale 218–219

Farfalle Pasta Bows with Asparagus Pesto and Spears 120–121

Farfalle [stricchetti] con pesto di asparagi 120–121

farro 23, 202

fava bean flour 23, 24

Fazzolette al papavero 156–157

fennel
Garganelli with Pork Cheek Ragu 124–125
Paccheri Tubes with a Veal Ragu 138–139

Fettucine di cioccolato 282–283

fish and seafood
Crab and Saffron Ravioli 212–213
Cuttlefish/Squid Ink Pasta Dough 17
Fish Stock 82–83
Fregola with Fish Stock and Clams 122
Half-moons of Pasta Filled with Grouper and Spinach 226–227
Minchiareddhi/Maccaruni with Mixed Seafood 134–136
Semolina Gnocchi with Lentils and Clams 200–201
Strozzapreti Pasta with Octopus and Cherry Tomatoes 174–175

flours 23, 72–73
00 flour 2, 3, 23
gluten-free flours 23, 24
semola flour (durum wheat semolina) 2, 3, 23

freezing pasta 67

Fregola with Fish Stock and Clams 122

Fregola with Milk and Blackberries 286–287

Fregula al vongole in bianco 122

fregula/fregola 50

fridge, storing pasta in the 67

Fried Pasta 123

Frittata di pasta 155

frittatas
Frittata of Leftover Pasta 155
Spaghetti Frittata with Aubergines 266–267
Tiny Baked Tagliolini Frittatas 272–273

Frittatine di tagliolini 272–273

Fusi Istrani con d'duja 148–149

fusilli 47

Garganelli ai ciococcolato, limone e strega 278–279

Garganelli al ragu di miale 124–125

Garganelli with Pork Cheek Ragu 124–125

gluten-free pasta 23–25

gnocchi 184
Asparagus Gnocchi 185
Grape-stuffed Potato Gnocchi 188–189
Polenta Gnocchi with Meat Sauce 192–193
Potato Gnocchi with a Parmigiano Reggiano, Speck and Cream Sauce 194–196
Potato Gnocchi with Spinach and Provolone Cream 196–197
Pumpkin Gnocchi with Sausage 198–199
Semolina Gnocchi with Lentils and Clams 200–201
Spelt Gnocchi 202–203

Gnocchi agli asparagi 185

Gnocchi de patate as Parmigiano Reggiano, speck e crema 194–196

Gnocchi di farina gialla con ragu di carne 192–193

Gnocchi di farro 202–203

Gnocchi di patate, spinachi e provolone fonduta 196–197

Gnocchi di semolia con lenticchie e vongole 200–201

Gnocchi di uva 188–189

Gnocchi di zucca con verza e salsiccia 198–199
gnochetti sardi 35
gnudi 184
 Naked Pasta Filling, Rolled and Served with a Cherry Tomato Sauce 190–191
Gnudi con sugo di pomodorini 190–191
Gorgonzola
 Cannelloni with Gorgonzola 249–250
 Gorgonzola and Cream Sauce 94–95
 Gorgonzola, Pear and Pecorino Pasta Filling 63
 Pici with Gorgonzola and Romanesco 166–167
 Roasted Butternut Squash and Gorgonzola Pasta Filling 62
Gossip Biscuits 287–288
grano arso 20, 23
Grano Arso Pasta (Burnt Wheat Pasta) 20
grapes
 Grape-stuffed Potato Gnocchi 188–189
 Linguine with Anchovy and Grapes 160–161
Grated Egg Pasta in Stock 126–127
Grattini all'uovo in brodo 126–127
grattini/grattoni 49
guanciale 75
 Casoncelli Parcels 207–208
 Penne Baked in Paper 260–261
 Spaghetti Carbonara 170

Hay and Straw Pasta with Peas and Prosciutto 158–159
hazelnut flour 23, 24
hazelnuts
 Chocolate Ribbons with Hazelnuts and Amaretto 282–283

Hazelnut, Chocolate and Frangelico Pasta 289
 Sweet Half-moons Filled with Ricotta, Hazelnuts and Chocolate 296–297
 Sweet Ricotta Pasta Filling 65
Hemp Pasta 21
honey
 Angel Hair Pasta Twists 277
 Fregola with Milk and Blackberries 286
 Garden Tomatoes and Honeyed Ricotta 92–93
 Pasta Coins with Ricotta and Honey 145–146
 Sweet Sardinian Ravioli with Orange Blossom Honey 298–299

jam
 Chickpea Oven-baked Ravioli 280–281
 Jam-filled and Baked Ravioli 290–291
 Spaghetti Tart 294–295

kamut 23

La mollica 109
larder and pantry ingredients 71–75
lasagne 36
 Baked Lasagne with Radicchio 241–242
 Celebration Lasagne 251–253
 Lasagne with Spinach and Pesto 256–257
 Solidea's Egg Layered Lasagne 264–265
 Vincigrassi Lasagne 274–275
Lasagne al radicchio 241–242
Lasagne con pesto 256–257
Lasagne Molisana 264–265
lentil flour 23, 24
lentils: Semolina Gnocchi with Lentils and Clams 200–201

Linguine on acciughe e uvetta 160–161

Linguine with Anchovy and Grapes 160–161

lorighittas 39

maccheroni al ferro 48

Mafaldine al pesto di pistacchio 162–163

Malfadine with Pistachio Pesto 162–163

malloreddus 35

maltagliati 51

Maltagliati con radicchio, speck e crema 111

Maltagliati con rucola e speck 130–131

mascarpone 74
  Filled Pasta Parcel Shoes with Browned Butter and Fresh Peas 220–221
  Pea, Mascarpone, Ham and Lemon Cappellacci 232–233
  Tagliatelle with Mushrooms, Thyme and Mascarpone 178–179

meat, cured 74–75

Mezzalune di cernia e spinaci 226–227

Mezzalune dolci ripiene di ricotta con nocciole e cioccolato 296–297

Milk Pasta with Beetroot and Ricotta 228–229

Minchiareddhi alla pescardore 134–136

Minchiareddhi/Maccaruni with Mixed Seafood 134–136

mozzarella 74
  Anelletti Pasta Pie 239–240
  Baked Lasagne with Radicchio 241–242
  Celebration Lasagne 251–253
  Mamma's Baked Pasta Shells 258–259

Rigatoni and Aubergine Cake 262–263

Solidea's Egg Layered Lasagne 264–265

mozzarella water 25, 76–77

mushrooms
  Baked Tagliatelle Lattice Pie with Béchamel and Porcini 245–246
  Cavatelli, Mushrooms and Sausage 119–120
  Celebration Lasagne 251–253
  Mushroom Pasta Filling 60
  Open Mushroom Raviolo 230–231
  Stuffed Pasta Shells with Mushroom and Ricotta 270–271
  Tagliatelle with Mushrooms, Thyme and Mascarpone 178–179
  Vincigrassi Lasagne 274–275
  Wide Pasta Ribbons with Autumn Mushroom Bolognese 182–183

My Papa Rocco's Spaghetti with Garlic, Oil and Chilli Intensity 171

n'duja: Pinched Triangle Pasta with N'duja 148–149

nettles: Tagliarini with Spring Nettles and Egg Yolk 176–177

nut flours 23

nut milks 25

oils 71

olives
  Garden Tomatoes and Honeyed Ricotta 92–93
  Pinched Triangle Pasta with N'duja 148–149

oranges
  Angel Hair Pasta Twists 277
  Handkerchiefs Dressed in Sugar, Clementine and Poppy Seeds 156–157
  Sweet Sardinian Ravioli with Orange Blossom Honey 298–299

orecchiette 41

Orecchiette with Chickpeas, Smoked Pancetta and Celery Leaves 136–137

Orecchiette con ceci, pancetta affumicata e sedano 136–137

Paccheri al ragu di viletto 138–139

paccheri tubes 40

Paccheri Tubes with a Veal Ragu 138–139

Paglia e fieno 158–159

pancakes

Baked Pancake Pasta with Radicchio and Béchamel 243–244

Italian Pancakes Bathed in Stock with Celery Leaves 128–129

Pancake Pasta 140–141

pancetta

Bolognese Ragu 86–87

Frittata of Leftover Pasta 155

Hay and Straw Pasta with Peas and Prosciutto 158–159

Orecchiette with Chickpeas, Smoked Pancetta and Celery Leaves 136–137

Pasta and Bean Soup 142–143

Penne Baked in Paper 260–261

Pinched Triangle Pasta with N'duja 148–149

Polenta Quadretti [squares] with a Bean and Anchovy Sauce 150–151

Potato-filled Tortelli Parcels 234–235

Spaghetti Carbonara 170

Pappardelle al funghi Bolognese 182–183

Passatelli in brodo 116–117

pasta

definition of pasta 2

dried pasta (*pasta secca*) 2, 3

fresh pasta 2, 3

gluten-free pasta 23–25

history of 1–2

pasta shapes 2–3

Pasta al gianuiotti 289

Pasta al ragu piccante 152–153

Pasta alla Norma 146–147

Pasta Cake 292–293

Pasta Coins with Ricotta and Honey 145–146

Pasta Crackers 118

pasta dough

Basic Gluten-Free Pasta Dough 26

blended pasta dough 23

Brown Rice Gluten-Free Pasta 27

coloured and flavoured pasta 8–22

Egg Pasta Dough 6

Enriched Egg Yolk Pasta Dough 7

gluten-free 25–28

hydration 8

liquids 25

liquid/flour ratios 8, 23

Quinoa Gluten-Free Pasta 26

Semola Pasta Dough 4–5

Standard Gluten-Free Pasta 26

Vegan Spinach Dough 28

see also flours

Pasta e fagioli 142–143

Pasta e patate 144

pasta fillings 59–65

Breadcrumb Filling 64

Gorgonzola, Pear and Pecorino Filling 63

Mushroom Filling 60

Roasted Butternut Squash and Gorgonzola Filling 62

Sweet Ricotta Filling 65

Tortellini Filling 61

Pasta fritta 123

Pasta fritta alla siracusa 277

Pasta lorda 216–217

pasta machines 29, 69, 70, 77

pasta wheel 70

pasta-making

edible flower and herb lamination 31–32

sfoglina method (hand-rolled pasta sheet) 29–30

shaping pasta 33–59

striping pasta 32–33

using a pasta extruder 31

using a pasta machine 29

see also cooking pasta; flours; pasta dough

Pasticcio di anelleti 254–255

Patate dolce con prosciutto e pistacchio 204–205

pea flour 23, 24

pears: Gorgonzola, Pear and Pecorino Pasta Filling 63

peas

  Anelletti Pasta Pie 239–240

  Celebration Lasagne 251–253

  Earring Encased Pasta Pie 254–255

  Filled Pasta Parcel Shoes with Browned Butter and Fresh Peas 220–221

  Hay and Straw Pasta with Peas and Prosciutto 158–159

  Little Hats with Broad Beans, Summer Peas and Pistachio 132–133

  Pea, Mascarpone, Ham and Lemon Cappellacci 232–233

  Pea Pasta Dough 14

  Potato Gnocchi with Spinach and Provolone Cream 196–197

  Spinach, Prosciutto Cotto and Ricotta Roll 268–269

  Tiny Baked Tagliolini Frittatas 272–273

Penne allo zafferano in cartoccio 260–261

pesto

  Almond, Basil and Tomato Pesto 102–103

  Asparagus Pesto 104–105

  Basil Pesto 105

  Breadcrumb Textured Pesto 106

  Cavolo Nero Pesto 107

  White Pesto 108

Pesto alla trapanese 102–103

Pesto bianco 108

Pesto di asparagi 104–105

Pesto di cavolo nero 107

Pesto di mollica 106

Pesto Genovese 105

Pici al cavolfiore con la mollica 164–165

Pici with Cauliflower, Leaves and Breadcrumbs 164–165

Pici con Gorgonzola e romanesco 166–167

Pici with Gorgonzola and Romanesco 166–167

Pisarei e fasò 114–115

pistachio nuts

  Angel Hair Pasta Twists 277

  Little Hats with Broad Beans, Summer Peas and Pistachio 132–133

  Malfadine with Pistachio Pesto 162–163

  Sweet Potato Gnocchi with Prosciutto and Crushed Pistachio 204–205

Pizzocheri alla Valtellinese 247–248

polenta

  Polenta Gnocchi with Meat Sauce 192–193

  Polenta Quadretti [squares] with a Bean and Anchovy Sauce 150–151

Polenta quadretti con fagoli e acciuga [cresc'tajat] 150–151

Pomodorini e ricotta con miele 92–93

Poor Man's Parmesan (Breadcrumb Topping) 109

pork

  Anelletti Pasta Pie 239–240

  Celebration Lasagne 251–253

Earring Encased Pasta Pie 254–255
Filled Parcels with Rabbit, Veal
    and Pork 218–219
Garganelli with Pork Cheek Ragu
    124–125
Mamma's Baked Pasta Shells
    258–259
Rich Rib Ragu 96–97
Solidea's Egg Layered Lasagne
    264–265
Tortellini Filling 61
see also guanciale; pancetta;
prosciutto; sausage; speck
potato starch 24
potatoes
Buckwheat Pizzocheri with
    Potatoes and Cavolo Nero
    247–248
Culurgiones with a Simple
    Tomato Sauce 214–215
Grape-stuffed Potato Gnocchi
    188–189
Pasta and Potato Soup 144
Potato Gnocchi with a
    Parmigiano Reggiano, Speck
    and Cream Sauce 194–196
Potato Gnocchi with Spinach and
    Provolone Cream 196–197
Potato-filled Tortelli Parcels
    234–235
prosciutto 75
Asparagus Gnocchi 185
Baked Pancake Pasta with
    Radicchio and Béchamel
    243–244
Cavatelli, Mushrooms and
    Sausage 119–120
Hay and Straw Pasta with Peas
    and Prosciutto 158–159
Pea, Mascarpone, Ham and
    Lemon Cappellacci 232–233
Spinach, Prosciutto Cotto and
    Ricotta Roll 268–269
Sweet Potato Gnocchi with

Prosciutto and Crushed
    Pistachio 204–205
Tiny Baked Tagliolini Frittatas
    272–273
Tortellini Filling 61
Vincigrassi Lasagne 274–275
pumpkin flour 24
pumpkin and squash
Pumpkin and Amaretti Tortelli,
    Mantova-style 236–237
Pumpkin Gnocchi with Sausage
    198–199
Roasted Butternut Squash and
    Gorgonzola Pasta Filling 62

quinoa flour 23, 24
Quinoa Gluten-Free Pasta 26

rabbit
Chestnut Ravioli with Rabbit and
    Thyme 209–211
Filled Parcels with Rabbit, Veal
    and Pork 218–219
radicchio
Badly Cut Pasta with Radicchio,
    Speck and Cream 111
Baked Lasagne with Radicchio
    241–242
Baked Pancake Pasta with
    Radicchio and Béchamel
    243–244
Ragu di carne 96–97
Ragu di cinghiale 101–102
ravioli 53, 54, 55
Chestnut Ravioli with Rabbit and
    Thyme 209–211
Chickpea Oven-baked Ravioli
    280–281
Crab and Saffron Ravioli 212–213
Double Ravioli 55
Filled Skirtless Ravioli Coins
    with Stock 222–223
Fresh Egg Yolk Raviolo 54
Green Ravioli Parcels with

Burrata and Pine Nuts 224–225
Jam-filled and Baked Ravioli
290–291
Open Mushroom Raviolo 230–231
shaping 53, 54, 55
Sweet Sardinian Ravioli with
Orange Blossom Honey 298–299
Ravioli di granchio e zaffarano 212–
213
Ravioli ripieno di marmellata 290–
291
Raviolo aperto con funghi 230–231
Red Wine Pasta Dough 18
ricci 47
rice flour 24
ricotta 74, 77
Baked Pancake Pasta with
Radicchio and Béchamel
243–244
Bucatini with a Spicy Ragu and
Whipped Ricotta 152–153
Cannelloni with Gorgonzola
249–250
Chickpea Gnudi with Dressed
Tomatoes 186–187
Dirty Pasta Stamps 216–217
Garden Tomatoes and Honeyed
Ricotta 92–93
Half-moons of Pasta Filled with
Grouper and Spinach 226–227
Mamma's Baked Pasta Shells
258–259
Milk Pasta with Beetroot and
Ricotta 228–229
Mushroom Pasta Filling 60
Naked Pasta Filling, Rolled and
Served with a Cherry Tomato
Sauce 190–191
Pasta with Aubergine 146–147
Pasta Coins with Ricotta and
Honey 145–146
Potato Gnocchi with Spinach and
Provolone Cream 196–197
Potato-filled Tortelli Parcels

234–235
Ricotta Sauce 98
Spinach, Prosciutto Cotto and
Ricotta Roll 268–269
Stuffed Pasta Shells with
Mushroom and Ricotta 270–271
Sweet Half-moons Filled with
Ricotta, Hazelnuts and
Chocolate 296–297
Sweet Potato Gnocchi with
Prosciutto and Crushed
Pistachio 204–205
Sweet Ricotta Pasta Filling 65
White Pesto 108
Ricotta con pasta 98
rolling pins 70
Rotolo di spinachi, cotto e ricotta
268–269

Saffron Pasta Dough 16
Sagne Chime 251–253
Salsa al Gorgonzola e panna 94–95
sauces
Bolognese Ragu 86–87
Carmela's Bolognese Sauce 88–89
Crushed Cherry Tomato Sauce
90–91
Garden Tomatoes and Honeyed
Ricotta 92–93
Gorgonzola and Cream Sauce
94–95
Rich Rib Ragu 96–97
Ricotta Sauce 98
Simple Tomato Sauce 99
White Milk and Butter Sauce 100
Wild Boar Sauce 101–102
see also pesto
sausage
Bucatini with a Spicy Ragu
and Whipped Ricotta
152–153
Casoncelli Parcels 207–208
Cavatelli, Mushrooms and
Sausage 119–120

Pumpkin Gnocchi with Sausage
198–199
Tortellini Filling 61
Wild Boar Sauce 101–102
Scarpinocc con burro e pinoli e piseli
220–221
*Scialatelli con peperone, pomodorino
e noci* 168–169
Scialatelli with Yellow Bell Peppers,
Cherry Tomatoes and Walnuts
168–169
Scrippelle m'busse 128–129
Sebadas, gnocco fritto 298–299
Semola Pasta Dough 4–5
shaping pasta 33–59
filled pasta shapes 51–59
unfilled pasta 33–51
soffrito 77
sorpresa 38
soups
Biscuit Soup 112–113
Bread Pasta in Stock 116–117
Fregola with Fish Stock and
Clams 122
Grated Egg Pasta in Stock 126–127
Pasta and Bean Soup 142–143
Pasta and Potato Soup 144
Spaghetti, aglio, olio e pepperoncino
171
Spaghetti alla carbonara 170
*Spaghetti alla chitarra con polpettine
di pollo* 172–173
Spaghetti alla Norma 266–267
speck 75
Badly Cut Pasta with Radicchio,
Speck and Cream 111
Leftover Pasta with Rocket and
Speck 130–131
Potato Gnocchi with a
Parmigiano Reggiano, Speck
and Cream Sauce 194–196
spelt 23
Spelt Gnocchi 202–203
spinach

Chestnut Ravioli with Rabbit
and Thyme 209–211
Filled Parcels with Rabbit, Veal
and Pork 218–219
Half-moons of Pasta Filled with
Grouper and Spinach 226–227
Lasagne with Spinach and Pesto
256–257
Naked Pasta Filling, Rolled and
Served with a Cherry Tomato
Sauce 190–191
Potato Gnocchi with Spinach and
Provolone Cream 196–197
Spinach Pasta Dough 11
Spinach, Prosciutto Cotto and
Ricotta Roll 268–269
Stuffed Pasta Shells with
Mushroom and Ricotta 270–
271
Vegan Spinach Dough 28
spirulina powder 24
sterilising jars 76
stocks
Beef Stock 80
Chicken Stock 81
Fish Stock 82–83
Vegetable Stock 84–85
storing fresh pasta 67–68
strascinati 42
strozzapreti 37
Strozzapreti Pasta with Octopus
and Cherry Tomatoes 174–175
Strozzapreti pasta, polpo e pomodori
174–175
Sugo di pomodorini 90–91
Sugo finto 99
Sweet Potato Gnocchi with
Prosciutto and Crushed Pistachio
204–205
sweetbreads: Vincigrassi Lasagne
274–275

Tagliarini al ortiche 176–177
Tagliarini with Spring Nettles and

Egg Yolk 176–177
Tagliatelle con funghi, timo e mascarpone 178–179
Tagliatelle in crosta con besciamella ai funghi 245–246
Tagliatelle with Mushrooms, Thyme and Mascarpone 178–179
tapioca flour 24
Testaroli al pesto 140–141
Timballo di anelletti 239–240
tomato vines 76, 93
tomatoes and passata
  Almond, Basil and Tomato Pesto 102–103
  Anelletti Pasta Pie 239–240
  Bolognese Ragu ('Accademia Italiana della Cucina') 86–87
  Bread Pasta Dumplings and Borlotti Beans 114–115
  Bucatini with a Spicy Ragu and Whipped Ricotta 152–153
  Carmela's Bolognese Sauce 88–89
  Cavatelli, Mushrooms and Sausage 119–120
  Celebration Lasagne 251–253
  Chickpea Gnudi with Dressed Tomatoes 186–187
  Crushed Cherry Tomato Sauce 90–91
  Culurgiones with a Simple Tomato Sauce 214–215
  Earring Encased Pasta Pie 254–255
  Garden Tomatoes and Honeyed Ricotta 92–93
  Garganelli with Pork Cheek Ragu 124–125
  Minchiareddhi/Maccaruni with Mixed Seafood 134–136
  Naked Pasta Filling, Rolled and Served with a Cherry Tomato Sauce 190–191
  Orecchiette with Chickpeas, Smoked Pancetta and Celery Leaves 136–137
Paccheri Tubes with a Veal Ragu 138–139
Pasta and Bean Soup 142–143
Pinched Triangle Pasta with N'duja 148–149
Polenta Gnocchi with Meat Sauce 192–193
Polenta Quadretti [squares] with a Bean and Anchovy Sauce 150–151
Rich Rib Ragu 96–97
Rigatoni and Aubergine Cake 262–263
Scialatelli with Yellow Bell Peppers, Cherry Tomatoes and Walnuts 168–169
Semolina Gnocchi with Lentils and Clams 200–201
Simple Tomato Sauce 99
Solidea's Egg Layered Lasagne 264–265
Spaghetti Frittata with Aubergines 266–267
Spinach, Prosciutto Cotto and Ricotta Roll 268–269
Strozzapreti Pasta with Octopus and Cherry Tomatoes 174–175
Tomato Pasta Dough 12
Wide Pasta Ribbons with Autumn Mushroom Bolognese 182–183
Wild Boar Sauce 101–102
Torta di pasta 292–293
Torta di rigatoni e melanzana 262–263
Torta di spaghetti 294–295
Tortelli di patate 234–235
Tortelli di zucca e amaretti 236–237
tortellini 52
  Tortellini Filling 61
trofie 46

veal
  Anelletti Pasta Pie 239–240
  Bucatini with a Spicy Ragu and

Whipped Ricotta 152–153
Carmela's Bolognese Sauce 88–89
Celebration Lasagne 251–253
Filled Parcels with Rabbit,
    Veal and Pork 218–219
Paccheri Tubes with a Veal Ragu
    138–139
Solidea's Egg Layered Lasagne
    264–265
vegan pasta 25, 28
vegetable and fruit powders 9–10
Vegetable Stock 84–85
Vincigrassi 274–275
Vincigrassi Lasagne 274–275
vinegars 71

walnuts
    Bucatini with Walnut Sauce 154
    Pasta Cake 292–293
    Scialatelli with Yellow Bell
        Peppers, Cherry Tomatoes and
        Walnuts 168–169
    White Pesto 108
wheatgrass powder 24

whey 25
White Milk and Butter Sauce 100
White Pesto 108
Wild Boar Sauce 101–102
wine and liqueurs
    Baked Chocolate, Lemon and
        Strega Garganelli Tubes
        78–279
    Chocolate and Frangelico Pasta
        Dough 19
    Chocolate Ribbons with
        Hazelnuts and Amaretto
        282–283
    Hazelnut, Chocolate and
        Frangelico Pasta 289
    Red Wine Pasta Dough 18
    Spaghetti Tart 294–295
    Sweet Sardinian Ravioli with
        Orange Blossom Honey
        298–299

xanthan gum 24

Zuppa imperiale 112–113